FROM THE

Monastery TO THE World

FROM THE

Monastery TO THE World

The Letters of Thomas Merton and Ernesto Cardenal

Translated and Edited by Jessie Sandoval;

with Additional Notes and Translations by Jeffrey Neilson

Introduction by Robert Hass

COUNTERPOINT
BERKELEY, CALIFORNIA

The publisher wishes to thank and acknowledge the editorial efforts of
Jeffrey Neilson and Robert Hass in bringing this book to print.

Library of Congress Cataloging-in-Publication Data
Names: Sandoval, Jessie, editor. | Merton, Thomas, 1915–1968. Correspondence.
    Selections. | Cardenal, Ernesto. Correspondence. Selections.
Title: From the monastery to the world : the letters of Thomas Merton and
    Ernesto Cardenal / edited and translated by Jessie Sandoval ; with an introduction by
    Robert Hass.
Description: Berkeley : Counterpoint, 2017. | Includes bibliographical
    references and index.
Identifiers: LCCN 2017015890 | ISBN 9781619029019 (alk. paper)
Subjects: LCSH: Merton, Thomas, 1915–1968—Correspondence. | Cardenal,
    Ernesto—Correspondence.
Classification: LCC BX4705.M542 A4 2017 | DDC 271/.12502—dc23
LC record available at https://lccn.loc.gov/2017015890

Paperback ISBN: 978-1-64009-155-9

COUNTERPOINT
2560 Ninth Street, Suite 318
Berkeley, CA 94710
www.counterpointpress.com

Printed in the United States of America

Table of Contents

Introduction
by Robert Hass

vii

The Letters

3

Translator's Afterword

247

Appendix

Chronology and Landscape

255

From the Spanish of Ernesto Cardenal
Selections from Gethsemani, KY
(Translated by Thomas Merton)

261

From "A Letter to Pablo Antonio Cuadra Concerning Giants"
by Thomas Merton

267

Notes to the Text

277

Index

309

Introduction

It's hard to know where to begin to tell the story of the letters that passed between these two poets more than fifty years ago. Thomas Merton was forty-two years old, eight years a priest and fifteen years a contemplative under a rule of silence at the Cistercian Abbey of Gethsemani in rural Kentucky when the young Nicaraguan poet arrived there to become a novice monk in the fall of 1957.

Cardenal would stay in the monastery for two years. He left in 1959 and moved to a seminary in Cuernavaca, Mexico, and from there to another in Colombia to prepare for the priesthood with the intention of returning to Nicaragua to create a spiritual community and arts center among the peasants and indigenous peoples of his country.

This mission was a dream Cardenal and Merton came to in their time together, and one that was going to have consequences well into this century. Cardenal did found his mission, among peasants and fisherman on an archipelago in a vast lake in the center of his country. Cardenal encouraged his parishioners to read from the New Testament, to read passages aloud to those among them—the majority—who could not read, and to offer their own interpretations. He recorded these sessions and published the results in four volumes during the years of the emergence of an active liberation theology in Latin America. In 1977 the Nicaraguan dictator, Anastasio Debayle Somoza, sent his army to the island and burned the church and meeting halls at Solentiname to the ground. In 1979 Cardenal joined the Sandinista Revolution that overthrew the fifty-year Somoza family dictatorship, and he became minister of culture to the new government. In 1983 the Polish pope John Paul visited

Nicaragua and publicly rebuked Cardenal, a priest, for holding a government position. In the next year he defrocked Cardenal, stripping him of his priesthood. It was a turbulent time. Five years later, six Jesuit professors involved with liberation theology were murdered in their home by the right-wing death squads of a government in El Salvador supported by the United States. In 1994 Cardenal resigned from the government to protest an authoritarian turn in the ruling party. Twenty years later, in 2013 the Argentine bishop Jorge Mario Bergoglio became Pope Francis, the first Latin American to hold the papacy. In 2014 Pope Francis reinstated the priesthood of Father Cardenal.

This book is a record of the correspondence between the two men from the time of Cardenal's departure in 1959 until the time of Merton's untimely death in a hotel near Bangkok, Thailand, in 1968. He was attending an interfaith conference on monastic life with Buddhist and Hindu monks and scholars. Always interested in Hindu and Islamic and Zen Buddhist spirituality, he had been enormously excited to travel to Asia. When he died—electrocuted by the faulty wiring in a fan in his hotel room—he was the most revered, most widely read writer about spirituality in the English language.

✢

The Abbey at Gethsemani—where Merton and Cardenal met—was a communal farm founded by a group of French Cistercian monks in the middle of the nineteenth century about an hour south of Louisville, an hour and a half from the countryside of that other Kentucky poet, essayist, and farmer, Wendell Berry. The year was 1848, a time of political and social revolt in France, so that the founding of a monastery in the new world mimicked in some way the origins of monasticism. The Cistercian order had its beginnings in a movement that swept Europe in the years of the disintegration of the Roman empire, when some groups of Christian men or women withdrew into communities where they shared work, renounced worldly attachments, and devoted themselves to their spiritual lives. The Cistercians—also called Cistercians of the Strict Observance—also called Trappists for their abbey named La Grande Trappe, in the French countryside—followed the most demanding of the rules set down for monastic life. Trappist monks took three vows: a Vow of Stability, which meant that they were committing themselves to living in the monastery they were entering for the rest of their lives; a Vow of Obedience, which meant that they would do as they were told by their religious superiors; and a Vow of "Conversion of Manners," as it was called, which committed them to a life of celibacy, fasting, manual labor, separation from the world, and silence.

What "separation from the world" meant seems to have changed over time with regard to issues like communication with family and friends in the outside world, which was rationed, but it was certainly a vow of poverty and simplicity; monks entering upon the life were required to make a will disposing of their earthly goods. "Fasting" at Gethsemani meant a simple vegetarian diet and occasional periods of fasting in accordance with the Church's liturgical calendar. There were three exceptions to the rule of silence: one could do the speaking necessary to organize work; one could speak during organized group discussions; and one could speak when discussing one's spiritual life in formal meetings with one's confessor or spiritual director. The idea was to live simply, keep quiet, work hard, and disappear into one's relationship with God. Some American version of this medieval regimen was the one that these two distinctly twentieth-century poets had entered, Thomas Merton in the winter of 1941 and Cardenal in the fall of 1957.

What took them there? Thomas Merton first. He was born in 1915 in France. His father was a New Zealander; his mother was an American from New York. They were both painters, which was why Merton was born in the French village where his parents had chosen to live cheaply and work. Merton's mother died when he was six, his father when he was ten. He spent a good deal of his childhood in boarding schools in France and

England. In those years he and his younger brother spent summers at his maternal grandparents' home in the Douglaston neighborhood of Queens on the north shore of Long Island. Merton's grandfather worked for a publishing company in New York. Merton did high school in English boarding schools under the supervision of a London physician, a friend of the family and his legal guardian under the terms of his father's will. He has described himself in those years of late adolescence and young manhood as aimless, existentially adrift. He was literary. He read the novels of the 1920s that young men read in the early 1930s—D. H. Lawrence and Aldous Huxley. He undertook *Ulysses*. He does not say he felt orphaned, but he had been orphaned. He started university at Cambridge, and he didn't flourish. Before the year was out he had gotten a young woman pregnant, a matter his guardian seems to have settled; he had gone through his allowance; and he was a long way from distinguishing himself academically and was on the verge of losing his scholarship. Both the guardian and his grandfather recommended that he start over, and he did, enrolling in the fall at Columbia, where, for the first time since his parents' death, he found a kind of home.

Columbia University in 1935 was a place in ferment. Merton took classes with Lionel Trilling and the poet and Shakespeare scholar Mark Van Doren, who became his special mentor. The Great Depression was on. The world was moving inexorably toward war, the campus abuzz with politics. As a freshman at Cambridge, Merton had signed a peace pledge, vowing to refuse to fight "for King and Country." At Columbia he made a speech at a peace rally—"maybe," he would write later about his twenty-year-old self, "it was a speech on Communism in England—a topic about which I knew absolutely nothing." Most important, he made friends among the other literary undergraduates, especially the future poet Robert Lax, who would become a lifelong friend; Ad Reinhardt, later a well-known abstract expressionist painter; Ed Rice, who would come to write a biography of Merton; and Roger Giroux, later of the publishing house of Farrar, Straus and Giroux and one of Merton's publishers.

His grandparents died in those years—his grandfather, whom he called "Pop," in 1936, his grandmother in 1937. His mother's brother became his legal guardian, but he and his brother were now very much alone in the world. He had become editor of the college yearbook, he wrote with his friends for the college humor magazine, and around this time something else began to stir in him.

One of his friends, Jim Knight, gives us this portrait of the undergraduate Merton:

> *In terms of sophistication, he was miles ahead of most of us. He dazzled the country boy from the South, as well as the starry-eyed kid from Brooklyn. He did all the things we thought about but didn't do—at least, not yet. He drank a lot, partied, chased (and caught) women. He impressed the hell out of both of us by saying he had learned Hungarian in bed. Beyond these classical youthful, gallant boasts, he was also a very serious man. Looking back, it seems to me he was always right from the very start on the big issues of yesterday (most of which remain the big issues of today)—on racism in America, on social justice, war and peace, the trials of democracy that require us to work hard at it or lose it; the bomb; fairness; the value of the arts and the meaning of his own life and the lives of his fellow human beings, all of them.*

In *The Seven Storey Mountain* Merton tells the story of how, in 1937, at the age of twenty-two, more or less adrift intellectually, more or less an atheist, he came across a book in the window of Scribner's bookstore on Fifth Avenue in Manhattan and on an impulse bought it. It was *The Spirit of Medieval Philosophy*, by the French philosopher Étienne Gilson. "And," he wrote,

> *the one big concept which I got out of its pages was something that was to revolutionize my whole life. It is all contained in one of those dry, outlandish technical compounds that the scholastic philosophers were so prone to use: the word* aseitas. *In this one word which can be applied to God alone, and which*

expresses his most characteristic attribute, I discovered an entirely new concept of God—a concept that showed me at once that the belief of Catholics was by no means the vague and rather superstitious hangover from an unscientific age I had believed it to be. On the contrary, here was a notion of God that was at the same time deep, precise, simple, and accurate and what is more charged with implications I could not even begin to appreciate, but which I could at least dimly estimate, even with my own lack of philosophical training.

Aseitas—the English equivalent is a transliteration: aseity—simply means the power of a being to exist absolutely in virtue of itself, not as caused by itself, but as requiring no cause, no other justification for its existence except that its very nature is to exist. There can only be one such Being: that is God. And to say that God exists a se, of and by and by reason of Himself, is merely to say that God is Being Itself. Ergo sum qui sum. *And this means that God must enjoy "complete independence not only as regards everything outside but also as regards everything within Himself."*

This notion made such a profound impression on me that I made a pencil note at the top of the page: "Aseity of God—God is being per se." *I observe it now on the page, for I brought the book to the monastery with me. I marked three other passages so perhaps the best thing would be to copy them down. Better than anything I could say, they will convey the impact of the book on my mind:*

> *When God says that He is being [reads the first sentence so marked] and if what he says is to have any intelligible meaning to our minds, it can only mean this: that He is the pure act of existing.*

> *Pure act: therefore excluding all imperfection in the order of existing. Therefore excluding all change, all "becoming," all beginning or end, all limitation.*

About the consequences of this moment, Merton writes: "When I had put the book down and had ceased to think explicitly about its arguments, its effect began to show itself in my life. I began to have a desire to go to Church." That same spring he came across a new book by Aldous Huxley. *Ends and Means* begins as a polemic against war and ends as an examination of religious practice. Huxley, who had written the satirical novels about the bankrupt values of the British upper classes that Merton had devoured as a teenager, had taken an interest in Vedanta and the wisdom of Hinduism, which provided a rich, sensuous form of devotional worship to the mass of believers and a more arduous path for those who took the trouble to train themselves to achieve "direct experience of an ultimate reality that is impersonal." Huxley connected these interests in politics and religion in this way:

All of us desire a better state of society. But society cannot become better before two great tasks are performed. Unless peace can be firmly established and the prevailing obsession with money and power profoundly modified, there is no hope of any desirable change being made . . . If the work is to be done at all—and it is clear that, unless it is done, the state of the world is likely to become progressively worse—it must be done by associations of devoted individuals.

One of Huxley's two great tasks was modeling peace through war resistance and the practice of nonviolence, and the other was modeling a social life through which communities could cure themselves and the world of the obsession with money and power. Merton wrote a review of the book for the *Columbia Review*, and what caught his attention particularly was Huxley's prescription for "the spirit as a whole, the freedom of action which it must necessarily have if we are to live like anything but wild beasts, tearing each other to pieces . . . The big conclusion to all this was: we must practice prayer and asceticism. Asceticism! The very thought of such a thing was a complete revolution in my mind."

Merton graduated from Columbia in 1938 and began graduate work in the fall. He was going to write a thesis on the poet William Blake.

Summers he and his friends rented a country place in upstate New York and worked at writing novels. Back in New York he took an interest in the work that the Catholic Worker Movement was doing in Harlem and began to volunteer. He read a biography of the English Victorian poet Gerard Manley Hopkins. While reading about Hopkins's conversion to the Catholic Church, he came to understand that he was going to become a Catholic and announced it to his somewhat incredulous friends. The story of those years, as Europe hurled toward war, is of Merton falling in love with the Catholic Church. He was baptized. He began to think of becoming a priest. He began to write poetry. Able to take a vacation, he went to Cuba, the playground and brothel in those years for white, Anglo-Saxon America, and was thrilled to be in a Latin, deeply Catholic culture where he sated his appetite by attending three or four Masses and other religious services a day at Havana's many churches.

He received his master's degree, took a job at a small Catholic college in upstate New York, and thought about religious orders he might enter. His account of this period in *The Seven Storey Mountain* reads like the account of a man falling in love, only he had fallen in love with the idea of being a saint, and it drew him to the strictest of religious orders, the Cistercians. He apparently did not look to them like a likely candidate. He was a recent convert, so they would have felt a caution about enthusiasm. He had, he explained, a not-unblemished life and an illegitimate daughter living in England. (He would hear, after the war, that she perished in the bombing of London.) But he was eventually accepted to their novitiate, at just about the time he received a notice—in those jittery days—from his draft board. He had decided not to apply for the status of conscientious objector, but to find a way to serve in which he did not have to kill anyone. It turned out that the condition of his teeth—years of toothaches in an English public school—saved him. He received a medical deferment and entered Gethsemani on December 1, 1941, a week before the Japanese bombing of Pearl Harbor.

The Cistercian order did not have a tradition of valuing intellectual work. Before departing for Kentucky, Merton had left a manuscript of his poems with his teacher Mark Van Doren, and Mark Van Doren showed it to an adventurous young publisher named James Laughlin, who had started a publishing house called New Directions, in which he had begun to publish some of the most important modern writers—Ezra Pound and William Carlos Williams and Tennessee Williams, among them. Laughlin accepted Merton's poems in the spring of 1944. In November, *Thirty Poems* was published. Merton, who had been given the name of Brother Louis, had mentioned to his spiritual advisor in the monastery that the former person in his head, the writer Thomas Merton, wasn't going away. His advisor—to his surprise—encouraged him to write. He had the news around the same time that his brother, John Paul, who had enlisted in the air force, died when his plane went down in the Atlantic. The last of his family was gone. He was a monk and a published author. He wrote several books for Catholic publishers about the Cistercian Order, and then he set about writing an account of how he came to be a Trappist. It seemed an unlikely book for a New York publisher, and an especially unlikely one for an avant-garde press like New Directions. He sent it to one of his college friends, Robert Giroux, a junior editor then at Harcourt Brace, and Giroux took the book. It had to pass through Church censors—they wanted all references, except glancing ones, to his sexual life and his paternity removed so as not to give scandal—and in 1948, early in the postwar years, the book was published in an edition of five thousand copies—which turned out to be a miscalculation. In the first year it sold more than six hundred thousand copies, and it continued to sell at that rate for a couple of years after. So Thomas Merton became one of the best-known writers in the world, and the man who, eight years later, as Director of Novices, was assigned as spiritual advisor to the young novice Ernesto Cardenal. He had also, having taken a vow of poverty, generated a couple of million dollars in royalties to an old monastery badly in need of repair.

+

Cardenal's route to Gethsemani is a story dramatic in a different way. He came from an upper-class Nicaraguan family. He was born in the beautiful colonial city of Granada on Lake Nicaragua and grew up in the other old colonial city of León, which had been the home of Rubén Darío, the most important Latin American poet of the early years of the twentieth century and the founder of the style that came to be known as *modernismo*.

This was consequential because Cardenal's father read Darío's poems to his children and because the United States marines had occupied Nicaragua from 1909 to 1933 to support a government sympathetic to American commercial interests and because Darío had written a poem well-known to Nicaraguans addressed to Theodore Roosevelt. It was written in the style of Walt Whitman and addressed Roosevelt as the "invader of an innocent America / that has Indian blood in its veins / and prays to Jesus Christ / and still speaks Spanish." (Central Americans were not apt to be unclear about U.S. intentions since they had seen the United States corner the world sugar market in 1898 by seizing Cuba, Puerto Rico, and the Philippines from Spain.)

So Cardenal grew up in an atmosphere that both admired North American poetry and associated Latin American poetry with the Catholic Church and resistance to North American Protestant rapacity. It was during his childhood, from 1927 to 1933, that Augusto Sandino, a *mestizo* and a clerk for a gold mining company, emerged as the leader of a guerilla war against the marines. Sandino, who became a national hero, was killed in 1934 when he was invited to a parley with the government in the capital, Managua, and, as he was leaving, was executed, along with his father, his brother, and the rebel group's minister of agriculture, a poet.

By 1940 Cardenal, who knew this history, was attending a prep school in Managua. The next year he enrolled in the National University in Mexico City and took his degree in literature there. He had begun to write poems—mostly, he said, imitations of Pablo Neruda. In 1947, age twenty-two, he moved to New York and enrolled at Columbia (he was—though they didn't meet until years later—a classmate of Allen Ginsberg), where he began to read American poetry intensely, especially Walt Whitman and Ezra Pound, and where he studied with many of Thomas Merton's former professors, including Mark Van Doren, and heard news of Merton and read *The Seven Storey Mountain*. He had begun to write his own poems in a style he called *exteriorismo*, poems like "Raleigh" and "With Walker in Nicaragua," which described the lush beauty of his country through the eyes of explorers and exploiters and *filibusteros*. They were poems written in New York City and during the following year in Italy and Spain and Switzerland—perhaps implicitly political but full of homesickness and a kind of erotic nostalgia for his landscapes as he imagined they were seen through the eyes of strangers.

In 1950, at the age of twenty-five, he went home and settled in Managua, in the shadow of the dictatorship of General Anastasio Somoza. When the U.S. Marines withdrew from Nicaragua in 1933, they adopted a policy of training the Nicaraguan National Guard to fight the insurgency. Somoza became the head of that National Guard and used his position to depose his uncle and become ruler of the country. Cardenal in Managua fell in love and, under the spell of Ezra Pound's classicism, began to write epigrams in the style of ancient Roman poets, about half of them to his beloved and half of them against the dictator. One of the love poems (in Thomas Merton's translation):

> *Be careful, Claudia, when you're with me.*
> *Because the slightest gesture, any word or sigh*
> *Of Claudia's, the slightest slip,*
> *Will perhaps be pored over by scholars*
> *And this dance of Claudia's could be remembered for centuries.*
> *Just saying.*

One of the political poems looks like this:

We heard shots last night
Out by the burial ground.
No one knows who they killed, or how many.
No one knows a thing.
We heard shots last night.
That's all.

The poems, especially the political poems, could not be published, but they circulated in manuscript and in mimeograph (as some of the poetry magazines of the Beat generation in New York and San Francisco circulated in those years). Pablo Neruda published some of them in Chile, though he didn't know the name of the author.

Around this time, 1953, Cardenal became involved with a group of young men who were plotting to remove Somoza by coup. Cardenal actually went into the mountains and was trained to use a machine gun. The conspirators were betrayed by provocateurs inside the group, and several of Cardenal's associates were arrested. Somoza—his nickname was "Tacho"—turned the prisoners over to his son—his nickname was "Tachito"—who interrogated and tortured them. One of them was castrated before he was killed; another had his tongue cut out and was returned briefly to the prison population as an example. Others were jailed, exiled, or disappeared.

This was a time when poets all over South America were looking to the politics of their countries and looking at the role of the Catholic Church in supporting the dictators and their landed oligarchies against movements for reform and social justice. Pablo Neruda had included in his epic of the continent *Canto General* a fierce denunciation of "The United Fruit Company." In his *Zero Hour*, the poem that sums up his early work, Cardenal, who had not been arrested, begins with a look at General Jorge Ubico, the notorious military dictator of Guatemala:

Tropical nights in Central America
with moonlit lagoons and volcanoes
and lights from presidential palaces,
barracks and sad curfew warnings.
"Often when smoking a cigarette
I've decided that a man should die,"
says Ubico smoking a cigarette . . .
In his pink wedding-cake palace
Ubico has a head cold. Outside the people
were dispersed with phosphorus bombs.

And it was at this time, rather shockingly, that Cardenal's thoughts turned to the Trappist monastery in Kentucky. The precipitating event was the decision of his beloved—her name was Ileana—to marry a protégé of Somoza. He wrote about the event several times. Here is the account from his journals:

Saturday, June 2nd, twelve noon, on the hour of the wedding, I was in my library, without anyone else but the housemaid, when suddenly we heard in the street—Roosevelt Avenue—the thunderous sound of Somoza's motorcade paralyzing traffic, like firefighters or ambulances, as they ran by at maximum speed. It was Somoza who was coming to the wedding in the Cathedral on his way to the Presidential Palace. Those thunderous sirens rang in my ears like bugles of victory, victorious over me. As strange as it may sound, fast as a flash, my mind perceived a superimposed vision of God and the Dictator, as if they were one and the same; the one alone who had triumphed over me. The fact is that I felt dejected down to the very depths of dejection, and it was then that I surrendered myself to God. I felt that I had already fought enough, in vain. I had nothing left but to try God.

•

There is a stranger account in one of his late poems, "Telescope in the Dark Night," a poem about sexuality that is addressed to God:

> *When that midday on June 2nd, a Saturday,*
> *Somoza García in a flash of lightning sped along Roosevelt Avenue*
> *all horns blaring to ward off traffic,*
> *in that very instant, just like his triumphant motorcade*
> *you just as triumphant suddenly entered me*
> *and my poor defenseless soul wanted to cover my private parts.*
> > *It was almost rape,*
> > *but with consent,*
> > *how could it be otherwise,*
> > *and that invasion of pleasure*
> > *until almost dying,*
> > *and saying: that's enough*
> > *you're killing me.*
> > > *So much pleasure that produces so much pain*
> > *Like a kind of penetration.*

✝

Thomas Merton in 1957 in a letter to a friend: "My novices are doing very well. There is one, a Nicaraguan poet, a quiet man and agreeable, who spent some time at Columbia, I would say, about ten years ago." Cardenal has said that, though *The Seven Storey Mountain* had planted in him the thought of monastic life, he had not had any thought of meeting Merton, didn't know whether he was still at Gethsemani or not. But they found quickly that they had a good deal in common. In his mentoring of newcomers Merton was inclined to be a little laissez-faire: "A master of novices," he wrote, "(at least in my opinion) must above all be a man who does not meddle in affairs which are none of his business. A monastery is a *schola caritas*—a school of love—but it is not men who are the teachers of love." And in a later poem Cardenal remembers this of Merton's greeting of the novices:

> *And Merton: his last warning*
> *In the Guest House, before admitting me to the cloister:*
> *"The life of a monk is*
> *a semi-ecstasy and forty years of aridity."*
> *It didn't frighten me.*

But Cardenal's arrival was a gift to Merton, and clearly, not only because Cardenal was expected to report on his progress, they found occasions to talk, at a moment when Merton badly needed someone to talk to. He had come to, if not a crisis, a moment of intense restlessness in his life at Gethsemani.

His restlessness took two conflicting forms. One dissatisfaction for him was that the institutional routines of life at the monastery did not slake his hunger for solitude. There was a part of him that longed to be a hermit, and his religious superiors had not taken kindly to what they might have regarded as the desire for special treatment. The other source of his unease was the world. "In August 1957," according to his biographer Michael Mott, "Merton read one of the Mexican magazines in which Ernesto Cardenal had a poem attacking the United Fruit Company. After sixteen years of isolation from social issues, Merton was cut off from what he needed to know." In September the Van Dorens visited him and spoke of the racial struggle in nearby Little Rock, Arkansas. The governor of the state had sent in the National Guard to prevent the entrance to the high school of nine black students who had been recruited to desegregate the school in accordance with the Supreme Court decision of 1954. Images of an armed force blocking their way had been front-page news. President Eisenhower had sent in federal troops—a division of 101st airborne—to escort the students to their classroom. The governor had responded by shutting down the four Little Rock high schools, an action approved in a referendum by the citizens of Little Rock.

Between 1948 when he published *The Seven Storey Mountain* and 1957, he had published a stream of books praising the contemplative life and withdrawal from the world: *New Seeds of Contemplation* and *The Waters of Siloe* in 1949, *The Ascent to Truth* in 1951, *The Sign of Jonas* and *Bread in the Wilderness* in 1955, *The Silent Life* in 1957. And now the world was returning to him in a way that he responded to with his customary intellectual voraciousness. He read—they were just appearing—detailed accounts of the effects of the bombings of Hiroshima and Nagasaki. He read the stories of Buchenwald and Auschwitz in William Shirer's *The Rise and Fall of the Third Reich* and returned to the readings of Gandhi on nonviolence that Huxley's book had sent him to. He read, he said, "an orgy of books about South America" and began to translate some of the political poems of Cardenal.

The two poets met twice a week during Cardenal's first year, once a week during his second. "From the very beginning," Cardenal wrote, "there was great understanding between us, being that we were both poets." They spoke, he said, "about matters all conscientious men were concerned with in this era." Merton, trying to integrate in himself these conflicting impulses, was also reading Zen Buddhist and Taoist thought. He had some idea that the peasants and indigenous peoples of South America in their communal life could be a model for contemplative, nonviolent communities. He had the idea that the spiritualities of East and West, of Christianity and Hinduism and Buddhism and Islam and the religions of the native peoples of the Americas, needed to be brought together in some new unity. In his notebooks he tended to berate himself for grandiosity, and that intensified his desire for a purer solitude. Somehow out of their conversations the idea emerged of a new monastic order, a simple one, in Nicaragua, in the islands of a beautiful lake where the peasantry, fishermen and farmers, were the descendants of slaves.

Cardenal, meanwhile, was giving himself over to monastic life. The record of his experience that we have is a poem, or sequence of poems, *Gethsemani, KY*, and the written meditations that were an exercise required of novices and which later became a book, published in English in 1972 under the title *To Live Is to Love*. They do not record his struggles. His adjustment to the unwinterized winter and the monastery diet was not easy. He had headaches. He suffered from an ulcer. (Merton thought he was exacerbating the ulcer by suppressing the impulse to write poetry.) There are private journals from this time, not yet published. The meditations, full of the way he was internalizing his new life, are more like homilies, well-shaped thoughts. He was beginning to become a teacher. One of the surprises of them—coming from the 1950s—is their ecological vision. He was reading in cosmology and evolutionary biology, and they deepened his sense of wonder. In this passage, for example:

All things love each other. All nature is oriented toward a thou. All beings are alive in communion with each other. All plants, all animals, all beings are fraternally united by the phenomenon of mimesis. There are insects which mimic flowers and flowers which act like insects, animals which resemble water or rocks or desert sand or snow or woodlands or certain other animals. And thus all beings love each other and feed each other, and are united in a gigantic process of birth and growth and reproduction and death. In nature everything undergoes mutation, transformation, and change, everything embraces, caresses, and kisses. And the laws which rule all animate beings and to which inert nature is also subject (for nature, too, is alive and animated by a life that is imperceptible to us) are variants of the one law of love. All physical phenomena are likewise manifestations of the identical phenomenon of love. The cohesion of a snowflake and the explosion of a nova, the tumble-bug that clings to a heap of dung, and the lover who embraces his beloved, manifest the same phenomenon of love. Everything in nature seeks to transcend its own limits, to go beyond the barriers of its individuality, to meet with a thou to which it can give itself, an "other" into which it can transform itself. The laws of thermodynamics and electrodynamics, the laws of

*the propulsion of light, and the universal law of gravity are all manifestations of the
one law of Love.*

And there is in the writing also an intense drive inward, into himself.
Cardenal's conception of God originates in the intimacy of his solitude:

> *God who is hidden in the dark, is reality, and we cannot apprehend him with our
> senses, our imagination, and our intellect . . .*
>
> *God's presence is invisible and obscure, like the presence of another person in
> the darkness of our own home.*
>
> *We have felt this presence within ourselves many times without realizing it, in
> the belief that we are alone with ourselves. The presence may make itself known
> by a sensation of total silence or by a mysterious feeling of love that wells up
> from the depth of our being.*
>
> *. . . The will of God, which you have failed to obey, is not something external
> to you, something imposed upon your own will from without, but rather some-
> thing that is more yourself than your own will, a thou that is you, your most
> inward self, your true self-identity and the deepest willing of your being.*
>
> *God's love is lodged deeply within us; it draws us toward Him, toward the
> center of ourselves, which is He. For love always seeks union, the union of lover
> and beloved. Someone exists within me who is not myself. And we are made in
> such a way that God dwells in the center of our being, in such a way that to be
> centered in ourselves is to approach and approximate God. And yet we cannot
> reach him, because the distance between Him and us is infinite: He is infinitely
> around us, above us, and within us.*

Looking back, Cardenal wrote of his relationship with Merton: "He
taught me to be like him, for whom spiritual life was not separate from
any other human concern (racism, politics, literature, the nuclear question, etc.) Naturally, we had huge things in common outside the walls of
the monastery." Cardenal left Gethsemani with Merton's blessing. His

plan was to go to Mexico, to the seminary in Cuernavaca, to study for the priesthood and to return to Nicaragua, where he hoped Merton would be able to join him in the creation of a new community—if Merton was able to get the permission of his superiors; he had taken a vow to stay in the monastery for the rest of his life.

+

Their correspondence tracks some of the ways in which Merton struggled with this idea. His abbot, Dom James Fox, has been described as a hearty, outgoing man and a good manager. He was an ex-Marine, and he had an MBA from Harvard. Any permission for a change of status had to go through him, though a final decision would have to come from the head of the Cistercian Order in Rome. The monastery at Our Lady of Gethsemani was in those years a community of about a hundred monks and a hundred novices, the largest monastic community in North America, and it was, relatively, thriving, partly because of the royalties from Merton's writing—a subject that seems to have been of no interest to him—and partly because the eloquence of his writing about what he called "the waters that flow out of silence" had attracted many men in those postwar years to the idea of a monastic vocation. Dom James had to manage the place and his world-famous writer about whose future and reputation the Cistercian Order and the Church in Rome was sensitive. It seems to have been a mismatch. One gets the impression from the biographical accounts that Dom James resented Merton, and Merton, who had always been attracted to father figures, was also always inclined to question authority. The abbot was Merton's spiritual director. To complicate their relationship, Merton—Father Louis—was the abbot's confessor.

There was a rule in the monastery against what were called "Particular Friendships." The rule existed, no doubt, not only to discourage romantic and sexual relationships, but also because of the idea that ordinary friendships tended to divide the community and to be counter to the personally anonymous ideal of a monk's life. For some of these reasons the abbot was uneasy about the relationship between the two poets and at a certain point forbade correspondence between them. He later relented. But both Merton and Cardenal understood that their letters were apt to be read by their superiors. Merton was wry on this subject, commenting that Church authorities were concerned, on the one hand, that he was homosexual and, on the other, that he might run off with a woman.

His writing in the last decade of his life intensified both his studies in spirituality and his engagement with the world. In 1960 he published *The Wisdom of the Desert*, a collection of the sayings of the fourth-century holy men who left the cities of the late Roman empire to live solitary lives in search for communion with their God. This must have been born of his own hunger for solitude. In his introduction to the book he remarks that the cities they were leaving were becoming Christian and that "these men seem to have thought . . . that there is really no such thing as a 'Christian state.' They seem to have doubted that Christianity and politics could ever be mixed to such an extent as to produce a fully Christian society . . . for . . . the only Christian society was spiritual and extramundane." This has its interest because it was the argument that supporters of Pope John Paul would make twenty years later when he rebuked Cardenal for serving in the Sandinista government at a time when Cardenal was inclined to argue that, in Latin America, in order to be a Christian, you had to be a Marxist. The argument captures the ferment of these years. Cardenal knew very well the story of Father Camilo Torres Restrepo, a Colombian priest and professor of sociology who joined a revolutionary group in 1966 and was killed in an engagement between the rebels and the Colombian army. All of Catholic Latin America knew that he was said to have declared before he died, "If Jesus were alive today, he would be a *guerrillero*."

It was at this time, watching Martin Luther King Jr. and the civil rights movement closely, that Merton edited a volume of Gandhi's writings on nonviolence and wrote a long essay meditating on Latin America and the Cold War addressed as a letter to another Nicaraguan poet, Cardenal's uncle, Pablo Antonio Cuadra.

He was also writing new poems, and the poems were socially engaged. In 1962 he published *Original Child Bomb*, a long prose poem describing the effects of the bombings of Hiroshima and Nagasaki that became an important document of the anti-nuclear movement in those years. The 1963 volume *Emblems of a Season of Fury* contained *Original Child Bomb* and an elegy for the black children burned in a Birmingham church and a ballad—"There Has to Be a Jail for Ladies," which celebrates civil disobedience. It begins:

> *There has to be a jail where ladies go*
> *When they are poor, without nice things, and with their hair down.*
> *When their beauty is taken from them, when their hearts are broken,*
> *There is a jail where they must go.*

—and a prose poem, "Chant to Be Used In Processions around a Site with Furnaces," in which a supervisor of the death camps addresses the future:

> *Do not think yourself superior because you burn up friends and enemies with*
> *Long-range missiles without ever seeing what you have done.*

And, as the likelihood of his getting to join Cardenal in Mexico or Nicaragua grew more remote, he studied the classic Taoist and Zen Buddhist texts and engaged in a mental dialogue with the Zen teacher D. T. Suzuki, whom he had been reading for years. The books that came of these encounters, the last he wrote, were among his best-selling and most influential: *The Way of Chuang Tzu*, 1965; *Mystics and Zen Masters*, 1967; *Zen and the Birds of Appetite*, 1968.

Cardenal, having been ordained in 1965 and having established his community at Solentiname in 1966, where he said Mass and read scripture to the largely illiterate peasant and fisherman families on the island, received the news of Merton's death in the place they had dreamed of. It was a complicated time, the year before Jorge Mario Bergoglio, the future Pope Francis, was ordained in Argentina. A few years later in 1971, a Peruvian priest, Father Gustavo Gutiérrez, would publish *A Theology of Liberation*, and some part of the response to this challenge was the "Dirty War" in Argentina, when Father Bergoglio, a very young director of the Jesuit order in his country, witnessed the purging of left-leaning priests by the military junta. This was some of the context in which Cardenal watched his community be burned to the ground, in which he renounced Gandhian nonviolence and joined the Sandinista Revolution and its government. That was 1979. In the following year the American government and the CIA armed the remnants of Somoza's army and initiated a counterrevolutionary war. Stark days: in 1980 in neighboring El Salvador as the Archbishop Óscar Romero, a public advocate for the poor, was saying Mass in the cathedral in San Salvador, he was assassinated by a high-powered rifle. Two years later came the confrontation between Cardenal and the Polish pope.

Cardenal wrote and published many poems in those years, collected in English translation in the volume *Apocalypse, and Other Poems.* They include an elegy, "Coplas on the Death of Merton," which contains these lines:

> *At last you came to Solentiname (which wasn't practical)*
> *after the Dalai Lama and the Himalayas with their buses*
> *painted like dragons*
>   *to the "uncanny isles"; you are here*
> *with your silent Tzus and Fus*
> *Kung Tzu, Lao Tzu, Meng Fu, Tu Fu, and Nicanor Parra*
> *and everywhere; as simple to communicate with you*
> *as with God (or as difficult).*

Nicanor Parra was the great Chilean physicist-poet whom both Cardenal and Merton admired and whose poems Merton had translated a few of. In another late poem by Cardenal, "Trip to New York," there is a last appearance by Merton when Cardenal and his publisher share a bottle of Chilean white wine, brought to New York by Parra as a gift:

> *Laughlin is a door-high man, and*
> *(as I already knew through Merton) brimming with love.*
> *After we're inside he asks his wife about Nicanor's wine.*
> *Where's the wine Nicanor left? He takes from the refrigerator*
> *The Portuguese white wine, Saint What's-his-name that Nicanor left*
> *The last time he was here. We're holding our glasses, about to drink*
> *When Laughlin lifts his toward heaven like an Offertory:*
> *"To Tom, I'm sure he'll be enjoying this party*
> *wherever he is!" And I: "He's here." Nicanor Parra's wine*
> *is delicious. "It's a curious thing," says Laughlin, "after his death*
> *you saw that each friend believed he was Merton's closest friend."*
> *After a pause and a sip of wine: "—and each one really was."*

✝

The letters of the two men were first collected in a Spanish-language edition, entitled *Del monasterio al mundo*, edited by Santiago Daydi-Tolson in 1998. We have depended on his editorial work and his notes to the letters to make this edition. Summarizing the uses of this record from a Latin American perspective, Professor Daydi-Tolson wrote: "Ernesto Cardenal and Thomas Merton represent—in an almost paradigmatic manner—the potential brought about by an encounter between politics, religion, literature, and art during the 1960s; they are also examples of the dialogue made possible between the two hemispheres, from the same American continent, that Merton considered essential for its survival. The

intellectual friendship between them, and their deeply grounded spirituality and poetics illustrate a period of transformation that in part can be
understood by shining a light on the collaboration between the two poets,
who were determined to change a world they could not abandon despite
their contemplative vocation."

—Robert Hass

FROM THE
Monastery TO THE World

The Letters

The Letters

Cardenal to Merton letters were translated and edited by Jessie Sandoval, referencing *Del monasterio al mundo.*

Unless otherwise noted, all Merton to Cardenal correspondence is taken from *The Courage for Truth: Letters to Writers,* Thomas Merton, edited by Christine M. Bochen (Mariner Books, 1994).

Letter 1:   Merton to Cardenal, August 11, 1959

Letter 2:   Cardenal to Merton, August 9, 1959

Letter 3:   Merton to Cardenal, August 17, 1959 Ω

Letter 4:   Cardenal to Merton, August 25, 1959

Letter 5:   Cardenal to Merton, September 5, 1959

Letter 6:   Merton to Cardenal, September 12, 1959 Ω

Letter 7:   Merton to Cardenal, October 8, 1959 *

Letter 8:   Merton to Cardenal, October 17, 1959 Ω

Letter 8a: Cardenal to Merton, October 17, 1959 †

Letter 9:   Merton to Cardenal, October 24, 1959 Ω

            Note on Letter 9

Letter 9a: Cardenal to Merton, October 27, 1959 †

Letter 10:   Merton to Cardenal, November 18, 1959 Ω

Letter 11:   Merton to Cardenal, November 24, 1959 Ω

Letter 12:   Merton to Cardenal, December 17, 1959 Ω

            Note on Letter 12

Letter 13:   Cardenal to Merton, March 11, 1960

            Note on Letter 13

Letter 14:   Cardenal to Merton, February 27, 1961

            Note on Letter 14

Letter 15:   Merton to Cardenal, March 11, 1961

Letter 16:   Merton to Cardenal, No Date, 1961

Letter 17:   Merton to Cardenal, August 16, 1961 [Previously untranslated]

Letter 18:   Cardenal to Merton, August 30, 1961

Letter 19:   Merton to Cardenal, September 11, 1961

Letter 20:   Cardenal to Merton, September 30, 1961

Letter 21:   Merton to Cardenal, October 14, 1961

Letter 22:   Merton to Cardenal, November 20, 1961

              Note on Letter 22

Letter 23:   Merton to Cardenal, December 24, 1961

Letter 24:   Cardenal to Merton, March 4, 1962

Letter 25:   Merton to Cardenal, May 16, 1962

Letter 26:   Merton to Cardenal, May 22, 1962

Letter 27:   Cardenal to Merton, May 31, 1962

Letter 28:   Merton to Cardenal, June 7, 1962

Letter 29:   Cardenal to Merton, July 2, 1962

Letter 30:   Merton to Cardenal, August 17, 1962

Letter 31:   Merton to Cardenal, September 16, 1962

Letter 32:   Cardenal to Merton, September 24, 1962

Letter 33:   Merton to Cardenal, No Date, 1962

Letter 34:   Cardenal to Merton, October 3, 1962

Letter 35:   Cardenal to Merton, November 8, 1962

Letter 36:   Merton to Cardenal, November 17, 1962

Letter 37:   Merton to Cardenal, November 17, 1962

Letter 38:   Cardenal to Merton, December 22, 1962

Letter 39:   Merton to Cardenal, February 25, 1963

Letter 40:   Cardenal to Merton, February 27, 1963

Letter 41:   Cardenal to Merton, March 13, 1963

Letter 42:   Merton to Cardenal, April 8, 1963

Letter 43:   Cardenal to Merton, May 21, 1963

Letter 44:   Merton to Cardenal, May 29, 1963

Letter 45:   Cardenal to Merton, July 17, 1963

Letter 46:   Merton to Cardenal, August 1, 1963

Letter 47:   Cardenal to Merton, September 15, 1963

Letter 48:   Merton to Cardenal, No Date, 1963

Letter 49:   Cardenal to Merton, November 13, 1963

Letter 50:   Merton to Cardenal, November 23, 1963

Letter 51:   Cardenal to Merton, December 22, 1963

Letter 52:   Cardenal to Merton, February 29, 1964

Letter 53:   Merton to Cardenal, March 10, 1964

Letter 54:   Merton to Cardenal, May 8, 1964

Letter 55:   Cardenal to Merton, May 16, 1964

Letter 56:   Merton to Cardenal, July 12, 1964

Letter 57:   Cardenal to Merton, July 20, 1964

Letter 58:   Merton to Cardenal, September 26, 1964

Letter 59:   Cardenal to Merton, October 5, 1964

Letter 60:   Merton to Cardenal, undated, 1964

Letter 61:   Cardenal to Merton, undated, 1964

Letter 62:   Merton to Cardenal, December 24, 1964

Letter 63:   Cardenal to Merton, January 28, 1965

Letter 64:   Merton to Cardenal, February 8, 1965

Letter 65:   Merton to Cardenal, April 24, 1965

Letter 66:   Cardenal to Merton, April 30, 1965

Letter 67:   Merton to Cardenal, May 10, 1965

Letter 68:   Cardenal to Merton, August 7, 1965

Letter 69:   Merton to Cardenal, August 15, 1965

Letter 70:   Cardenal to Merton, August 24, 1965

Letter 71:   Merton to Cardenal, November 17, 1965

Letter 72:   Merton to Cardenal, December 15, 1965

Letter 73:   Merton to Cardenal, January 8, 1966

Letter 74:   Merton to Cardenal, January 18, 1966

Letter 75:   Merton to Cardenal, February 5, 1966

Letter 76:   Cardenal to Merton, February 22, 1966

Letter 77:   Merton to Cardenal, April 9, 1966

Letter 78:   Cardenal to Merton, June 20, 1966

Letter 79:   Merton to Cardenal, July 3, 1966

Letter 80:   Merton to Cardenal, October 14, 1966

Letter 81:   Cardenal to Merton, November 20, 1966

Letter 82:   Merton to Cardenal, November 26, 1966 (previously
              untranslated)

Letter 83:   Merton to Cardenal, January 2, 1967

Letter 84:   Merton to Cardenal, March 11, 1967

Letter 85:   Cardenal to Merton, April 15, 1967

Letter 86:   Merton to Cardenal, July 28, 1967

Letter 87:   Cardenal to Merton, August 14, 1967

Letter 88:   Cardenal to Merton, March 5, 1968

Letter 89:   Merton to Cardenal, March 15, 1968

Letter 90:   Merton to Cardenal, July 21, 1968

Letter 91:   Merton to Rev. Archbishop Paul Philippe, undated and
              unsent, October 1965

Letter 92:   Merton to Pope Paul VI, undated and unsent, October 1965

Ω Merton to Cardenal correspondence with Ω is taken from *The Courage for Truth: Letters to Writers* (1994) and includes omitted sentences that have been restored from "Time of Transition" (1995):

        3, 6, 8–12

* Merton to Cardenal correspondence with * is taken from *Witness to Freedom: The Letters of Thomas Merton in Times of Crisis*, edited by William H. Shannon (Harvest Books, 1995):

        7, 91–92

† Merton to Cardenal correspondence with † is taken from Christine M. Bochen, "Time of Transition: A Selection of Letters from the Earliest Correspondence of Thomas Merton and Ernesto Cardenal" *Merton Annual Volume* 8 (1995):

        i, ii

Letter 1

Our Lady of Gethsemani, Trappist, KY

August 11, 1959

Dear Ernesto:

I prayed a lot for you during the feast for St. Lawrence yesterday. I hope that you arrived in Mexico without any difficulty. You are probably staying with Mejía Sánchez, but I lost his address, and have to write to you at the [*Universidad Iberoamericana*].

I am now sending you the article about Pasternak ["Boris Pasternak and the People with Watch Chains"]—they are publishing it in Spanish translation in the journal *Sur*.

There is nothing new here. The [novice], Brother Paul of the Cross, spent a few days in the hospital—it seems that he too has ulcers, even though he denies it, emphatically. We completed the dormitory and Brother Gerard [illegible] is finishing the crucifixes. It seems that Father Abbot [Dom James Fox] is leaving for France and the Vatican at the end of August, and is returning by the end of September. I sent [Robert] Lax a few translations of César Vallejo's work for his leaflet—and *Jubilee* is printing one of my articles about Monte Athos, in the August issue.

I hope that you are well—and very happy to find yourself in Mexico. What do you think about Dom Gregorio's monastery [*Santa María de la Resurrección*]?

With great affection in N.S.

Father Mary Louis

Letter 2

Universidad Iberoamericana, Mexico, D.F.

August 9, 1959

Reverend, Father Mary Louis O.S.C.O.

Gethsemani

Dear Father Louis:

I have only just arrived in Mexico because my trip took one week. There were some errors with the itinerary that I was given, and it took two more days than I had been told. On top of that, I actually arrived on Friday night in New Orleans, and had to stay there until Monday because the Nicaraguan consulate, where I was to renew my passport, was closed on Saturday. Except for the boring wait in New Orleans, where I found absolutely nothing to do, there were no other delays.

The day after I arrived in Mexico (the day before yesterday), I went to visit the monastery [*Santa María de la Resurrección*]. There I spoke with Father Prior [Dom Gregorio Lemercier], and told him everything that I needed to say, and he is clear on everything. I agreed with him that I would return to the monastery in two weeks, and stay as a guest, or postulant, for a few months until I can clearly see what God wants from me.

The monastery is located in a very beautiful place, quite remote from Cuernavaca (about half an hour on foot) in an isolated area, surrounded by tropical vegetation, facing some forests, somewhat similar to the ones facing the monastery in Gethsemani. The monastery lies over a hill, from which a magnificent panoramic view of the entire valley of Cuernavaca can be seen with the city below, and beyond that, huge sierras and volcanoes.

They are constructing a very revolutionary church, in the style of Mexico's modern architecture. A young monk, who is an architect, is directing it. However, something very odd happened to me as I arrived here, despite everything that I have just described to you, and everything that I was enjoying. I felt sad and depressed, with a strange sense of melancholy that I never felt when I was in Gethsemani; wherein, from the first moment I had arrived there, I had felt invaded by an immense sense of happiness, which I never lost during the entire time. I spoke with this young architect, who is very charismatic, and found him radiant with happiness, as I had always been while I was in Gethsemani, and this made me realize the difference in my current emotional state.

I do not know if this could just be a brief psychological phase because, objectively speaking, I do not see any reason to feel depressed there. Either way, I am resolved to go and remain there [in Cuernavaca], sad or not, for as long as necessary, until God reveals to me what I am supposed to do— unless my health does not permit it. I am not worried about this because I am completely in God's hands, and I feel that He is with me, and that He is guiding my steps, and that He has brought me here. At the same time, I have no desire to return to the world, nor am I considering the slightest possibility of remaining in Mexico, even though I could give classes at the *Universidad Nacional,* or at the Jesuit university [*Universidad Iberoamericana*] because there is a great need for professors with university degrees, and I would be able to acquire a position immediately, if I wanted it. But I cannot live in the world, because I do not belong to it. Moreover, I know for certain that I have not lost my calling, and that I belong only to God, and that He will take me where He wants me to be, and I am at peace.

My stomach feels more or less the same as when I was in Gethsemani. There are times when I am doing well, and sometimes not. I was feeling worse during the trip, probably because I was more nervous, and probably due to the delays, and the unpleasant waiting in New Orleans. From the moment I entered the world, and arrived in Louisville, I discovered that the world is truly a horrible and inhospitable place, especially city life in the United States. Life in Mexico, even Mexico City, is still more humane. In New Orleans, aside from the library and the Tulane museum, which were closed during almost the entire time that I was there, and the churches (always closed, or empty), I had nowhere else to go. I spent most of the time inside my hotel room. On the street, there are only shops, restaurants, and movie theaters. Wherever you fix your eyes, all you see are ads for sex and food. There is nothing more boring than to walk through those streets, once you have lost all interest in such things.

There were many moments in Gethsemani when I thought that our lives were monotonous, but there is no comparison between that exterior monotony, which is accompanied by a very intensive internal life, and the horrid monotony of modern city streets—all horrifically identical, with absolutely nothing interesting to do. What made me sadder was thinking about all those many novices leaving Gethsemani to live in these cities. It does not surprise me that so many of them decide to return, so soon after leaving. I am certain that if I had gone to live out in the world, of my own accord, I would have immediately asked for reinstatement back in Gethsemani. I tell you all of these things because perhaps you might want to pass along my message to them during your conference with the novices in Gethsemani. I am always remembering them, and keeping them in my prayers. I wish you could tell them that my experience of the world is that it is unlivable, and if they leave because they think that the world is more interesting, they will regret it immediately, as soon as they leave.

When I arrived in Louisville, I went to a restaurant to eat some sandwiches because it was already noon, but as soon as I opened the door, I turned around and left, horrified by the earthshaking jukebox music. It was horrible, and so loud, that I thought it better to starve to death than to eat with that music. From the outside, behind the glass windows, there appeared to be a profound silence, but the inside was hell. I decided to enter another restaurant, but only after reassuring myself that there would be no music; but just as soon as I ordered my food, the jukebox began to blare. I had no choice but to resign myself. In this, I have seen a preview of the world. From the stillness of the monastery, in can appear to be calm and serene, but once we enter, it is a living hell.

I received the telegram that you sent to the address of Ernesto Mejía Sánchez. I am lodging at the Jesuit university because it is more monastic, with more facilities for Mass, etc., and staying with Father Martínez, and with another Nicaraguan Jesuit, who is also a very good friend of mine. The university rector is also another Nicaraguan Jesuit, and also a friend.

The translations of your poems are ready for publication, and we are only waiting for the illustrations by Armando Morales. I wrote to him and asked about them, before leaving [Gethsemani]. The young guys in charge of the university press are good friends of mine, and they are very happy with the poems. They really like them, and are very impatient to publish the book [*Poemas*]. Apart from this, I am sending you an issue of a magazine with Pasternak's letter, and the latest issue of *La Revista Mexicana de Literatura*, with a few of my poems from *Zero Hour*. They are also going to publish this collection in a small book. I have also been told that my *Epigrams* are about to be published. Mejía Sánchez has read my anti-Somoza poems in conferences, and I have been told that they have been greatly applauded. These poems have also been published in various revolutionary magazines, including a communist one in Chile, directed by Neruda. The translation for [Robert] Lax [*El circo del sol*] will appear in the university magazine [*Revista de la Universidad de México*].

Father Martínez received your letter and will be writing in response in the next few days. He tells me that your letter has made a great impression on him, and has given him much to think about. He sees that my case is like his, and tells me that his own case is like the one of Gerard Manley Hopkins. Father Martínez has suffered much, like Hopkins, and is still suffering; but he tells me that Hopkins resolved his problem in the wrong way. I do not know if Father Martínez will be able to resolve his.

The disturbances continue in Nicaragua. On the day that I arrived in Mexico, there were articles in the newspapers with news about two invasion attempts by the two different fronts—the *Olama* movement, and *Mollejones*—but we do not know if this is true. There are two movements that are preparing invasions in Nicaragua: one, infiltrated by communists, and the other is democratic. There have been protests and rallies in Leon and Managua, students have been shot, many have died, and other people injured. This has now provoked new rallies and protests. The clergy have acted courageously, and the priests have denounced the government from their pulpits. There was also a priest, acting as chaplain, who had gone along with one of the groups, and he has been imprisoned, too, with the rest. All this makes the archbishop's pro-government declarations, which I have included with this letter, all the more inexplicable. My cousin [Pedro Joaquín Chamorro Cardenal], who had been missing in the jungle, has now been found after fifteen days. He has been recognized by the police, and is now in prison. By sheer miracle, it seems to be true that the prisoners have not been tortured this time.

I will write again, once I have more things to tell you about. Please do not feel obliged to respond, if you do not have time. But I count on your prayers, as I always keep you in my own humble ones. I also keep the novices in my prayers too.

In Christ,

Ernesto Cardenal

[P.S.] I am not too sure about the train ticket price. The ticket says, $50.84, but I find it strange that it would be so cheap, because I had it in mind that it was more expensive. Since my family has sent me $50.00, I am sending this to Gethsemani, in case this was the cost of the trip. If this was not the case, I beg that they let me know, so that I can send the difference. OK.

Letter 3

Dear Ernesto:

Thank you for your letter. I was relieved to hear you had finally arrived, because I thought interiorly that the plan would very probably not be quite as simple as it looked on paper. Certainly when it was expected that you would reach Mexico City from San Antonio in eight hours, I knew it was impossible. And so you had two days in New Orleans: they must indeed have been miserable. I think the weariness of the journey and the other effects of your leaving here, with the inevitable letdown, must have been chiefly responsible for your sadness. I know of course how you would feel, and it was to be expected.

You came here under ideal conditions, and everything was of a nature to make you happy and give you peace. You had given yourself completely to God without afterthought and without return, and He on His part had brought you to a place where the life was unexpectedly easy and pleasant and where everything went along quite smoothly for you. Hence in reality the first real Cross you met with, in your response to God's call, was the necessity to *leave* this monastery, under obedience, after having been told that it was not God's will for you to stay here.

You must not regard this as the end of your vocation, or as a break in the progress of your soul toward God. On the contrary, it is an entirely necessary step and is part of the vital evolution of your vocation. It is a step in your spiritual maturity, and that is why it is difficult for you. Certainly it would have been pleasant to remain in the state of almost passive irresponsibility here—that is one of the qualities and one of the vices of this monastery: everything is geared to keep one passive and, in a certain sense, infantile. This is, from a certain point of view, excellent, and it can quickly bring many souls into a state of detachment and peace, which favors a certain interior life. But unfortunately also the peculiar circumstances of this monastery prevent real spiritual growth. Underneath the superficial and somewhat false good humor, with its façade of juvenile insouciance, lie the deep fear and anxiety that come from a lack of real interior life. We have the words, the slogans, the notions. We cultivate the pageantry of the monastic life. We go in for singing, ritual, and all the externals. And ceremonies are very useful in dazzling the newcomer, and keeping him happy for a while. But there seems to be a growing realization that for a great many in the community this is all a surface of piety, which overlies a fake mysticism and a complete vacuity of soul. Hence the growing restlessness, the rebellions, the strange departures of priests, the hopelessness which only the very stubborn can resist, with the aid of their self-fabricated methods of reassurance.

Your own interior life was perfectly genuine. God gave you many graces and brought you close to Himself, and perhaps you would never have come so close to Him anywhere else. For these last two years, Gethsemani was ideal for you, and you must regard it as a great grace that God brought you here. It is something that has changed the whole direction of your life. But at the same time if you had remained here, the general spirit of unrest in the community and the growing fear of falsity which have disturbed so many of our best vocations and made them leave, would have reached you too. And by that time you would have been professed, and in a very difficult position.

The fact that you were in danger of developing a stomach ulcer was a warning sign of the very painful and harmful experiences that would have awaited you if you had stayed here, and I assure you that the happiness you had known in the novitiate would not have lasted long.

What next? You must wait patiently, prayerfully, and in peace. No one can say yet whether you should enter another monastery. I do not know if you will be happy in the choir anywhere, since you do not sing. I advise you not to think too much about whether or not you are happy. You will never again reduplicate the feeling of happiness that you had here, because it is not normal to do so. You would not have known such happiness even if you had remained. Your life now will be serious and even sad. This is as it should be. We have no right to escape into happiness that most of the world cannot share. This is a very grim and terrible century, and in it we must suffer sorrow and responsibility with the rest of the world. But do not think that God is less close to you now. I am sure you are closer to Him, and are on the path to a new and strange reality. Let Him lead you.

J. Laughlin tells me that he is publishing my translation of your Drake poem ["Drake in the Southern Sea"] in the New Directions annual. Along with some poems of Pablo [Antonio Cuadra]. [Robert] Lax will be glad to hear that *The Circus [of the Sun]* is being printed in Mexico. Have you contacted Mira?

I have little time now, so I will finish and write you again later. Keep me posted, and let me know when you enter at Cuernavaca [Benedictine Monastery of the Resurrection in Mexico]. I told the novices your message, that the world was unlivable, and they received it with awe. I am sure they do not doubt it. If one wants a pleasant and harmless existence, certainly Gethsemani is the place for it. And I don't think the average novice who enters here will ever be deeply affected by the sense of nullity and falsity that underlies the façade. Yet it is strange how some of them remark on the tension. A more mature postulant, who stopped at a French monastery on the way here, says he felt no tension at all in the French monastery, but feels it here. It is very strange, and I think very significant.

Please give my best regards to Dom Gregorio [Lemercier, O.S.B., Superior at Cuernavaca], and say I pray for him and for his monastery. Your description of it sounded very beautiful.

And now, God bless you. Best regards also to Fr. Martínez, to Mejía Sánchez, etc. And here is a letter from Morales, in Peru. Nothing from Pablo Antonio yet about the islands. With all affection, in Christ,

F. Louis

[P.S.] The magazines just arrived—many thanks.

Letter 4

[Handwritten]

FEAST OF ST. LOUIS [AUGUST 25, 1959]

REV. F. LOUIS O.S.C.O.

GETHSEMANI

Dear Father Louis:

Today, the feast of St. Louis, is my second day in Cuernavaca. On the evening before coming here I received your beautiful letter of the 17th—quite auspiciously, with the miraculous opportunity with which the Lord sends all things to me. In this letter you admirably prepare my spirit to enter here. You instilled a great peace inside me, and I received your letter as if it had been seen directly by God himself—dictated by Him. I have been left feeling grateful to Him, and to you for this letter. It is the most important one that I have ever received in my life. It reminds me of the first letter that you sent to me when I was about to enter the Trappists, the one that I did not dare respond to because, thinking that you did not know Spanish, I found myself incapable of adequately responding to such a letter in English. Now, again, I also feel incapable of answering your letter, even in Spanish.

The following morning I went to say "good bye" to Father Martínez, and helped him out with his Mass, and after the Mass, I also showed him your letter and had him read it. He read it with much thoughtfulness and awe, and asked me to leave it with him, in order to read it over and over again, and meditate more about it on his own, and later, he brought it back to me in a taxi.

I am convinced about what you told me, that I should not place so much significance on the happiness I experienced as a novice in

Gethsemani, or assume that this should be recaptured in some way, or believe that it must be necessarily related to my union with God. Still, I am happy, not with the drunken exaltation with which I entered Gethsemani, but with great peace. The oppressive experience that I had when I first visited here has not presented itself again this time. But still I feel no attraction to become Benedictine. I am feeling a peaceful happiness, and with a kind of indifference, but void of repugnance or attraction for them. About the only thing that I am certain of is that I do not want to return to the world.

Upon saying goodbye, Father Martínez said the same thing that you believe, and that I also believe with more conviction every day: that I should be a priest. The Jesuits have recommended the seminary in El Salvador, which they run. They tell me that I would probably not be able to advance my studies in Nicaragua because there is a shortage of professors, and I would have to conduct my studies along with everyone else there; however, in El Salvador, they would make sure I could study philosophy within one year. Also, they are offering me free enrollment, otherwise this financial matter would be another problem. Adapting to Jesuit training will be difficult for me, but any seminary will be difficult, so I gladly accept this if it is God's will. Classes in El Salvador begin in February. I could wait here in Cuernavaca: my tourist visa in Mexico expires precisely in February. They are also recommending a late-entry vocation seminary in Salamanca, but I do not want to go to Spain.

Dom Gregorio has not yet called me to speak with him, and I have yet to lay out all of these plans before him, nor have I given him your letter to read. Today, he was going to Mexico City for the day.

I am staying in the guesthouse, in a marvelous room with a large window, the width of the entire room, from which you can view the entire valley, and the city of Cuernavaca. It is a city of about eighty thousand people, and during the night, it is quite a beautiful spectacle to gaze down, there below—as if from the sky—all the city lights, lit.

I think that the first negative sensation that I had when I first arrived here was due to a kind of fixation that I had in mind of the memory of the Trappists, which was keeping me away from reality. I did not like the Office [Hours of the Holy Office] in Spanish because the cadence was different from the one in Gethsemani, but I have now grown accustomed to it, and enjoy the Office very intensely, even more so than in Gethsemani. I also did not like the habit here because I found it ugly, in comparison with ours, which had so much aesthetic beauty—I still miss it. Moreover, all I saw here were strangers' faces, instead of a community where I had settled in. Here were none of my novice peers, for whom I had felt great affection, and still do, including for those who had already departed before I left, but inside me, they still continue to be present in my memory of the Trappists. Please tell the novices that I am always praying for them, as I did when I was there.

I am *Proustian*, and live through memory. More than anything, I will feel nostalgia for those days—the days when I lived less from the past, more than in any other time in my life, and rejoiced in the beauty and happiness of the present. As time goes by, I begin to forget the difficult details, and only remember the happiest moments—the most poetic aspects of the Trappists. However, this does not matter because I know that these days in Cuernavaca will later equally turn into unforgettable memories.

Dom Gregorio is building small groups of cells in the community of the monastery, and said that he will transfer me to one of them, just as soon as they are finished constructing them. With time, he plans to put the entire community into little groups of five or six isolated cells— something more similar to *Subiaco* than *Montecassino*—and leave the actual monastery solely for the guests, the novices, and the community projects.

They are finishing up the church built by a monk, which is the most beautiful and unique church that I have ever seen in my life. It is round and made up of odd-shaped stones of different sizes, with no windows, like a well. In the center, over a circular base made up of black stone, lies the altar, like a small stadium. The light shines in directly from the sky through a pierced opening in the ceiling made from mica stone—it looks like a circus tent. One has the sensation of being inside a hole in the ground, or inside a volcanic crater, or a prehistoric cavern.

My Mexican friends, all of them left-wing, and some of them still communists, have welcomed me with great enthusiasm. They were very interested in my experiences with the Trappists and would not tire of asking questions, and I did not tire from telling them all about it. All have asked to come and visit me in Cuernavaca, and I have told all to come. Leon Felipe is the most interesting case of all—one of the best Spanish poets living in exile. He had always been religious, but heretical, and even blasphemous, and especially resentful against the Church over the question of Franco. Now he is more religious than ever after the death of his wife, and with his friendship with Father Ángel Martínez he is practically a convert. We have given him your books, and he is reading them avidly, staying up all night. Felipe is coming to visit me with Father Ángel next week. I will send you a few of his poems. We also gave him your essay to read about Pasternak, "Boris Pasternak and the People with Watch Chains." This is a stupendous essay. Father Ángel Martínez likes it very much. Mejía Sánchez wants to see if he can publish it in Mexico, even if it already appears in *Sur*, because he considers it very important.

I am sending you back the letter by Morales that you gave me to read. The book [Cardenal's translation of Merton, *Poemas*] is ready, and now they are only waiting for the illustrations. I have written to Pablo Antonio Cuadra, urging him to send them. *La torre de Babel* will be published with a collection of theatrical works of the university, and we gave "Prometheus: A Meditation" and the "Signed Confession" to the *Revista de la Universidad de México*. Robert Lax will appear in the next volume of *Revista Mexicana de Literatura*. Mejía Sánchez has been very instrumental in making all of these arrangements. I am very pleased with New Directions' publication of "Drake in the Southern Sea."

Father Martínez meant to write you this week when he had some free time. They overwhelm him with so much work that he does not even have time to perform his *Acción de Gracias*. Many times he must collapse in bed with pain from his ulcers. I think he suffers very much.

Forgive my abuse with this very long letter. I am praying for you a lot, especially today, and every single day, and for the novices too. Please give them my best.

An embrace in Christ,

Ernesto Cardenal

Letter 5

Dear Father Louis:

I am sending you some poems about Gethsemani, copied down in haste. There I had them in notes, and here, I have more or less given them a more definitive shape and form. I am not too sure about them. They seem to me somewhat mediocre. I think the ones I wrote before joining the Trappists were better. For me, these mainly have the value of serving as documentation from those days. I am writing others that I will send to you much later. If I publish them, I am thinking of titling them: *Gethsemani, Kentucky*. What do you think?

I have just finished reading your article about Mt. Athos in *Jubilee*, which the monks have lent me, and it is very interesting. Especially the ending.

My stomach is doing well. Every day I am doing better. So I think that I am getting cured. My spiritual life remains the same: very passive and very simple, so simple that I almost do not feel it. I only know that God dwells inside me because I feel myself detaching from everything, and when I am alone and in silence, I am happy. While I was in Mexico, I felt strangely impervious to all city life, and also happy. During those days in Gethsemani, I almost could not perform a single prayer, nothing more than a tacit prayer, because just as I attempted to make it more formal, I would feel my stomach aching. This does not happen to me now. I also attend all the hours of the Divine Office without feeling any aches.

I think that the smoking has done me good. Ever since I left Gethsemani, I have been smoking, but only very little, as you advised: about seven cigarettes a day.

Armando Morales held an exhibition in Lima with tremendous success. Painters, critics, and all the newspapers have been unanimous in saying that he is the biggest thing in painting that they have seen in a long time, and the sales of his paintings have broken all the records.

Father Jacinto Herrero has written me to say that his superiors have advised him to perform his ministry in Avila for a couple of years, and that he should decide later in regards to his contemplative vocation. He tells me that this is how he will do it, and charges with me sending his regards. I think Mira is coming in a few days, because he has already been admitted.

By chance today I read a Mexican newspaper, and found out that a friend of mine was in the Argentine rebellion against the Argentine president. He is General Carlos Toranzo, who had been ambassador to Nicaragua. He had lived near my house, and we had been very good friends. Carlos had been one of the principle leaders in the revolution against Perón. Now the new president has decommissioned him, but the military is rebelling because he is very popular among them, and they refuse to follow the president's orders. I do not know what is going to happen. He is very Catholic, is very democratic, and a great person.

In Nicaragua they continue to prepare a bigger invasion than the first one. The failure of this one was due in part because the Nicaraguan communists prevented Fidel Castro from sending the help that he had once offered my cousin, Pedro Joaquín, with whom he had sympathized a great deal. They told him that my cousin was a reactionary, and a big American sympathizer, and so then Fidel did not help. There are still two different groups fighting in the mountains of Nicaragua. One of them appears to be helped by Castro because he is a Nicaraguan, who had fought with Castro, and had given him a lot of money for his revolution. However, I do not know what kind of political leanings he has. My brother Gonzalo is currently leading the underground movement inside Nicaragua, taking part in dangerous activities, like the smuggling of arms, communicating with revolutionaries abroad, and building dynamite bombs and placing them inside Somoza's buildings and those belonging to *Somocistas*. I have only recently found out about all of this, when my brother-in-law stopped by here, in Mexico, and came to visit me in Cuernavaca, because they had not been able to inform me of these things before by letter. They are in great need of our prayers.

You are always my first intention in Mass and throughout many hours of the Divine Office. I also pray a lot for the novices. Did the pieces of ceramic that I sent to the kiln of St. Meinrad arrive [in Gethsemani]?

In Christ,

Ernesto Cardenal

Letter 6

Dear Ernesto:

Not only have I received two good letters from you but a charming one also from your dear grandmother thanking me for helping you, etc. I can see indirectly from her letter and from what she says people say of you that your stay at Gethsemani made a very great difference in your life and that you have changed and developed remarkably. It is my own experience that God did much work in your soul when you were here and I believe He will continue to carry on this good work, all the more so when you are passive and quiet and content to let Him work without desiring to see anything that He is doing.

I am very pleased to hear that your stomach is better. That is a good sign also, but you must expect that in times of stress you will have the same trouble. It may happen that trouble in the stomach may come when you are evolving toward a change or a new step—when a new phase of your life is beginning to come into being. When the step is made, the stomach will be quiet.

Both Dom Gregorio and I agree that it is utterly providential that the Jesuit Fathers have offered you hospitality in their seminary and will educate you for the priesthood without charge. This is another evident sign of God's love for you, and with all peace and joy you should accept it, with no anxiety and care about where or how you will exercise this priesthood when the time comes. Simply receive the necessary education and seminary training, with great humility and love, and do not fear the effects of a different kind of formation. If for some reason it is insisted upon that you behave officially as a Jesuit-formed spirit, let your conformity with the party line make contact with only such men as [Jean Pierre de] Caussade, [Jean Nicolas] Grou, Lallemente, etc. who are all strong on peace, passivity, abandonment, and not aggressive or systematic at all. But I am sure any director will recognize in you the value of your tendency to silence, childlikeness, and peace.

The pieces of ceramic work returned from St. Meinrad and the larger crucifix is definitely one of your very best works. It came out a deep brick red, and has a very heavenly and spiritual joy about it, which I like greatly. I am having Fr. Gerard put it on a walnut cross, and it will hang here in our room. I will have a picture taken of it if I can. The other smaller pieces are all good. Should I try to send you any of them?

Dom G. showed me pictures of the church of the monastery at Cuernavaca and it is certainly very interesting and effective. I should imagine that saying Mass there with the roof open to heaven must be a wonderful experience. His visit here was a great success and we had some good talks. It is good to find someone who agrees so completely with one's views on the monastic life. I am sure your stay there will be very profitable and that it will carry you forward, far beyond what you reached when you were here. Gethsemani is a very limited place, in its way. The Holy Spirit is certainly working here, but there comes a point where further development is frustrated or impossible and where truth becomes seriously falsified. Of course I suppose that is true wherever human institutions are found.

Your poems about Gethsemani [*Gethsemani, KY.*] are very effective and have a special meaning for anyone who knows the scene and the incidents. The simplest ones are the best—for instance the little song "*Hay un rumor de tractores . . .*" and the other one about the smell of the earth in the spring in Nicaragua, and the ones that bring to mind contrasts and comparisons with Nicaragua. The one about the snow is very effective: perhaps it is the best. Though once the statement is made here, it loses force when repeated, more diffusely, in the other poem where the pigs and the motor horn come in. The paradox there is good, but less successful.

I think you are right in saying that these are less good than the ones you wrote before coming here. Certainly they have less power. But they should be what they are, simple and quiet and direct. And with that charming Chinese brevity. On the other hand your poems in the *Revista de la Literatura* are splendid. They constitute some of the few really good political poems I have read—they have the quality, and even more, that the left-wing poets had in the thirties. They are powerful and arresting and I am very happy with them. I wish I knew more about the background and the story. I think they are clearly your best poems.

I have been reading some more of [Jorge] Carrera Andrade and think I will have to translate some of them. He is very good.

Stephen Spender's wife came through here and we had a very fine conversation together. She is a splendid person, very interested in religion, liturgy, St. John of the Cross, yoga, etc. etc. I told her about Corn Island [an island off the coast of Nicaragua where Cardenal and Merton thought about founding a monastery] and she was enthusiastic. I have had no information about it though, and do not know whether the bishop will stop by to talk about it.

Morales's letter was deeply moving and I can see part of the reason why his exhibit was a great success. The news fills me with joy and I hope to hear more about it, see some reproductions of the pictures. I hope the book of poems is coming along, with the illustrations. I am returning his letter. I pray for him as well as for you and Pablo Antonio every day at Mass, not forgetting Mejía Sánchez and P. Martínez.

Fr. Paul of the Cross left, but I am forwarding your letter to him.

I shall keep Gonzolo in my prayers and Masses. It is dangerous work but I hope it will be fruitful. I think you must all go a little slow, and don't depend too much on [Fidel] Castro. I think he is a little out of his depth and there is danger that he may make decisions and gestures that have no basis in reality, in order to salvage something of his own position, which will be more and more menaced. Take it easy. There is great danger that the revolution in Nicaragua may serve as nothing but a cat's paw for the Communists. Let *them* get burnt. However, I cannot claim to know the political situation.

I value and appreciate your prayers. Keep them up. I am sure God will hear them. I have great confidence in the future, though I do not know exactly what will come out. I think there is considerable hope of a really constructive answer and solution to everything. More later.

God bless you, and please mention to your grandmother that I was very happy about her letter, which I will try to answer when I get time.

With all affection, in Christ,

F. Louis

Letter 7

Though the extant copy of much of this letter is cut off at the right margin and therefore incomplete, it is possible to reconstruct the gist of the letter. Merton had received "good news" from Dom Gregorio Lemercier; it seemed to him that the dispensation permitting Merton to leave Gethsemani would be granted. Though Merton did not yet know whether or not Rome had contacted Abbot James Fox, who was at the time hospitalized in Bardstown, Merton was taking the opportunity to write "a conscience matter" letter detailing his plans for traveling to Mexico via Albuquerque, New Mexico, where he could look at Indian pueblos and perhaps "make a kind of retreat in the desert." He wondered about what papers he would need (passport, visa, tourist card) and alerted Cardenal that he would be sending packages of books, from time to time, to be held for his arrival. One "small trial" was his health (Merton was later hospitalized for an operation in mid-October). Sickness, he noted, could be providential, slowing down a man when he was about to turn an important corner. This move was "such a wonderful opportunity" to "realize in actual fact" the simplicity of the monastic life, get away from "all the artificiality," and find the ideal in true purity and solitude. To the typed letter, Merton added a note in his own hand.

OCTOBER 8, 1959

Dear Ernesto:

I have received very good news from Dom Gregorio in Rome. He has seen Father Larraona and it seems that the dispensation will be granted, but still the Superiors of the Order must be consulted and this may be quite an obstacle. But it seems as if in the long run the move will be completely successful. This is very fine and encouraging news, and is certainly the result of much prayer, including your own prayers, for which I thank you. Keep them up; they are more necessary than ever.

I have written Dom Gregorio a letter, which was mailed in the usual way, open, and so I was not able to speak very freely. Father Abbot does not know all the details as yet, as far as I can tell, though I have told him in a general way that since I cannot obtain a leave of absence from him, I am appealing to Rome. I do not know whether or not Rome has yet contacted Father Abbot. At the moment he has been in the Bardstown hospital with a hernia operation.

Since I can more easily write you a conscience matter letter, I think I will take this opportunity to send you some important remarks, which you can convey to Dom Gregorio at the proper time.

First of all, about entering Mexico. I think it would be safer if I got a passport and a regular visa to enter as a permanent resident. This will take time. If there is some special difficulty I will simply enter, as you did, on a tourist card. I imagine that to obtain a visa I would have to have some kind of document or affidavit from Dom Gregorio. I hope he will know what to do, and will take steps to produce the necessary evidence that I will have a home and support in Mexico. This could be sent when it is definite that I am to come.

The plan I thought would be most convenient would be, when I get the indult, to leave here and go to Albuquerque, New Mexico, and take up the question of the visa with the Mexican consul there. While I am waiting for things to materialize I could then take a look at some of the Indian pueblos in that region, which would be very interesting. I could even perhaps spend a few days on one of the missions and make a kind of retreat in the desert.

If Dom Gregorio thinks best, I would simply come to Mexico as fast as possible on a tourist card and then get the visa later, as you have done.

From time to time I will send you packages of books—they will be *our* books and perhaps you could keep them for me. I think there is still one book of yours here, Max Jacob. I will enclose that in one of the packages.

One small trial is my health, at the moment. There have been some complications in my usual infirmities. I hope I do not have to spend any time in the hospital. I think it is just a providential event that will help me prepare for a new step. Often sickness has the function of slowing a man down when he is about to turn a corner. Please pray that it may be no more than this and that everything will go well. This is such a wonderful opportunity to reach out for a more simple and solitary life, and to put into practice the ideas that have come to me for so many years. It would be a shame to spoil it. I am very happy that things are turning out well, and I want to correspond perfectly with the opportunity. It is so important to try to realize in actual fact the simplicity of the monastic ideal, and to get away from all the artificiality that grows up in the monastic institution. Let us pray that we may find the ideal of a simple, non-institutional, contemplative life in the mountains, in true poverty and solitude. Meanwhile I hope there will be a little house available soon, when I get there.

[Vertical by hand in the lefthand margin] How are you? I have not heard anything from you since Dom Gregorio brought your poems [*Gethsemani, KY.*]. I am wondering if a letter of yours has failed to reach me. If you answer this one, it had better be a matter of conscience. Let me know any other advice or suggestions you think would be useful. When traveling in Mexico, perhaps I ought simply to dress as a layman. I will need prayers in the next two or three weeks as the struggle with Father Abbot [James Fox] may be quite difficult, though there is nothing he can do now, at least as far as I am concerned. Keep well, and may God bless you. Faithfully in Christ our Lord,

F. Louis

Letter 8

[Letterhead]

ST. ANTHONY HOSPITAL

ST. ANTHONY PLACE

LOUISVILLE, KY

OCTOBER 17, 1959

Dear Ernesto:

I am in the hospital for a few days, but it is only a matter of a minor operation and everything will be all right. I hope to be fully recovered in a day or two.

So far there is no indication that Father Abbot has heard anything from Rome. At least he has not said anything to me about it, and his attitude does not indicate that he feels upset about anything. I should be very surprised if he had heard from Rome, and at the same time I presume that nothing will be done until he is consulted. Hence I may have to wait quite a long time. But it is worth being patient about.

Before I came to the hospital I got all the Carmelite nuns at the Louisville Carmel to pray for this intention. I also had the happiness of saying their proper Mass of St. Teresa on the Feast day—which was the day of my operation. I am sure their prayers will be very powerful.

[D. T.] Suzuki is finally sending his preface to my Desert Fathers' book. It has not arrived yet but it should be very interesting. I am very happy about it.

Naturally I look forward very much to coming to Mexico, and continue every day to pray that this venture may be successful for the glory of God. One must expect obstacles and difficulties but there seem to be so many indications that this is God's will and I trust He will bring it to completion in His own way. I look forward to hearing news from you when Dom Gregorio returns from Rome. I am very pleased that his requests were successful and that Cuernavaca is now established as a priory.

I remember you every day at Mass, along with Pablo Antonio and all your intentions for Nicaragua. And I know you will not forget to pray for us. I am expecting to return to the monastery tomorrow or the day after. There is no special news at Gethsemani—everything is as usual. There are very few new postulants, but Fr. Robert made his profession on October 4.

With all best wishes to you, and all affection in Christ our Lord,

F. Louis.

Letter 8a

Dear Father Louis:

I have just received your stupendous letter, which has given me much joy. I am extremely happy and am giving many thanks to God because everything is turning out so well, as we have asked. During the Mass and all the hours of the Office I have been asking most especially for this intention, and it seems that it is God within me who has been seeing to it that I have this intention permanently in the Office, and I will do so even more during these last remaining days.

I am also very grateful to you for your other letter, after mine in which I sent the poems. I had not written you again since then because I thought that Dom Gregorio would pass through Gethsemani again on his return, and I was waiting to see what new news he would bring—and in the meantime I had nothing new to tell you. Apparently Dom Gregorio was not going to pass through Gethsemani again on his return since you have sent me this letter for him. We expect him this week and I will give him the letter as soon as he arrives.

Pablo Antonio has just sent me Morales's illustrations. They seem marvelous to me, as they do to him. I sent them to Mejía Sánchez so that he would take them to the university. They would proceed immediately to publish the book since they were eager to begin, and I told them that while they prepared to publish the text they could send you the illustrations so that you could see and approve them (which approval I was sure you would give). If they no longer had time because they were going to publish the illustrations immediately, [I asked] that they would at least send you the page proofs. I do not know if they will do one or the other. But perhaps neither the one nor the other is now necessary since you are coming soon and can see them here yourself.

A guest who came to the monastery told me that some friends of his have made some translations of your poems and were expecting to publish them around December. He told me that they would bring them first to me so that I could review your translations.

I suppose that you will want to stay a few days in Mexico City before coming to Cuernavaca to see some important things (Our Lady of Guadalupe, murals, bookstores, the pyramids of Teotihuacán, some persons, etc.). In that case I would want to go spend those days in Mexico to be your guide in the city. You would have to notify me of your exact date of arrival so that I may go to meet you.

I suppose it will be best for you to come in completely secular clothes. Some priests use the Roman collar, but it is not necessary, nor is it common.

I will keep here those books of yours that you send me. Please send the copy of the poems of Gethsemani that I sent you with Dom Gregorio, if you still have them, since I have lost one of them. You do not need to send me any of the ceramic figures that I made there, since I have the molds and can make them over again. But I would like—if you can—a photo of the crucifix in the novices' chapel.

I am sending you a letter that Pablo Antonio wrote me. Everything he says about Ometepe [another possible location for a contemplative foundation] seems very good to me. But it also seems to me that Corn Island is a marvelous place. The ideal would be to live for some time in both places. I wrote to the bishop of Bluefields [Carthusian Bishop Matthew A. Niedhammer] when I left Gethsemani, as you had told me. I do not know if he got to talk with you. He did not respond to me, but he had no reason to do so.

I hope your illness will be nothing serious, and I will also be praying a lot for your health during these days. I have again begun to feel bad as before; at times I am better and at times worse. When Dom Gregorio comes I will ask him if I can see a doctor, since he offered me medical treatment should I need it. I do not know if this will be an obstacle to entering the seminary in February as I had planned. I will see what the doctor says, and also what you advise me. Whatever happens does not worry me because, since it is something outside my control, it will be God's will and, that being so, it will also be what is best for me. I will write Father [John] Eudes [Bamberger], because he told me to let him know how I was doing once I had been here a while, and because if I still did not feel well he could advise me what to do.

I have no apparent reason for not being well, because in every other way I live a life of total peace and much happiness, of perfect solitude and silence. I spend time on the Office, lectio divina, Latin, some literature, prayer, scripture, and a new translation of the psalms into Spanish, which we are doing in the monastery, and I think it is turning out to be stupendous. I do not have problems or anything that worries me. I do not think of the future, I am one with the will of God, and I live completely in the present.

I am reading *The Sign of Jonas* for the third time. I read it the first time when it was published, with a purely literary interest. I read it again, with a different interest, when I was about to enter Gethsemani. Now it has a new interest for me after having lived, more or less, the whole book. I was planning to read only certain passages because I had already read it twice, but I found that all of it interested me and I could not skip even one line.

Mira is here in the guesthouse waiting for Father Prior in order to enter the novitiate. He is very happy to have come here and not to Gethsemani. Also in the community is Franco, the one from Oaxaca, who applied for admission to Gethsemani and you advised him to reenter this monastery. He is very happy to have done so. He says he is very happy and is very grateful to you for your advice, and he has asked me to give you his best. I hope that God will continue to hear our prayers. In Christ.

Ernesto Cardenal

Letter 9

Dear Ernesto:

I got your letter of the 17th safely yesterday when I returned from the hospital, so everything is OK. Father Abbot left this morning for California and will return before November 1st. Things are evidently going to move quite slowly, but I have every hope of success, though I have not the slightest idea what is taking place. But that is very well. The thing is in the hands of God and we must let Him work it out as He pleases. Certainly our prayers are being answered, in due season. The only thing that surprises me is that so far nothing difficult or unpleasant has occurred, and somewhere along the line there is going to be a hard and nerve-racking obstacle to negotiate, in the very difficult rupture that will have to made with Gethsemani and with its Father Abbot. That is what I most dread and feel will be most difficult, because of all the personal ties and even obligations that exist. This is what . . . will now require the most prayers and the greatest help of the Holy Spirit. A work of God can often and usually does demand a complete uprooting that is extremely painful and disconcerting, and which requires great fidelity in the one called to do the work. The difficulty comes in the darkness and possibility of doubt, in the mystical risk involved. I am very glad that the danger and the risk appear very clearly to me, and I am resolved to be faithful in this risk and not cling to the security of the established position I have here. But I dread going off with imprecations hurled after me, and being treated as a traitor, etc. This must not be allowed to affect things so much that I become influenced by it. Yesterday I had a very fine long conversation with the prioress of the Louisville Carmel [Mother Angela Collins] who is a fine person and who has her nuns praying for our project. But we will all have to be very determined and struggle without discouragement, trusting in God and accepting difficulty and delay.

That brings me to the question of your own health. I certainly do not think that the stomach trouble you had here will necessarily be an obstacle to your entering the seminary, and I would not let it become an obstacle by worrying about it. The reason for your leaving here was that this life puts an exceptional pressure on one who tends to have ulcers: but seminary life is closer to normal and it would hardly burden you more than an ordinary life would. You will doubtless always be molested with stomach trouble in one form or another so I would just make the best of it; do not let it deter you from undertaking the things that are for God's glory; accept the handicap He has willed for you and take the normal care of your health that will enable you to support the work you have to do.

Pablo Antonio's letter contains a lot of wisdom, and I agree with him that a place like Ometepe has about it all the elements that are called for in a contemplative foundation that is to play a really vital role in Latin American culture and society. It will take a little time before we might be ready for Ometepe but that is the kind of thing that really makes sense. Corn Island has natural advantages, but that is all. I feel, as does Pablo Antonio, that one must also be rooted in the Indian and Latin cultural complex in a very definite way. Besides that, the bishop of Bluefields [Carthusian Bishop Matthew A. Niedhammer], when he finally got around to replying to my second letter, became very timorous and told me that he could not take me unless I were actually *sent* by my superiors. My explanation of this is that I sent the letter to him open, with permission of Father Abbot, and Father Abbot evidently enclosed a letter of his own that put the fear of God into the good bishop and told him, in no uncertain terms, to steer clear of anyone who wanted to leave Gethsemani. The bishop really sounded frightened.

It would do no harm to send proofs of Armando Morales's pictures, as I may yet be a month here, if not more. I am glad that they are very good, and think the whole edition sounds very promising.

I will certainly let you know when I can hope to come to Mexico and it would be wonderful to look at the city and its environs together. I shall want to see all the best things and meet your friends. It will be necessary for me to really soak in the atmosphere of Mexico and get thoroughly acclimatized, though naturally I am not looking for a lot of hectic social life. But it is certainly a duty to become quietly and gradually really a part of the nation and of its life and not simply be a gringo tourist. I just want to look and learn and be quietly receptive for a very long time, and become integrated in the whole cultural atmosphere of the city and the nation. Above all I hope no one will expect me to come as a kind of celebrity with something to say and a part to play, because that would be very harmful to the whole project. Everything should be done quietly and discreetly, for very many reasons—first of all for my own personal and spiritual good, and secondly for the success and right working of the plan. Because it is very important that no publicity be given to the fact that I have left Gethsemani and the Order, but that even those who know about it should understand it simply as a normal leave of absence. Later when the new venture begins, it will make itself understood on its own terms. Above all nothing must be said about new or special projects, and the worst thing that could happen would be for me to be surrounded by eager inquirers and prospective postulants ready to join a "new Order." That would be fatal.

I am glad to hear of Mira and Franco being there, and the fact that they are happy about it sounds very good and augurs well for the future. Give them my best wishes and my blessing, and I will keep praying for them.

I shall take your advice about wearing plain secular clothes. I don't even want to wear black. If I don't look like a priest, at least I don't want to look like a Jehovah's Witness. But of course it all depends what I can get. The suitcase they gave me, to take to the hospital, fell open in the middle of a street in Louisville and I was scrambling around to put books, shirts, etc. back in. It was raining, too. I haven't sent the books yet but I am getting together a package today.

My regards to Dom Gregorio—he will have received the letter from you and one I wrote the last day at the hospital. I still am not sure whether the indult is to be sent to him or to me—or both. The simplest would be, if he gets the original, to send me a photostat. But he doubtless has thought out what he intends to do, and I leave the whole thing in his hands and those of God. When I told the Carmelite prioress how Dom G. had come here and proposed his plan etc., all unexpectedly, her simple comment was: "He who is sent by God speaks the words of God."

So let us keep up our hope and our desire to serve Him truly and sincerely, devoting our limited and fallible wills to Him with all purity and fidelity of heart. It is not a question of building a great edifice, but of living a simple life and preserving as much as possible of the values we already have found, in experience, here and elsewhere—eliminating as far as possible the great defects and obstacles of a highly organized life. A woman wrote recently to the monks: "We would have expected the Trappists more than anyone else to put Christ back into Christmas, and instead you have put cheese into the Mass."

With all affection and blessings, and with great gratitude for your prayers. I remember you every day by name in the memento, with Pablo Antonio, Mejía Sánchez, Armando Morales, etc. God bless you all.

F. Louis

Note on Letter 9

After this letter, and until March of the following year, Merton stops corresponding with Cardenal. Two of Cardenal's letters from this period, dated October 17, 1959, and October 27, 1959, respectively (included in this volume), are not included in the archives of the Thomas Merton Studies Center and thus not available in *Del monasterio*. However, these two letters are published in "Time and Transition," in *Merton Annual*, Vol. 8 (1995): 162–200. In a letter from December 5, 1959, to Father Jean Daniélou, Merton comments on his situation: "My letters are very carefully controlled. Until recently, one of our former novices, Ernesto Cardenal, a Nicaraguan poet, who went to Cuernavaca, had permission to write me conscious-matter letters for direction in his own problems, and messages from Dom G. could come through in that way. Two days ago Father Abbot informed me that a conscious matter from Cardenal had arrived and would be *sent back* to Mexico without being given to me. He pretended to have no other reasons for this than 'it is too much work and Trappists are not supposed to give direction by mail.' He completely ignores the bona fide fact that Cardenal has a very valid reason for consulting me about his own personal problems, which are serious, and which, as a poet, artist, etc., can be well handled by someone who understands those things. Of course he is also my contact with Dom G." (*Witness to Freedom*, 210).

Letter 9a

Dear Father Louis:

I have just received your letter of the 24th, and I have also [received] the one you wrote me from the hospital. I am very happy [. . .] that your stay there was very short because it indicates that [. . .] operation was not serious.

Dom Gregorio came two days ago. I gave him your letters and have just spoken with him today. He told me to write you that you should come with a tourist visa, since the other was currently very difficult to obtain and one would have to wait an extremely long time. Being here, it would be very easy to renew this visa, or, as well, exchange it for a residency visa. He has done this with some foreigners staying here. But it would not be advantageous to give the address of this monastery to the Mexican authorities, because these procedures for exchanging visas are somewhat illegal, and it is best if they do not know the foreigner's place of residence; that way, they will be unable to carry out any vigilance or to maintain any records on him (records and vigilance that hardly exist in any case).

I can only imagine how difficult the departure from Gethsemani must be for you. I had been thinking about that for days. It is a very great test, which very few religious have. It is like leaving one's home and family for a second time. But I was also thinking that perhaps God would make this departure unexpectedly easy for you. As was my departure from my home, which I had feared so much, and which nevertheless was later, by some miracle, so easy that I felt as if I had taken some sort of drug (and my departure from Gethsemani, which was already for me like a second home, was equally simple). I am fully convinced of the immense good that your coming will do for Hispanic

America. As are the three or four persons in this monastery who are aware of your visit (the superiors, since the community knows nothing), and who are waiting for you with extremely intense interest and a great deal of prayer.

It was precisely yesterday that, during the Mass, I was inspired to offer up all my stomach ailments for your plans. But don't think that these ailments are very great, because, on the contrary, they are extremely easy to tolerate. Nevertheless, they are the only ones I can offer up since I have no others, either physical or moral or of any kind; and I think that few people—religious or otherwise—suffer less than I do.

Next Sunday Mejía Sánchez will come to visit me. He will bring the illustrations and poems so that here we can make arrangements for their distribution. I understand that soon he will be able to send you copies of the illustrations, since the university told him that he should personally be in charge of making the prints and I suppose that he was going to proceed to do so immediately.

Morales has just returned to Nicaragua after his trip through South America, where he had great success. He was in the São Paulo Biennial Exposition and there received an award as the best Hispanic American painter, or something like that. He has participated in five international expositions and has received awards in all five.

It is possible that [José] Coronel [Urtecho] will also come to Mexico soon. Fortunately for him, he no longer has a diplomatic post in the government, and he has a son in jail as a revolutionary. He currently does not have economic opportunities in Nicaragua and it is possible that he will come to Mexico in December, where he could give classes in both universities, the national university and the Jesuit university. It would be great if his stay in Mexico coincided with yours.

I have been thinking about which place of residence would be most suitable for you during your stay in Mexico City. Perhaps in a small hotel, discreet and quiet? Or perhaps also in the Jesuits' *Universidad Iberoamericana*, which will be quiet and empty since the students are leaving on vacation in November. There you could choose to live in two parts: in the university itself, staying in the Jesuit community, which is small since there are only five or six living there and some of them will also be on vacation; or in the student residence, where I stayed, which is directed by a Nicaraguan Jesuit who is a very good friend of ours, and which will also be empty. They could give you an apartment there by yourself; in both places you would have a chapel to celebrate Mass.

It would be much better if you came in common, everyday, colored clothing, which is how the Jesuits dress, and that way your presence will be more inconspicuous. It seems to me that we will be able to avoid all undesirable and sensationalist publicity. For that, it would perhaps be advisable that you come with your maternal last name, or simply as Father Louis. Several friends of ours work in the newspapers, and we could later make arrangements with them for a serious, official version of the news, and when it is opportune.

I want to tell you again that the good which your presence will do here is incalculable, especially among certain people—the leftists which are the most important and most energetic groups in Mexico (the Catholic groups are mediocre and reactionary and it is necessary not to mix with them or collaborate in their publications so as not to lose one's reputation). When I have spoken with them I have been impressed with how they go about seeking God along odd paths, or how God mysteriously seeks them within themselves. All they need is the apostolate of a presence such as yours, without preaching, since it is the preaching which has alienated them.

Father Prior has told me that he will make me see Dr. Garza, a famous psychoanalyst in Cuernavaca, a friend of Suzuki, and a disciple of Dr. [Erich] Fromm (though they have told me that Dr. Fromm himself has not been able to cure his own ulcer and, not long ago, was very ill because of it). I think all I need is some orientation talks so that I can treat myself, and so my ailments will not interfere with my vocation, since I do not pretend to be without any suffering.

My cousin Luis Cardenal escaped from the prison in which they were holding him strictly incommunicado, at the foot of the presidential mansion, leaving at night in military dress. Pedro Joaquín Chamorro and one hundred others are being tried in a War Council, which has already become long and tedious.

This morning the monastery is marvelous because the whole community went to some priestly ordination in Cuernavaca and the only ones left in the house are a postulant and myself. I end this letter in order to pray a while for the things that I write you about here, in this empty monastery. I embrace you, in Christ.

Ernesto Cardenal

P.S. Dom G. asks me to tell you that the normal procedure for the indult is that they send it to you. In case it comes to him, he will send it to you immediately. And in case there is some delay, he will get in touch with their procurator in Rome in order to accelerate the process.

Also that I tell you that he spoke with Father [Jean] Daniélou in France and that he is in complete agreement with all the steps you have taken and approves it all.

Also that you should look at number 50 of the *Supplément de La Vie Spirituelle*, where there appears an article on the statutes for hermits, and in which it is stated that the only solution to this problem is exclaustration.

I have received a very charming and friendly letter from Laughlin asking me about you and your plans. I have just answered him bringing him up to date on how things are going.

Odilie Pallais, in Nicaragua, who is interested in this, is offering many prayers for the success of your plans (from her sick bed). And surely also offering up much suffering, because her best prayer is her illness.

Affectionately in Christ,

Ernesto Cardenal

Letter 10

Dear Ernesto:

When your letter [of October 17] arrived three, or maybe two weeks ago, Father Abbot made a lot of difficulty about giving it to me, but he eventually did so. There was not much else he could do, since it was a conscience matter letter. I was glad to get it. And I made known to him that I thought such correspondence should not be interfered with. At the same time I told him that I would assure you that he was unfavorable to it. In a word, there is considerable opposition to the correspondence. But still the rights of conscience remain, and if there is something important then I think he is bound to allow a conscience matter letter to pass. He probably will not pass any other kind of letter, that is from you at Cuernavaca.

The other day Rev. Father left quite suddenly for Rome. I have no doubt his journey was intimately connected with the matter which interests me closely. At first I thought he had left of his own volition. Later I realized that he had been summoned to Rome, in actual fact, by the Abbot General [Dom Gabriel Sortais]. No one knows exactly what is the purpose of this journey, but if he was summoned to Rome against his own will, that puts a different complexion on the matter. However, prayers are certainly needed at the moment. I just learned today that Fr. Larraona, the head of the Congregation of the Religious, has been made a Cardinal. That seems to be very good news, as far as I am concerned. I am sure Dom Gregorio will be equally pleased by it.

I was very interested to hear of the progress on the book of poems. New Directions is bringing out a paperback of my *Selected Poems*, almost the same selection but not quite. Mark Van Doren has written a very fine preface. I wonder if you heard about the trouble his son Charles got into. That TV program, on which he won so much money last year, was "rigged" and Charles was an accomplice to the whole thing, which was very unfortunate. I don't think he clearly realized where it would lead, and he was not the most guilty one. Still, there has been a big fuss about it, with a lot of self-righteous speeches by senators on the shame of lying! As if senators were notable for telling the truth.

I am very happy to hear of the wonderful success of Armando Morales and I hope he will keep it up, though success is not the important thing, but the spiritual work of the artist. And I look forward to receiving copies of his illustrations from Mejía Sánchez—they have not yet arrived but I will inquire about them. It is a pleasure to know that [José] Coronel [Urtecho] may be in Mexico soon. Incidentally, Laughlin will probably be stopping here in December. I will be glad to see him.

About your own difficulties: I hope and pray that your conversations with Dr. Garza will be helpful. Of course, you understand that you will never be completely without difficulties, and I would not be discouraged at all from continuing at the seminary or at the monastery, whichever you prefer. You certainly have a vocation, but not necessarily a conventional type of vocation. Whether you are actually called to the priesthood cannot be decided without further trial, but the important thing is that you have clearly a vocation to a contemplative life, in a general way, and the only thing that needs to be found out is exactly how or where. And that is not too important because wherever you are you will be tending to the same end. The only problem about the priesthood is whether you can be a priest without getting too involved in an exhausting and time-consuming ministry. That is the question. But for the rest you need have no doubts and no fears. God is with you. Incidentally I am touched by the simplicity and kindness with which you offer your troubles for me. With so many friends praying for me I am sure everything must inevitably go very well with me, and no matter how dark and obstructed things may sometimes appear, I have great confidence that everything will eventually work out well. But there is need for patience. I am glad too that Odilie is praying for me. I greatly value her prayers.

Prayers are the most important thing at the moment. And deep faith. The inertia of conventional religious life is like a deep sleep from which one only awakens from time to time, to realize how deeply he has been sleeping. Then he falls back into it. It is true that God works here also, but there are so many influences to deaden and falsify the interior life. A kind of perpetual danger of sclerosis. The psalms become more and more of a comfort, more and more full of meaning when one realizes that they do *not* apply to the conventional situation, but to another kind of situation altogether. The psalms are for poor men, or solitary men, or men who suffer: not for liturgical enthusiasts in a comfortable, well-heated choir. I am sure you have greatly enjoyed the work of translating them.

In a couple of days they will dedicate at Washington the immense new shrine of the Blessed Virgin which looks like a big substantial bank. Strictly official architecture, and the thing that strikes me most forcibly is its evident Soviet quality. There is a kind of ironical leveling process that makes Soviet and capitalist materialism more and more alike as time goes on. Who is more bourgeois than Khrushchev? And he made a very "good" impression in the U.S.A., except on the fanatics who refused to see him as one of their own. A successful gangster, who is now affable and a good family man in his declining years.

I will not continue this letter, as there is not much more news. We wait in silence and in peace for the coming of the Savior—in an advent atmosphere. I pray constantly to Our Lady of Guadalupe. Thank you again for all your prayers and your faith. I agree with everything you said in your letter, everything hopeful and all the positive outlook you express for the future. I think the university would be the best place for the stay you plan in the city.

Trusting that nothing will happen to prevent this letter reaching you, and with all blessings and regards to you—kind memories to Dom Gregorio. I wrote him the other day, and wonder if he received the letter.

With all affection, in Christ,

F. Louis

Letter 11

[Letterhead]

THE BROWN HOTEL, LOUISVILLE

NOVEMBER 24, [1959]

Dear Ernesto:

I told Fr. Abbot I would write you a conscience matter letter and did so at Gethsemani but I don't know if it was sent. Do not be misled by the stationery. I have *not* started on the trip. The indult has not yet arrived and I have no news of it. But Father Abbot has *gone to Rome* and is evidently opposing everything with his power. But I also think he has been called to Rome to answer some questions. He may be back this week.

If the indult is coming, it should come about next week. If you do not hear from me soon—say by December 8th—then perhaps there is something wrong. J. Laughlin is coming here in the middle of December and if you write to him he might get it in time to relay information to me. Father Abbot is very difficult about conscience matter letters now, but I still think he will *have to* let one through. Put not only "conscience matter" on the inner envelope but also "sub gravi."

If all goes well I hope to be there before Christmas. I will come by plane, I hope, and will arrive in the evening about 6:30 or 7 and we can go to the university. If you are not at the airport I will go to the university by taxi and ask for Fr. Martínez.

Gethsemani is *terrible*. Tremendous commerce—everybody is going mad with the cheese business. I want to leave very badly.

Today I said Mass for the [feast] of St. John of the Cross at Carmel. The nuns are praying very hard.

My mind is completely made up to totally cut off all ties that attach me here. It is *essential* not just for my own peace but for the glory of God. I must advance in the way He has chosen for me and I am sure He will make everything easy.

My best regards to Dom Gregorio—it is impossible to say all the things I want to say to you and to him. Pray that we may meet soon. I pray to Our Lady of Guadalupe.

I'll send a telegram to Cuernavaca as soon as I am ready to leave and have freedom to do so.

If things get very difficult, I can be reached via Fr. [Jean] Daniélou, who can always get a conscience matter letter to me, but I think yours will still get through—but there may be difficulties.

God bless you all—pray for me. Thanks for offering your suffering.

If things get *very bad*—I will be in Louisville in January for one day and can be reached through the Prioress of the Louisville Carmel, 1746 Newburg Road, Louisville.

With affection, in Christ,

F. Louis

The letter from Rome for which Merton was waiting was sent on December 7 and arrived on December 17. The indult Merton had sought was not granted.

Letter 12

My Dear Ernesto:

Fr. Prior has given me permission to write Dom Gregorio in the absence of Rev. Father and this is my last chance to get a note to you also. As Dom G. will tell you, a letter from Rome has given absolutely final negative decision of my case. Or at least, a decision so final that I am not at liberty to take any further steps on my own behalf, but can only accept and obey. I must stay here until the Church herself places me somewhere else. I still believe that the mercy of God can and perhaps will accomplish this, but I can only wait in darkness and in faith, without making any move. I have hopes that Dom Gregorio will still be able to do something for me. But what?

I think the reason the Congregation swung in favor of Dom James is that he told them a lot of irresponsible remarks about me by Gregory Zilboorg, a famous Freudian psychiatrist who is respected in Rome and has died recently. Zilboorg said of my desire of solitude that I just wanted to get out from under obedience and that if I were allowed a little liberty I would probably run away with a woman. I don't pretend to be an angel, but these remarks of Gregory Zilboorg were passing remarks made without any deep knowledge of me—he had seen me around for a week at a conference at St. John's [University, Collegeville, Minnesota]. We had not had much to do with each other, he never analyzed me, and Fr. [John] Eudes [Bamberger] said that Z. frequently made rash statements on the spur of the moment, which he later changed. Well, anyway, I think that is why Rome rejected my case, for certainly Dom James will have made everything possible out of these statements of Zilboorg. He has probably made enough out of them to queer my reputation in Rome forever. I remember now that you may have seen Zilboorg when he came here—or was that before your time?

I have seen the illustrations of Morales and they are fabulous—I wrote Mejía Sánchez about them. I think Mejía Sánchez will be able to reach me still with correspondence about the poems. I would like half a dozen copies of the book at least, and be sure to send me yours when they appear. Could I have a subscription to the *Revista Mexicana de Literatura* and to the *Revista de la Universidad*? I think they will still get through. Of course there is always Laughlin, if there is something important. He will be down in January. However, as I say, for my own part I can only obey the Congregation and remain passive and I have no hope of making any move to leave this Order. I have in fact promised not to leave, but will only await the action of the Church to move me elsewhere if she sees fit.

So many people have prayed hard for me: their prayers will not be lost. I received the decision of Rome without emotion and without the slightest anger. I accept it completely in faith, and feel a great interior liberty and emptiness in doing so. This acceptance has completely liberated me from Gethsemani, which is to me no longer an obstacle or a prison, and to which I am indifferent, though I will do all in my power to love and help those whom God entrusts to me here. I know we will always be united in prayer, and I assure you of all my affection and of the joy I have had in our association. Do continue to write poetry, or above all continue with your art. Everyone thinks highly of your poetry. Laughlin will probably come and see you some day. I must now get this letter out before Rev. Father returns. I suppose Pablo Antonio will still be able to write. I close with all love to all of you—all my affection in Christ Crucified and Risen. *Christus Vincit, alleluia.*

F. M. Louis

Merton's exchange of letters with Cardenal was interrupted when Dom James Fox prohibited him from corresponding with Cardenal. Merton resumed writing to Cardenal in March 1961. (From *Time of Transition*)

Note on Letter 12

In his letter to Dom Gregorio Lemercier, of the same date, December 17, 1959—which he attaches to this letter to Cardenal—Merton mentions to him the prohibition of maintaining correspondence with Cardenal: "Besides, I should tell you that when Dom James wanted to forbid me to correspond with Cardenal, and I advanced my reasons, saying that I considered Cardenal as an intimate friend, at that moment I could see Dom James's expression. He was triumphant. To say that I had an intimate friend was quite simply to acknowledge a particular friendship. How happy he was. He was totally vindicated. I was a homosexual . . ." (*Witness to Freedom*, 213). At the end of the letter, referring to Cardenal and their friendship, Merton adds: "I regret very much that I cannot write him even a brief word" (*Witness to Freedom*, 214).

Letter 13

Dear Father Louis:

This letter is to give you news about the publication of your book [*Poemas*] at the University of Mexico. The publishing has not started yet because everything here runs very slow, and it appears that the university press has many books to publish; so ours has probably been held up. However, they have promised me that it will come out in the next couple of months (the same has happened with the other two books that the university is publishing for me: my epigrams, and the translation of the Latin epigrams [*Epigramas*]). I have already signed the contract for your book of poems, and the university is going to pay $300 for the author's rights, which will be awarded to me in a few days. What do you think about splitting the money between you, Armando Morales, and me, each receiving $100? I beg you to write me, if this division seems fine to you.

The university will also award us thirty copies of the book, that we can also divide among the three of us (ten copies for each). Another fifty copies will be distributed throughout the university, and to other writers or institutions that we may suggest.

I think Mejía Sánchez will also write to you, telling you all about these details regarding your book. He sent you a few publications a few months ago. I also sent you a few books a while ago, published by the university, and a copy of my poems from *Zero Hour* that came out a while ago. It looks like these poems have been very well received here in Mexico, especially among certain people on the Left, which pleases me very much because I think that with these people, this is a kind of apostleship. They are also publishing for me the poems I wrote here in Mexico about the Trappists. It is a little book called *Gethsemani, KY*, and I will send it to you, as soon as it is published. My grandmother wrote to you, to give thanks for sending the Christmas book, which she had enjoyed immensely.

I continue here in the Monastery because they are providing me with philosophy classes, and it has not been necessary to go to a seminary. I will do it in two years, and afterward, I will go finish up theology at a seminary—I still do not know where, perhaps here in Mexico too. I still continue to suffer from stomachaches. I am under medical treatment, but they still do not know what it is. They think that it might be a form of gastritis, and that it is not psychosomatic as Father Eudes believed, but they still have not cured me. Nevertheless, I am happy because these ailments have drawn me closer to God, and have now become a form of prayer and way of life in the presence of God. I keep you always in this prayer and in this presence of God.

Affectionately in Christ,

Ernesto Cardenal

Note on Letter 13

This letter from Cardenal, the only one from 1960, does not receive a response, which suggests that the ban on Merton's communicating with Cardenal is still in place. Cardenal is conscious of this and careful not to make reference about this occurrence.

Letter 14

February 27, 1961

My Dear Father Louis:

The University of Mexico has already printed my translations of your poems, and I have sent to you, by ordinary mail, the ten copies that were due to you plus twenty more which I have bought with the money paid by the university. The rest of the money ($79.00) I am sending you with this letter in a check.

I would have preferred that the illustrations were full-page, but the publishers thought otherwise (they thought that putting them horizontally across the page would be a bit confusing for the reader and very difficult to understand). But I think they look good anyway.

I read your beautiful and interesting letter to Pablo Antonio, when I was in Nicaragua spending some days with my family. I think some parts of that letter will be published in the next number of *El Pez y la Serpiente*. Thanks for that wonderful edition of *The Ox Mountain Parable*. I am going to translate it for some magazines here, as well as some of the other material you have sent to Pablo Antonio for *El Pez y la Serpiente*.

I will have one more year of philosophy here, and next year I plan to enter the Seminary for the theology (probably here in Mexico City).

Praying for you as always and with all affection in Christ,

Ernesto Cardenal

Note on Letter 14

With this letter from Cardenal at the beginning of 1961 (written in English), correspondence is reinitiated between him and Merton, more than a year after Merton's superiors decide against his plans to leave Gethsemani. The brevity of the letter, as well as the silence regarding the incident that led them to lose contact—along with the previous letter of March 11, 1960—makes one wonder about Cardenal's insecurity regarding Merton's situation and his relationship with Cardenal. During these dates, the prohibition against writing to Cardenal no longer makes any sense, as Merton now desisted from all attempts to leave Gethsemani. After this letter, which Merton responds to almost immediately on March 11, their correspondence develops without difficulty and on a relatively regular basis.

Letter 15

Dom James Fox prohibited Merton from corresponding with Cardenal, discounting the claim that Cardenal was in need of Merton's advice on spiritual matters (see Michael Mott, The Seven Mountains of Thomas Merton, *pages 339–40). Merton resumed writing to Cardenal in March 1961, though he periodically wondered whether they were "still fully in communication" (for example, see Merton's letter to Cardenal dated December 15, 1965).* (From *The Courage for Truth*)

MARCH 11, 1961

Dear Ernesto:

I have received all the copies of the *Poemas* [Spanish translation of *Selected Poems*] . . .

Personally I want to say once again that I think your translation of the poems was a magnificent and truly creative job. It is seldom that a poet is so fortunate in his translators. Reading the poems again I am once again struck by the fact that they have a life of their own in Spanish, almost as though they were destined to be in Spanish as well as in English, by a kind of nativity or *natura* within themselves. In any case, you have found that *natura* and given it expression.

Again the illustrations of Armando Morales are perfect for the book. I agree it is a shame they could not take up the full page in each case, but of course one has to remember the limitations of the ordinary reader and his confusions. The book is very effective even with this limitation. I am glad the three of us could work together to produce this very individual book with all that it says and means. In many ways the pictures are the most powerful and significant part of the book.

I have received the first copy of *El Pez y la Serpiente*, which I think is very fine and I am proud to be a part of it. There are great possibilities here. I am sending on to [Robert] Lax your fine translation of his *Circus* [*The Circus of the Sun*]. Have you seen the whole book? I will get him to send you a copy. It is truly magnificent, a whole cosmic meditation.

Soon *New Directions* 17 will finally appear with the poems I have translated, including one of yours. You will see also the dialogue with Suzuki. I will make sure that copies are sent to you as soon as they are available.

Much has taken place since you left us. There has been a great deal of work in the renovation of the interior of the monastery. The whole chapter room wing is being renewed from within, new floors and everything. It will be very comfortable. Other wings will be renovated in the same way. It takes time.

For my own part, in strange unforeseen ways I have suddenly found myself in a kind of hermitage. Not that I live there or even sleep there, but I have some time during the day to spend there two or three days out of the week. It is very beautiful [and was] built primarily as a quiet place in which to receive Protestant ministers who come in small groups for retreats, a few times during the year. It is on the hill behind the sheep barn, hidden from the novitiate and the monastery by the pine trees, at the head of the field where the cows used to pasture, looking out over the valley. It is a small white house of cement blocks, very solid and with a fireplace and a nice porch. It is completely quiet and isolated, the only trouble being that I am seldom there. The Abbot General was here and visited the monastery and saw this hermitage, which he approved, saying that he felt it was the solution to a problem. Perhaps it may turn out to be so; I hope it will. My chief concern now is to try to arrange things so that I can at least use this house fairly often for contemplation and prayer. My life is one of deepening contradictions and frequent darkness, the chief effect of which is to produce much interior solitude. I try as far as I can to see and do God's will, which certainly leads to solitude. So for the moment this interior solitude is certainly right.

I appreciate all your prayers and those of all the others who pray for me. I hope you will not forget me, and I know you will not. I remember you often in Mass, with all our friends in Latin America and especially in Nicaragua.

I shall continue to send things for *El Pez y la Serpiente*. They will probably have received by now a small piece on the atomic bomb [which Merton rewrote and published as *Original Child Bomb*].

Sudamericana has probably already written you concerning *The Tower of Babel*. Did they tell you if they are going to do it? Did they send you *The Behavior of Titans* by New Directions? It should also go along with *The Wisdom of the Desert*.

It was good to hear that your studies were progressing, and I hope that all will go smoothly. Be patient and follow the way of simplicity with which God has blessed you. But things cannot help sometimes being filled with anguish, for all of us who seek to love Christ. Life is never in any way as simple as it ought to be: there are so many conflicts, not between good people and bad only but between the good and the good. This is worse, and produces unending confusion. We must seek peace in the underlying simplicity that is beyond conflict: and here we seek the naked presence of God in apparent nothingness. If only we find Him, the emptiness becomes perfectly full, and the contradictions vanish. But in order to do this we must be faithful to a will that is inscrutable, which does not reveal itself in simple and clear-cut decisions as we would like to think. Rather than try to find all the nuances of meaning and morality in each case, we must seize hold desperately on the first available indication and trust in God for all the rest.

I especially liked the psalm translations in *El Pez y la Serpiente*. They are filled with the true spirit of the Psalter, and chanting these versions every day must be a fine experience. I remain united to all of you in prayer, that God may lead us all by His light to Himself.

Very cordially in Christ,

Tom Merton

P.S. I have in the hermitage a very small delicate ceramic cross of yours, one of the most primitive and "poor," a Christ of one single narrow line like a neolithic string or worm, *vermis et non homo*, yet all the more *homo* because *vermis*. I like it very much.

Letter 16

Merton wrote the following note by hand below the typed manuscript of "An Elegy for Ernest Hemingway." Hemingway died on July 2, 1961.

[NO DATE, 1961]

Dear Ernesto:

The death of Hemingway was announced in the monastery. I presume you know about it. If Pablo Antonio wants this poem, he is welcome to publish it. Or anyone else you know. I have rewritten the piece on the Atomic Bomb [*Original Child Bomb*]. It is longer and more complete and a few errors have been checked. I will send the new version when it is printed.

The political news from Latin America is bad and confused—or rather it indicates the inner confusion of the U.S. Let us hope that the truth can still be found and vindicated.

With all blessings and best wishes; greetings to all my friends out there. Cordially in Christ,

F. M. Louis

Letter 17

[Handwritten]

AUGUST 16, 1961

Dear Ernesto:

I don't know if I sent you this poem about Auschwitz, "Chant to Be Used in Processions Around a Site with Furnaces." I don't think so, only Hemingway's, "An Elegy for Ernest Hemingway." Ferlinghetti is publishing this one in a new magazine in San Francisco, *Journal for the Protection of All Beings*—and also the text about the atomic bomb, "Original Child Bomb." You can use this one wherever you want.

It is very important to work and pray for peace. Political methods will have no effect because the confusion is too great. The risks are terrible, and the emptiness of men is flourishing in a perfect destruction—but God will not abandon us.

Everything is the same here. *New Directions* 17 should be coming out soon. Laughlin is headed out here this weekend.

With my best wishes to you and Dom Gregorio.

F. M. Louis

Letter 18

[Originally in English]

AUGUST 30, 1961

Dear Father Louis:

Thanks for your Elegy to Hemingway and your CHANT that you sent me. Both are very good. I translated the Elegy, and it was published in the literary supplement of a Mexican newspaper, *México en la Cultura*, which I sent to you. Pablo Antonio published it also in his newspaper in Nicaragua, and I think it will appear in *El Pez y la Serpiente* and also in an anthology of American poetry that is going to be made in Mexico. Many people have liked that poem very much. I also translated your OX MOUNTAIN PARABLE and sent it to a magazine, but it has not appeared yet, I think. I am glad to hear about your publication by Ferlinghetti ["Chant" in *Journal for the Protection of All Beings*]. The anthology of American poetry that I translated with Coronel is going to be published very soon in a big publishing house. The University of Mexico is now printing an early book of poems of mine (*Epigramas*). I am glad to hear about *New Directions* 17.

I have always been sick with my headaches, in spite of medical treatments, but I think I will be able to enter the seminary for theology. I will probably enter the Nicaraguan seminary, and I will go there around November. It is a good seminary now; its spiritual formation is especially good, and at the same time a permanent visa in Mexico is a problem (I see that visa difficulty as a sign of the Will of God to go there).

My life here is always very peaceful, in the love of God and the submission to His Will.

Philip Lamantia, the Catholic beat poet, is temporarily living here at the monastery. We have become great friends, and he is deeply religious now, and very interested in the contemplative life. He has great esteem for you and has liked your recent poems very much. [He] told me to give his regards to you. There have been some conversions here among American beats living in Mexico, Lamantia's friends, and they too sometimes come to the monastery. I instructed the two of them for Baptism, and one is going to become a monk. You have done a lot of good for them through your books.

I am sending you some books that may interest you. Praying for you always,

Yours in Xto.

Ernesto

Letter 19

Dear Ernesto:

It was very good to hear from you, and I am grateful to you for translating the Hemingway poem. It was well presented in the paper and I am glad it is to be reproduced in other publications. It has not yet been printed in the U.S., but I have not been very active about promoting it. The death of Hemingway seemed to me to be a let down (which I indicated in the poem), a final manifestation of the emptiness of his generation. In the poem, the words "unready dynasty" refer to this fact: that the U.S. of the twenties was proud and confident and seemed about to take over the whole world. But when the chance came in 1945, they were not "ready." Hemingway has all along manifested the ambiguities and falsities of this generation, and what followed him is even worse. There was much sincerity there but in the end there was more sham than truth. The great problem of American writers is that they find it easy to attain to a superficial kind of reality simply by setting themselves over against the unreality of the "squares." But this is not enough. It is not sufficient merely to be moons illuminated by the sun of a square society that is almost extinct. Yet that is not true either. There is a lot of disordered animal vigor in the U.S., a huge abundance of it still, rambling and incoherent, discontented, baffled by its own absurdity, and still basically seeking something. I think the search has almost been given up: hence the tragedy of Hemingway, as a sign of the eventual despair of all of them.

Nevertheless there was a solemnity about his death, and about the way he too entered the shades almost as a classic figure in Hades, and passed through our midst by an announcement in the Chapter Room. It was very stirring.

I have been very interested in your translations of the beats and am glad to hear that some of them are visiting you or staying at the monastery. Any poems I have seen of Philip Lamantia lately I have liked. Another ex-novice, poet, since your time (he was a young boy from California, a kind of prodigy) sent some of Lamantia's poems and that was my first acquaintance with him. I don't know if [Lawrence] Ferlinghetti's magazine [*Journal for the Protection of All Beings*] is out yet, with the poem in it. It should be. The Chant ["Chant to Be Used in Processions Around a Site with Furnaces"] was also in *The Catholic Worker,* and some Mennonite magazine is picking it up. An English Dominican wants to print it in England, so I guess it will get around as a peace poem. Some people are shocked by it and cannot stand it. I think it is a little difficult for some readers to accept.

I almost wrote a long letter to Pablo Antonio and think I will do so tomorrow: it will be not only a personal letter but also perhaps a kind of statement of my position in the face of the present situation [published as "A Letter to Pablo Antonio Cuadra Concerning Giants"]. And he can use it in his magazine if he wishes. I think it might be worthwhile to attempt this, and it might be of some interest. For my own part I get so impatient with the stupidity and the inexorable descent into confusion that takes place everywhere, especially in the U.S., that I think it is a moral obligation to say something intelligent if I possibly can.

The shocking thing is that the whole world is being pulled this way and that by two enormous powers that are both practically insane and both insane in the same way, with the same paranoid obsession with power, the same fascination with technological expansion, the same vulgarity, the same brutal stupidity and insensitivity to human and spiritual values (although in the U.S. religion is cynically supposed to be blessing the whole system), the same callous addiction to super-myths, and the same helpless immersion in materialism. The trouble is that because the U.S.

happens to be more inept, more confused, addicted to myths that are more vague and more patently absurd, everyone now begins to respect the other paranoiac because he is more calculating and more efficient. This, in point of fact, only makes him all the worse.

Since beginning this letter I have written the piece I intend to send to Pablo Antonio. It is being typed out now, and it will be mimeographed so I can send you a copy. I don't see any necessity for being tragic about the world situation. It is still a war of nerves rather than of bombs, but [it is] a war of nerves *with* bombs. In such a situation one has to remain objective, without, however, cultivating the fake technological objectivity of the engineers of death, who talk of the extermination of millions as if it were a matter of killing flies. Or those who relish weapons systems the way an aesthete relishes the ballet.

Thank you for sending the interesting books, particularly [Jorge Luis] Borges and Octavio Paz. Also the Indian material and Salomón de la Selva, whom I will read with pleasure. I liked your article on the Nicaraguan poets very much and it reminded me that I am still a great admirer of [Alfonso] Cortés: someday I want to translate some of his poems, if you can send me some. I thought you were much too modest about yourself. I have been in correspondence with a Moslem student of mysticism in Pakistan [Abdul Aziz], who sends very fine letters and interesting books on Sufism, some of which are admirable. I am also working on some versions of parts of the Chinese Taoist Chuang Tzu, without knowing Chinese, but using different translations. John Wu, the Chinese scholar, will come down and help to go over them, and I think we could make an interesting book out of it [*The Way of Chuang Tzu*]. Also I am doing some versions of parts of Clement of Alexandria [*Clement of Alexandria*, published in 1962]. Did I send you the little piece on the atomic bomb [*Original Child Bomb*]? It is coming out with interesting illustrations by Lax's good friend [Emil] Antonucci, who illustrated the *Circus*. Did you get his complete *Circus* book? He was very happy with your translation.

Here are a couple of poems that might interest you. The one on the Moslem angel ["The Moslems' Angel of Death"] is based on an Islamic text, which is splendid and dazzling. I have been very much in contact with Louis Massignon, the scholar most reputed for Islamic studies. Père Daniélou was here. Also Dom [Jean] Leclercq. They were very interested in the hermitage, which is still very fine and the center of my life here.

I should finish now, but I wish you good health and happiness. I know that now you should probably bear with your headaches: they are evidently part of your life. If you can continue to accept them without worry and in peace they will not hurt you. But I wish you all the best and many blessings. We are united in prayer. Please send all my regards to all my friends and tell Pablo Antonio that I will write him soon and send him the article.

With cordial best wishes in Christ,

F. Louis

Letter 20

[Originally in English]

SEPTEMBER 30, 1961

Dear Father Louis:

Thank you for your very good letter, and the two poems that you sent me (both of them are very beautiful, strange, and profound) and for your wonderful LETTER TO PABLO ANTONIO, which I liked very much. I think it is one of the most important pieces of writing that you have done (although you have written many important things), and I am sure it is one of the most important statements that has been made about the present situation and the present age. It will be very good, especially for Latin America. Many intellectuals here are worshipers of Gog; they think that the rejection of Magog must be the acceptance of Gog. Most of them think according to the "party line"; that is, they don't think. Borges has now been condemned by the Literary Left because he had an independent position in the case of Cuba: he was not with Magog, but he was not with Gog either, and he said so. And that has been the Cuban case: they changed one imperialism for another, one slavery for another, and the new one has been worse than the other. Cuba is truly a Soviet country now. But on the other hand, the U.S. policy has been stupid. In Nicaragua there was great hope in Kennedy. The Kennedy men had promised they would help against the dictatorship. But they made the Cuban invasion with the help of Somoza instead. The planes departed from Nicaragua, and one of the Somozas was there saying farewell to the invaders. There is little hope now. The dictatorship is as bad as always. The communist underground is getting stronger every day. That is why your present statement is so important now, in the present confusion.

One of the young American poets who was baptized here, and one who wants to enter the monastery, Howard Frankl, has been so kind to me as to translate into English all my poems of GETHSEMANI, KY. (I hope you received the booklet that I sent to you), and he wants them to be published in the U.S. We have thought about New Directions. Well, I am not sure how they sound in English, nor how they will sound for Laughlin. I have decided to send them to you. If you think that they can be given to Laughlin (or to some other publisher if you have some other one in mind), you may send them. Act according to your judgment, whatever you think is best. Lamantia also translated two of these poems, and we are going to send them, together with some of the others translated by Howard, to *Evergreen Review*. Lamantia married here at the monastery, and he is living in Mexico City now. He will teach and live there for some time.

I just received the Circus [*of the Sun*]. It is a beautiful book, and very good poetry also. I think he is one of the best poets in the USA now. I don't know the [*Original Child*] Bomb yet; I want to see it; it must be very good. I will send you Cortés's poems. Lamantia was very much impressed by him also, and he said he wanted to make some translations of him too.

Everything else is going well here. My headaches don't bother me very much. I am habituated to them, and I am at peace as long as it is the will of God. But I am seeing a famous stomach specialist and he says he is sure that he will cure me. In fact, I am better with him now. I tried psychoanalysis before, under the advice of F. Eudes but it didn't work. The doctor was an atheist and he didn't seem to understand my religious experience. He said that I wanted to be a Trappist for masochism and nonsense like that. He said also that I was an acute neurotic case, and needed many years of deep psychoanalysis. That my whole emotional life was dead. I don't know if that is true. I know that I am *dead* to the world, but I don't think that is pathological because it is a direct effect of my conversion to God. But as he said so many other things that were nonsense, and he didn't want to take into account the religious aspect, I could not trust him. Father Prior advised me to stop seeing him, and to see a stomach specialist, which is what I am doing and I think that is better.

My friend Howard Frankl would like to have a copy of your "Letter to Pablo Antonio." He was very much impressed, and he wants to show them to other people in the United States. And if you have some other copies that you could send to me, I would like to give them to some people in Mexico also.

Always united with you in prayers,

Ernesto Cardenal

Letter 21

Dear Ernesto:

Recently I sent you various copies of the letter to Pablo Anotnio ["Letter Conerning Giants"] for Frankl and other friends. Did I send you a separate one of a dialogue with Suzuki ["Wisdom in Emptiness, A Dialogue: D. T. Suzuki and Thomas Merton"]? In any case, I am sending one now. I believe you will be interested.

The translation of your poems arrived, and it is excellent. Would you like me to send it on to J. Laughlin? It would make a fine little book as it stands (I also received the Spanish version, which was superb). However I think it may be a little hard to persuade him to publish it immediately. He might want it in the same series of pamphlet-poets as Pablo Antonio, whenever that will be. In any case I hope to write an introduction to it, wherever it is published. If Evergreen Review will not use the selection made by Frankl, let me know and I will try it at Jubilee. Or at best, they can make another selection.

There is a very fine new poet, Denise Levertov. I forget whether you translated some of her work or not. She is splendid, one of the most promising. I will try to remember to get New Directions to send you a copy of her new book. You will like her very much. She has lived a bit in Mexico, I think.

I have had a very nice letter recently from Carrera Andrade, who is now ambassador of Ecuador in Venezuela. I hope I can go on making more translations of Latin American poets. I tried hard to get some copies of some of the poets referred to in the publications that have been sent from down there, but Laughlin does not seem to be able to get most of them in New York. I will look forward to getting something of Cortés from you, and I will translate some of him.

What do you know of the Spanish poets writing now? They do not seem to have as much life, but they are trying to stir themselves into new life, so it would appear. Manuel Mantero has been writing to me a lot and sending his stuff. It seems good, but nowhere near as good as your work and Pablo Antonio's, or that of other writers in Central and South America, especially Octavio Paz.

Lax has printed the "Original Child Bomb" [in *Jubilee*] and Laughlin is making a small book out of it, which you will see soon.

God bless you always. We must live always more and more in the purity and light of the Gospel, with simplicity and trust in the God Who has loved us and chosen us. This reality is more and more forgotten, and the state of the world is due to the fact that men have become almost incapable of understanding it. It seems to me that now Kennedy is trying by pressure and force to maintain or encourage a mentality of violence. This is not surprising, and I suppose it is inevitable. But it is very dangerous. However, everything is dangerous. When everything is dangerous, one no longer minds much about it, but is free to care for the essentials.

Always cordially in Christ,

F. Louis

Letter 22

[Handwritten]

NOVEMBER 20, 1961

Dear Ernesto:

Thank you for your good letter. I will write longer soon. This is only to tell you that I have sent the manuscript of your poems [*Gethsemani, KY*] to Laughlin, and that Lax wants to see them for *Jubilee Pax* [*American Pax*]. Do you have another copy to send to Robert Lax?: Jubilee: 399 Park Ave. South, New York 16, N.Y. Pray for us, we are starting an American Christian Peace Movement. It will be very difficult. We are, alas, very late! I will write later and send more material that might be of interest. With all blessings in Christ,

F. M. Louis

P.S. Victoria Ocampo wants to use "Letter about Giants" in *Sur.* Do you think there is any objection to this?

Note on Letter 22

The letter from Cardenal that Merton refers to here in this note—the one following September 30, 1961—is missing. From the commentaries that Merton makes in his next letter of December 24, one can infer that Cardenal must have mentioned that he was leaving to study at the monastery of La Ceja, in Colombia; he must have also made a reference to his plans of publishing *Vida en el amor* and two new books of poetry.

Letter 23

Though Merton did not designate any of his letters to Cardenal as "Cold War Letters," the subject matter of the following letter certainly is representative of Merton's thinking during the period between October 1961 and October 1962, when he wrote the 111 letters that he himself issued in a mimeographed collection entitled Cold War Letters.

DECEMBER 24, 1961

Dear Ernesto:

Though I do not have any definite news yet about the poems, I want to write to you now because Christmas week, as you know, is very busy here. As usual, the novices are decorating the novitiate. We have two very small Christmas trees, and the decorations have been somewhat restrained so far, but there is still one more afternoon and the Lord alone knows what monstrosities will make their appearance during that time.

I sent the small group of poems to Lax at *Jubilee* and have not heard from him about them, but probably there is a letter from him being held up with the Christmas mail, and I will not see it until Tuesday. J. Laughlin has them, but together with another manuscript of mine he has not yet reported. The one thing he has been working on hardest with me, at the moment, has been a paperback anthology of articles on peace [*Breakthrough to Peace*]. This we both feel to be quite urgent, and we are giving it a lot of time and thought; also we want to bring it out without delay. I am sure he will soon have news about your poems, but we must keep after him. It will not hurt for you to write to him again, and I will also remind him. I am meanwhile very interested in the meditations you mention, based on notes you made while here. I think this ought to be a very valuable little book, and Laughlin might want to look at it. Or in any case it ought not to be hard to find a willing publisher.

To *Jubilee* I sent some pictures of Gethsemani that might conceivably go with your poems; I do not know what the issue will be. I have no copies of the Christmas issue, which has a short thing of mine ["The General Dance"], but I will send it if I get one, [and] also the book from which it is taken: *New Seeds of Contemplation.*

I was glad to get the magazine with the Spanish version of the "Ox Mountain Parable," and the other publications that came along at the same time. Cortés has not yet put in his appearance. Is he, by the way, still living and writing? I know you said something about that in your article on the Nicaraguan poets, but I am not sure I remember correctly.

Probably you are now down at Río San Juan. I think of that often, and of Ometepe. Curious that Corn Island should have been the jumping-off place for the abortive Cuban landing.

There is no telling what is to become of the work I have attempted with the Protestant ministers and scholars. Evidently someone has complained to Rome about my doing work that is "not fitting for a contemplative" and there have been notes of disapproval. The contacts will have to be cut down to a minimum. I do not mind very much, personally. I have the hermitage and would rather use it as a hermitage than as a place for retreat conferences. In all this I remain pretty indifferent, as a matter of fact. There are much wider perspectives to be considered. My concept of the Church, my faith in the Church, has been and is being tested and purified: I hope it is being purified. Even my idea of "working for the Church" is being radically changed. I have less and less incentive to take any kind of initiative in promising anything for the immediate visible apostolic purposes of the Church. It is not easy for me to explain what I feel about the movements that proliferate everywhere, and the generosity and zeal that goes into them all. But in the depths of my heart I feel very empty about all that, and there is in me a growing sense that it is all *provisional* and perhaps has very little of the meaning that these zealous promoters attribute to it. So about any contacts I may have had with Protestants. I have had just enough to know how ambiguous it all becomes. The only result has been to leave me with a profound respect and love for these men, and an increased understanding of their spirit. But at the same time I am not sanguine about the chances of a definite "movement" for reunion, and, as I say, I am left with the feeling that the "movement" is not the important thing. As if there were something more hidden and more important, which is also much easier to attain, and is yet beyond the reach of institutional pressures.

I am deeply concerned about peace, and am united in working with other Christians for protest against nuclear war; it is paradoxically what one might call the most small and neglected of "movements" in the whole Church. This also is to me terribly significant. I do not complain; I do not criticize; but I observe with a kind of numb silence the inaction, the passivity, the apparent indifference and incomprehension with which most Catholics, clergy and laity, at least in this country, watch the development of pressure that builds up to a nuclear war. It is as if they had all become lotus-eaters. As if they were under a spell. As if with charmed eyes and ears they saw vaguely, through a comatose fog, the oncoming of their destruction, and were unable to lift a finger to do anything about it. This is an awful sensation. I hope I am not in the same coma. I resist this bad dream with all my force, and at least I can struggle and cry out, with others who have the same awareness.

The thousand and one paradoxes and contradictions inherent in the position of so many Catholics are really confusing and in the end leave one paralyzed. For while insisting with more and more emphasis on "the Church," they also at the very same time emphasize more and more a morality that destroys and dissolves the substance of Christian life and of the Church. Apart from a few token issues that are defended with complete intransigence, like birth control, sexual morality, etc., the whole trend seems to be toward the supine acceptance of the most secular, the most debased, the most empty of worldly standards. In this case the acceptance of nuclear war. Not only that, but it is glorified as Christian sacrifice, as a crusade, as the way of obedience. So much so that now there are many who insist that one is not a good Christian unless he offers a blind and unresisting obedience to every behest of Caesar. This is to me a complete nightmare. And I realize that I have to be very careful how I protest because otherwise I will be silenced. And no doubt sooner or later I will be silenced. It is very difficult to get articles on peace past the censors.

However, it is consoling that there is at least a minority that is waking up and beginning to react. Mostly among non-Catholics, but also among a few chosen Catholics. Of course, Dorothy Day, and *The Catholic Worker*, whom everybody dismisses with a shrug of the shoulders. But also Father Daniel Berrigan, the Jesuit poet, and some others. I think I told you we are founding a Fax movement. It turns out that the leaders are all in a small circle. Lax, [Ed] Rice, myself, Fr. Berrigan, the *Catholic Worker* people, some other priests, many of whom I already know. And the rest of the clergy? Alas, a great number of them have either joined the John Birch Society or sympathize with it. So you see what I mean.

Yet fortunately also there was an articulate group within the totality of the American bishops who gave out a semi-official reproof to this kind of thing and declared that they were opposed to the J. Birchers.

I will have to review the matter of translations in Buenos Aires. I believe that the correct translations probably will appear in *Obras completas [de Thomas Merton]*. I have never known anything about *The Tower of Babel*. Why not try it somewhere else? I wait with interest to see your two new books of poems and I believe that the seminary in Antioquia sounds like a good idea. Did you finally receive the dialogue with Suzuki ["Wisdom in Emptiness, A Dialogue: D. T. Suzuki and Thomas Merton"]? I will send another copy with translations of *Clement of Alexandria*. Did I tell you

Victoria Ocampo is going to publish "Letter to Pablo Antonio" in *Sur*? I hope that this will go well. I believe that it will probably be prudent to cut the following passages:

On page six, cut the entire second paragraph ("It is a Christianity of money . . .") and in turn, add to the end of the first paragraph what follows ("We have a Christianity of Magog that doesn't protest against war, against crime, against greed, but only against Gog").

On page seven cut line eleven of the prayer, "Surely our mission is truly for the world . . ." until "hidden in them." Is this ok? I hope it will not be too late.

I haven't heard anything from Pablo Antonio about this, but I know he is busy. I only mention it because he might have sent me a letter I didn't receive.

All my blessings for you in the New Year. I remember you especially in my Masses for Christmas, as I remember you every day. Best wishes and blessings for all, especially Pablo Antonio and Armando Morales, and to Otilia Pallais above all. I still need your prayers, from all of you, now more than ever. Do not stop staying in contact with me.

With all cordial best wishes in the love of Christ our Lord,

F. M. Louis

[Handwritten P.S.] I will let you know as soon as possible what I hear from Lax or Laughlin concerning the poems.

Letter 24

MARCH 4, 1962

Dear Father Louis:

I am now here at the seminary for late vocations in Colombia, in a very beautiful place within the mountains of Antioquia, next to a very picturesque little colonial town named La Ceja. The seminary is in the countryside and the landscape here is majestic with large mountains, and one has the sensation of being in a large country. The people of Antioquia are the most religious in Latin America. There is a priest in almost every family, and the whole countryside breathes a religious peace. The peasants of La Ceja look frozen on the corners and in the plaza, like monks in meditation (the "ponchos" they use to wrap themselves look like monks' habits), and I think that in a certain way they are in a state of Zen. I feel myself content to be here. Without a doubt, God has brought me. All seminaries are hard, especially for me, given my circumstances, but I think that this one is one where I will be able to fit in well, and the place is beautiful and peaceful.

There are one hundred and thirty seminaries. Almost all of them are young university students or professionals. The daily regimen is very free. I will be able to dedicate myself to writing and to sculpture (I am giving sculpture classes to some), and the Father Rector has a very generous spirit, with great understanding, which reminds me a little of you and Dom Gregorio. The emphasis here is placed on charity, as in Gethsemani and in Cuernavaca. There is much love between everyone, and there is also much joy and freedom.

When I was in Nicaragua, I received many of your packages with wonderful items: *New Seeds of Contemplation*, which is so amazing, especially with the new sections you added. All these new sections are all so very crucial. José Coronel Urtecho read it and was very excited about the book. He also liked very much *Disputed Questions*, and was especially interested in the last part of the essay that I showed him, *El Espiritu Primitivo del Carmelo*, regarding the Carmelite order. Also, the various articles regarding the Peace Movement seem very good to me, and I can see that all the work that you and they are doing with this movement is very important. I also really liked your article "Christian Action" and will be translating it. I want to make these issues known in Latin America. They will awaken much interest here; the bad thing is that there are few places to publish. We have *El Pez y la Serpiente*, but the bad side of this is that Pablo Antonio does not bring it out often enough: *de tarde* and *tarde*. He has too much work in *La Prensa* and does not have a lot of time for the magazine—but he told me that *El Pez* number 3 with your "Carta a Pablo Antonio" ["A Letter to Pablo Antonio Cuadra Concerning Giants"] will finally come out in a few days.

The political situation in Nicaragua is very interesting. The Somozas must now relinquish power because there must be elections within one year, and the USA has told them that not one single Somoza can be elected as president. The most that they would be able to do is commit fraud in the elections, so that the one elected would not turn out to be in opposition to them. Most likely, this would also expel them from the country because he would not be able to govern with them [present in the country]. However, it is also very possible that they will not even be able to commit fraud, because their party is crumbling and the opposition is stronger every day, and therefore perhaps they will fall before those very elections take place, and there will be true free elections. The most interesting part is that with free elections, the winner would surely be Pedro Joaquín Chamorro, the director of *La Prensa*, for whom you once interceded with President Somoza when he was imprisoned, and [who is] my and Pablo Antonio's cousin. He is not the most popular person in

Nicaragua, with the prestige of his imprisonments, exiles, and tortures, and the biggest adversary to the Somozas. His ideas call for very radical social-Christian reform—to be a Christian Fidel Castro; that is to say, what Castro could have been and was not because he gave himself to Marxism.

Pedro Joaquín Chamorro's group is from the most highly regarded and best educated Christian young men in Nicaragua (with the ideas of Maritain, *Catholic Worker*, etc.) and most importantly, Pablo Antonio would be our Minister of Culture, with whom we would have a real literary renaissance in Nicaragua with journals, magazines, etc. It appears that Providence is deciding these things for Nicaragua, because everything is happening in such a way that more and more often favors Pedro Joaquín, while everything is turning out badly for the Somozas, and every time, their power is crumbling more and more. Since things are happening there very quickly, it could be that the Somozas could fall very soon and we will have free elections. The U.S. government also seems to want these elections.

I always have the same plans for when I return to Nicaragua. I will start our own little group there, in some place like Ometepe, as described in *Disputed Questions*. Howard Frankl, the ex-beatnik poet who translated my poems and just recently entered the monastery of Cuernavaca, would go there also; there is another young poet in Nicaragua who also wants to go, and a young Father [Father García], who is a professor in the seminary of Managua, who is also planning to write to you in the next few days, to consult with you regarding his vocation. We would naturally be above politics, but we would help them with advice, letters, etc., and with a place of retreat where they could go to think and meditate. I have spoken a lot about all of this with Coronel, and he too has planned these things a lot with me, and would be a very permanent guest. He already leads a very eremitic life in Río San Juan, even though he lives with his wife; every day he reads the Rule of Saint Benedict, and his life is very Benedictine. He says that he is not going to participate in the new government, that this is for Pablo Antonio, and that it will be up to us to help them with advice and prayer. I was in Ometepe because my grandmother has some properties there and I went to take a look. They do not seem very good to me, and I told her that it is best to sell them, but there are also other similar places there where I could do some work after being ordained a priest.

I continue to suffer from headaches, but I think that I can handle study; I will do everything possible for it, and if it is God's will that I enter the priesthood here, that is how it will be, if he has destined me for that. If not, may it also be God's will, whatever else it may be.

I suppose you have received my book of *Epigramas* that the University of Mexico published for me, and also the book of *Poesía revolucionaria nicaragüense*, that Mejía Sánchez and I prepared in Mexico. Inside are many of my poems that are also included in the book of *Epigramas*, and in my poem *La hora 0*, but in this anthology, they all appear as anonymous. Also, there are many different poems by Pablo Antonio from *Jaguar y la Luna*, and from all the Nicaraguan poets, but this book cannot be circulated in Nicaragua. I hope that you have received both of these books. I have another book of poems that will be published for me in Nicaragua. *La antología de poesía Norteamericana* is also being published now, and soon I will also publish my little book of religious meditations from Gethsemani [*Vida en el amor*], which is like a kind of *Seeds of Contemplation*, basic without the elevation of the great heights of mysticism in *Seeds of Contemplation*, naturally.

Pablo Antonio is going to send you a copy of the *Antología Laurel*, of Hispanic American poets, which cannot be obtained anywhere else, and an Argentine writer, a friend of ours, will send you other books from Argentina, especially the last ones from Borges. He promised to do it. You can also write to Italy and ask for a very good Hispanic American anthology that has been published there: *Poesía Hispanoamericana del 1900*. Guanda, Editor, Parma-Italy. I think that it is inexpensive.

United with you always in my prayers, in Christ,

Ernesto Cardenal

Letter 25

MAY 16, 1962

Dear Ernesto:

A letter that arrived the other day from Fr. García at the Seminary in Managua reminded me that I had not answered your own fine letter from Colombia. I was glad to hear you were in the seminary there, and the place sounds grand: La Ceja, with its good, quiet, primitive people. That is wonderful. Such places are getting fewer and fewer on this earth. It is a grace for you to be there. But I have no doubt at all you will find the seminary life a bit difficult. I am glad the rector is a good and understanding person. That is most important.

I am glad you liked the books. Alceu Amoroso Lima has written a tremendous preface for the Brazilian edition of *Disputed Questions*. I hope all the good things he says about me are at least half true. But it should help the book very much in Brazil. I knew you would like the "Primitive Spirit of Carmel" ["The Primitive Carmelite Ideal"] and its implications. It has had some effect on the Carmelites in this country who are even starting a project something like what was suggested, but I believe it will soon turn into something different. Who can tell? In this country everything tends to be corrupted by the propaganda methods and the "promotion" that it undergoes. Promotion will end by ruining everything.

The "Letter to Pablo Antonio" has been having quite an effect in various places. It has been translated into German for the magazine *Hochland*, by a German who has gone to live with the Jews in Israel to make reparation for the sins of Hitler. He writes very poignant letters about his love for the young Jews who were in concentration camps when they were children, and their love for him. It appeared in *Sur* (the letter to PA), and I got a nice letter about it from a poetess in Uruguay (Esther de Cáceres, I suppose you do not know her. She was a friend of Gabriela Mistral). I also wrote a short notice to be inserted in a volume of homages to Victoria Ocampo ["To Friends of Victoria Ocampo"]. If the Church people do not like her, this may upset them a bit, but I don't care. There is too much stupidity and prejudice and plain narrow-mindedness, and it is ruining the Church in many places.

The versions of the peace articles I have sent you are not the best ones, and if you have not had any translations published, it would be best perhaps to correct them by other versions, which I will send. "Christian Ethics and Nuclear War" was revised and appears in *Jubilee* as "Religion and the Bomb." I will try to get a copy of this to you soon, but I have no copy even for myself at the moment. I am trying to do a book on peace but I am not sure it will be permitted. I am sending a copy of *The Catholic Worker* with a long article on peace, which is more or less correct except for a couple of misprints. ["We Have to Make Ourselves Heard" was published in *The Catholic Worker* in two parts in May and June 1962.]

Also with New Directions I have done an anthology of articles on nuclear war [*Breakthrough to Peace*] by various authors, [Erich] Fromm, [Lewis] Mumford, etc. etc. It looks very good and I hope it will soon be out, that is in three months or so. Do pray for both these books to do good.

Unfortunately I have not got such good news for your Gethsemani poems [later published as *Gethsemani, KY*]. Laughlin does not want to risk bringing them out as a book. They are, he feels, too slight a collection with which to introduce you and in any case he does not want to publish these poems by themselves. I suppose the most practical thing would be for him to gather into a volume *all* that you have done so far. Otherwise I have *not* received your *Epigramas* nor have I received from Mejía Sánchez the book of revolutionary poetry [*Poesía revolucionaria nicaragüense*]. He asked me if they arrived and I have not received them. Maybe they did not even get here. Nor did the books from Argentina arrive. Maybe they haven't had time to arrive.

I have begun to translate some poems of Alfonso Cortés and have even written a little poem about him ["To Alfonso Cortes"]. I will type out some of the translations and the poem and send them all later. For the rest I do not remember if I sent you the poem about the Ladies Jail ["There Has to Be a Jail for Ladies"], but I know you do not yet have the peace prayer ["Prayer for Peace"], which I enclose. It was requested by a member of Congress [Frank Kowalski] who had been military governor of the prefecture of Hiroshima and who helped the inhabitants there rebuild their city after the war. I have received many touching letters from people interested in peace, especially from some who are interested in the women's peace movement, which I think is more important than it looks. Also from a young Quaker who with two others is to sail in a twenty-five-foot boat to Christmas Island to protest the renewal of atomic testing.

It is most important that we pray for peace, and detach ourselves more and more from the futile and lying values of the world of men who are moving toward war carried by the momentum of enormous sins and lies. The society of man, particularly in the West, is burdened by a history of infidelity and crime that are enormous, and all we do is excuse and palliate our falsity, trying to blame someone else who is as guilty as we are. We are all guilty, but that means that we must in a very special way avoid the final guilt of violence or of despair. Hence the importance of truly Christian values.

I will write to Father García, and I believe that it will be good for him to come here, if he can, to discuss his vocation. Although I wonder if this is the place for him. Maybe even better, he should stay with you in Central America. Yet it would neither be bad for him to pass some time here. I will not be able to promise him much time, but I will at the least be able to see him as a postulate and regular novice. The frequent retreats of Protestants and others keep me unusually busy. The hermitage is fine. I take advantage of it as much as possible. This life takes on a new dimension when one actually has time to begin to meditate! Otherwise it is not really serious, just a series of exercises which one offers up with a pure intention and with the hope that they mean something. That is not what the monastic life is for.

I think often of you. I am very happy at the canonization of St. Martin de Porres. I think often of all my good friends in Latin America, to whom I am so close, and in many ways more close than I am to the people I live with here. Send my regards to Pablo Antonio. If you see Bishop Medellín, send my regards (if he is the same Bishop who wrote here in 1958). We continue to be united in prayer and faith, and we trust in the light of Christ. He has conquered falsity and violence, but he must also conquer in his and through us.

With cordial best wishes always, in Christ the Lord,

Tom Merton

Letter 26

MAY 22, 1962

Dear Ernesto:

Yesterday your essay on Alfonso [Cortés] arrived and last evening I read the first few pages. It is most impressive. I will probably add to the poem on Alfonso about which I told you in my letter of a few days ago, on the basis of the extraordinary picture you give of him. I think he is a most absorbing and wonderful figure, in some sense prophetic.

The thing that strikes me most about his poems, and you may yourself have said this in pages that I have not yet reached, is his extraordinary ontological sense, his grasp of objective being. He is much more than a surrealist. Indeed he is the only true surrealist, for instead of going like them to the heart of a subjectivity which is at the same time all real and all unreal, he plunges to the heart of a transobjective subjectivity which is the purely real, and he expresses it in images as original and as eloquent as those of Blake. He is one of the most arresting poets of the twentieth century, and in my opinion certainly one of the very greatest. He really has something to say. I want to work more on his poems, and I will send you the rough drafts. There is a very good new magazine, *Second Coming*, in which I hope to arouse interest in him. Who knows, perhaps after some poems they might print a translation of your essay? We shall see.

I have not received any extra copies of *Jubilee* but as soon as I do I will mail you one by air, for it contains the essay "Religion and the Bomb," a longer and more detailed as well as corrected version of the one you have translated. It is this *Jubilee* version that should be printed. Perhaps you could use the version you have done as a tentative offering to some magazine, and when accepted, do the other version. You could explain that easily enough, or perhaps also show them the other article in English. I would not want you to do the translation twice over without guarantee that it would be printed. But you be the judge.

A Spanish publisher, Editorial Guadarrama, Lope de Rueda 13, Madrid, is interested in some of my work. Perhaps you could send them the translations you did of parts of *The Behavior of Titans* and also "The Tower of Babel." Sudamericana is never going to do anything with these works; the people in Spain might; unless you can find someone in Bogotá who is interested. That might be even better, I don't know.

I certainly envy you going to Bogotá; it must be a stimulating place. If you pick up anything interesting in the way of literary magazines, I hope you will send them along to me after you have finished.

There is a great deal of action for peace here, at last, though I do not think it can really affect those who are so deeply involved in the enormous war machine. This is the most fabulous war effort in history and I do not see any chance that it can be carried on at the present rate without ending in a tremendous explosion. The mentality of the people seems to be utterly confused and stupid, they seem to have no grasp on the real nature of the issue or its seriousness. They are prisoners of a completely quantitative view of life and consequently, having no sense either of essence or of existence, are out of touch with reality: and first of all with their own reality. It is a culture of well-fed zombies. May God deliver us from the consequences of all this. And yet too when one sees the earnestness and the integrity of some of those who do speak out, it is very encouraging. Leo Szilard, the atomic scientist, has an interesting peace movement that comes closer than anything else to carrying out the program outlined by the Popes. If I can get my book on peace [*Peace in the Post-Christian Era*] published, I hope to devote at least part of the royalties to that movement. Pray that it may be permitted.

Today I said Mass especially for you, and for Ometepe: also for Pablo Anotnio, Coronel, and all my friends in Nicaragua, without omitting Alfonso. Is he still around? It's too bad that he cannot write more, but it is also significant and prophetic in a sense. With all my blessings and well wishes in Christ.

Tom Merton

[Handwritten] P.S. I am sending a copy of the course on Mystic Theology that I dictated last year.

Letter 27

Dear Father Louis:

I was so glad to receive your last two letters; they were such good letters. I am also very glad that you are interested in Alfonso and doing those translations in English, and that poem about him: "To Alfonso Cortés." I hope to see them. Your assessment of him is very interesting. In Nicaragua, we are also convinced of his greatness and importance, as you say. He is in good health, and always writing verses, but for the past few years the ones he writes are all bad. I think that his madness has finished eating away at his brain, and perhaps a psychiatrist would be able to improve his mental condition—even if he could not cure him entirely, he would be able to write again, as he did during his better days. But the government does not want to spend on him; and there, where he is, no one provides him with treatment. But it is still possible to speak with him. Recently, when I was in Nicaragua, I went to see him, and he recognized me, but said he could not understand how I could be Ernesto Cardenal, since he knew that Ernesto Cardenal was in a monastery, and later added: "Surely there must be two Ernesto Cardenals."

I had only started the translation of "Christian Action in World Crisis," and did not continue with it because you had mentioned in your first letter [from May 16, 1962] that you had a new version. I am waiting to receive this in order to continue. Instead, I have translated the "Prayer for Peace," which I liked very much, and will be taking it to Bogotá. I will also send it to the *Magazine of the University of Mexico* (they are leftists and almost communists, but I think they would like this Prayer) and to

Nicaragua, as well as Antonio Cuadra's *La Prensa*. A few days ago I wrote to Sudamericana requesting "The Tower of Babel," since it looked like they were not going to publish it. I hope they send it to me—otherwise I will ask Pablo Antonio for it (I think he has a copy in Nicaragua) and will send it to Editorial Guadarrama, which is a very good partner.

I have also written to the friend from Argentina, who was going to send you those books, to find out if he has, or still has not, and to remind him to do so. I have also written to Mexico to remind them to send you those other books, which they most likely have not sent. I will also send you any interesting publications that I find in Bogotá. I have not kept up with the latest ones because no one else here in the seminary is interested in these things, and they do not receive them; but I will put myself in touch with the best young writers there. This is why I believe that this trip is very important (there are twenty days of vacation next June).

If Laughlin does not wish to publish those poems now [*Gethsemani, KY*], it is fine, I am not sorry. Everything that happens is lovely because it is God's will, and in this case, I think perhaps it is right not to publish them. I have not been too happy with the way these poems sound in English, despite the fact that the translations are very good, and do not know how they could possibly be improved. Perhaps in the future, a more compete edition could be suggested to Laughlin, as you say. I have two new unpublished books of poetry. One of them is a long poem, *The Doubtful Strait*, a narrative of 150 pages, about the events in the discovery and conquest of Central America (Columbus, Cortez, Las Casas, Balboa, Cuauhtémoc, etc.), which I wrote last year in Mexico, and which perhaps Pablo Antonio might publish in a special edition of *El Pez y la Serpiente*. A fragment appeared in *The Plumed Horn / El Corno Emplumada*, a magazine that the Beats in Mexico publish, and I think that it has arrived for you, or it will arrive.

Have you continued receiving the *Magazine of the University of Mexico*? The director promised that they would be sending it to you after I came

back from there. The university is also going to publish a volume of translations of Pound and Coronel that I made. And now in June, Coronel is
publishing the two first volumes of a very large work that he is doing about
the history of Nicaragua [*Reflexiones Sobre la Historia de Nicaragua*], and that
he will be sending to you. You will be interested in that work, especially
the first volume, which is a magnificent study about colonialism, the
Indian, *mestizaje*, etc. All of this also applies to the rest of Latin America,
and [it is] therefore a very important work to learn about the shaping of
these lands.

I think that we can propose a volume to Guadarrama with these last
essays of yours, which we have translated as "A Letter to Pablo Antonio
Cuadra Concerning Giants"; "Boris Pasternak and the People with Watch
Chains"; "Let the Poor Man Speak"; "Religion and the Bomb"; "Prayer
for Peace"; and "Prometheus: A Meditation," which Pablo Antonio has
and is planning to publish next time in *El Pez y la Serpiente*. It seems to me
that the campaign for peace that you and those friends are undertaking
will be greatly transformative throughout the world and the Church, and
I do not think that it is preaching to the desert; these are voices that one
way or another will be heard. I will pray for that campaign that you are
waging.

I really appreciate the Mass you offered for us, and the intentions, and
I am very happy knowing that you have done this. Pablo Antonio has
made a trip to Europe and had sent me a postcard all the way from Maria
Laach. He was thinking of seeing the Pope and telling him about the
problems in Nicaragua.

Are you still the master of novices? According to your letter, it seems to
me that you are still, despite the hermitage retreat. Father García has not
written to me yet, and I do not know what decision he is going to make.
I have not seen the bishop of Medellín, and I will give him your regards
when I see him, although I do not know if he is the same one who wrote
[to Gethsemani]. My life here is very happy, as it had been in Gethsemani

and Cuernavaca. I do not have the difficulties that one would expect from a seminary. I have a lot of free time at my disposal to dedicate myself to my own work, and I can also lead a very contemplative life of silence. I am writing a lot and taking full advantage of the time very well. I also do some work in sculpture, and I am giving some classes in this to some seminarians.

I have not received "There Has to Be a Jail for Ladies" and I hope that you will send it to me.

United always in prayer,

Ernesto Cardenal

Letter 28

[Handwritten, never before published]

June 7, 1962

Dear Ernesto:

I will answer your fine letter in a few days. I am sending you copies of the letter and the list that I am sending first to Guadarrama. These will make interesting books, I think.

God bless you. Here is the poem "There Has to Be a Jail For Ladies," and many others.

In Christ,

Tom Merton

Letter 29

Dear Father Louis:

I have just returned from Bogotá, which has been an interesting experience. It is a city with a lot of character and a great historical past, which it still conserves, and a lot of literary tradition. In this sense it is too traditionalist, but there is a fine group of young poets with whom I have made friends and have been in touch, and this will be very useful for the future, since I am putting them in touch with our other friends in Nicaragua, Mexico, etc. They gave me a few publications and magazines that I will send to you next time.

Upon my return here, I found your letter and the copy of the manuscript for the Editorial Guadarrama. I am very pleased with our plans to publish with that publisher, which is very good and has a wide distribution in Latin America. But I have also received a letter from Sudamericana wherein they tell me that they want to publish "The Tower of Babel." Could we do it so that it is published at the same time with both publishers? If it can be done this way, that would be best. If Sudamericana does not allow the other publisher to do it, I think it would be best to leave it to them and let Guadarrama only publish the other essays; then this way there would be two books. I have just written to Sudamericana asking them if they do not object to the publication of "The Tower of Babel" in the other volume of Guadarrama.

I do not know exactly what is in the content in the English version of *The Behavior of Titans* because I am not familiar with the book. I suppose that "Prometheus: A Meditation" is part of it; I do not know what other parts there are. Do you think that "A Prayer for Peace" could also go in this book? I have already translated the essay "Christian Ethics," and it will be published in a Columbian newspaper and in *La Prensa* of Nicaragua.

It seems a good idea to me to publish the book of poems with the translations by José María Valverde and me, and any others that can be added, similar to another very good one that Coronel Urtecho made, etc.

I am sending a book of meditations that I spoke to you about before, *Vida en el amor*, to a good friend of mine in Spain for him to publish there, wherever he thinks is best.

A friend of mine from Argentina, Zuleta Alvarez, has written to me that he has already sent you those books he promised, and that he has also written to you to let you know about this package—which will be delayed in arriving.

An anthology of Hispanic American poetry has just been published in the United States that I think should be very good: *Literatura Hispanoamericana*—[edited by] Anderson Imbert and Eugenio Florit ([published by] Holt, Rinehart and Winston). I think that you can easily obtain it, and I think that it is the only anthology of Hispanic American poetry that has been published in a long time.

United always in Christ,

Ernesto Cardenal

Letter 30

Dear Ernesto:

Thank you for your letter and for the card by Sudamericana. I have been very busy and have not been able to answer your wonderful letter about the trip to Bogotá. I have always thought of it as an unusually interesting place and there must be plenty of life there. I am eager to see some of the material you have gathered from the poets there.

As to business: here is a copy of my letter to Llausas [of Sudamericana]. You will judge the situation by its content. They have violated the contract and I believe that we will have to sort out the problems before moving on. This, by the way, will leave me free to work with Guadarrama. I have now sent them *The New Man* together with various other things, including of course *The Behavior of Titans.*

A very fine young Jesuit poet, Daniel Berrigan, has been here for a week, and has given some magnificent talks to the novices. He should be represented in *El Pez y la Serpiente.* He could do some fine things, and he writes excellent articles on the present spiritual and social situation. We are much in agreement about war and so on. He is one of the few who are really alive and awake on all these questions, here. The majority remains asleep.

I have been in contact with Henry Miller. He has written some extraordinary essays recently, especially a book called *The Wisdom of the Heart,* from which Pablo Antonio could also extract some really great material.

This is only a note; I must get to other things. I will write more fully later. I still haven't typed the poem about Alfonso Cortés, or the translations. I intend to do a few more translations before typing them all. I have been reading [César] Vallejo again, and hope to translate more of him too.

Here is a poem about a child's drawing of a house ["Grace's House"], and a copy of a letter to Hiroshima [Cold War Letter 98 to The Honorable Shinzo Hamai; see *The Hidden Ground of Love*], which you can publish anywhere if you like. And some *estampillas* [stamps].

Everything is well. Let's be aware of the profundity of hope that Christ has given us, and the reality of the presence of the Holy Spirit in our hearts. Let us grow in faith and strength.

With all my blessings, cordially yours in Christ,

Tom Merton

Letter 31

SEPTEMBER 16, 1962

Dear Ernesto:

A pair of new developments. First, I have arranged with Sudamerica to publish *The Tower of Babel* separately, at the same time that it can be included with other material by Guadarrama in Madrid. I haven't heard anything from them in months, however, and I don't know how things are there. I suppose things are going along as planned. Sudamericana might be in contact with you. The have said they sent contracts. Can you arrange with them what you find to be the most adequate participation, since you can probably use any income more than we? Why don't we divide the rights in half? I haven't mentioned this to them, but I can if you want.

The books have just arrived from Argentina. I am very grateful and will read them with interest.

I still haven't typed out the poems of Cortés that I have translated. They are here on the desk, but I will try to get to that tomorrow or the day after. They are only a few, and it would not take long, but I am always getting tied up with other jobs, in the limited amount of time I spend here in the office. I try to get to the hermitage every afternoon, now. This is the best thing I can possibly do. All the rest is more or less illusion and waste[d] motion. It grows on me more and more how much the activity we indulge in is really a kind of game of reciprocal delusion: especially when it takes place in a solemn and formal institutional framework in which everything is of the utmost seriousness and is, at the same time, almost incomprehensible. But always serious!

The state of madness in the most developed human societies is, it seems to me, almost incurably grave and acute. The total unreality of the thought and the statements one meets everywhere here is almost unbelievable.

The other day I met a young Spanish Jesuit who is on his way to Ecuador and then to Colombia. He is Father Feliciano Delgado. You will like to meet him. He writes for *Razón y Fe* and other magazines over there.

The publication of a large "Merton Reader" [*A Thomas Merton Reader*] is well under way. It contains some of the things I am most anxious to say and is fairly complete except that one of my publishers let me down and would not allow the other one to have rights to the material printed by them. But we were able to compensate by digging up articles and essays that were in unusual places, and the book may well be all the better for it. I have asked the publisher to send you a copy. It should be out in October.

Also the anthology *Breakthrough to Peace* is out, and I do not know if the publisher has sent you a copy, or if I have. If you do not receive it after a couple of weeks, please let me know.

There are a few "peace candidates" trying desperately to get themselves elected to Congress. Their efforts are significant in the sense that they have *no party* to support them and are being put into the race purely by individual efforts of people who are aroused by the issue, mostly by intellectuals. Their election is of course unlikely, but at least their presence in the campaign has a modicum of meaning. But that is very little, and when one considers the vastness of the issue and the stupidity and truculence of the vast majority of the people, one might well feel a little negative about it all. I hope South America is more intelligent than we are. I hope you are well. Father Sylvanus is now in a hermitage in Martinique, but I don't know if he'll last long with this. All my blessings, in Christ,

Tom Merton

Letter 32

Dear F. Merton:

I have just received your letter from the 16th and I am happy that the publishing has now been arranged with Sudamericana. Many thanks for telling me that we should split the rights half and half—they had told me that they would pay approximately seventy dollars for the translation. It might be good for you to write to them and tell them this, and I will write this to them too. I really appreciate your suggestion because it will help me to buy books.

I received the package with *The Wisdom of the Desert* and *The Behavior of Titans*, both very beautiful editions. For the publication of Guadarrama: Do you have copies of the translations for "Atlas and the Fatman," "Letter to an Innocent Bystander," and "A Signed Confession of Crimes Against the State"? Because I have the other translations, but I do not have these three, I think that you must probably have them.

I am preparing a mail package for you with a few publications from Colombia and a few from Nicaragua. There are very few interesting publications from Colombia because the most valuable writers are only in a very tiny minority, with huge economic difficulties for publishing (like everywhere else). The only really good magazine is the magazine *Mito*; unfortunately I cannot send you the volumes that the editors promised to send me from Bogotá, and still have not sent me. I hope to send them to you next time. Colombia is a very traditional country, the most traditional in America, very loaded with tradition, with all the good and the bad that this signifies. In literature, the great (neoclassical) tradition that they had in the past carries great weight, and among the public there is a great affinity for literature, but they continue to stay attached to those forms. The same happens with Catholicism; it is probably the most Catholic country in America, but it is a very conservative Catholicism, with a lot of clericalism, etc., and needs reform, or else it will be swept away by Communism.

I am also sending you these items: a few of my poems and fragments of one long poem about the history of the Conquest of Central America [*The Doubtful Strait*] that I composed last year, and that have appeared in a few newspapers and magazines.

I still have not received *Breakthrough to Peace*. I am reading your notes about asceticism and mysticism with great interest and avail. I was also very interested in your Cold War letters, and through them I have learned about the great apostleship and great good that you have been doing through letters to so many different people in so many places. "Hagia Sophia" and "Grace's House" are two very beautiful poems.

It would be very good if you could put us in touch (or put Pablo Antonio in touch with Father Berrigan for *El Pez*). The same in regards to Henry Miller's *The Wisdom of the Heart*. How could we obtain a copy in order to publish something of his in the magazine? Perhaps you could send me Miller's address, and I will write him asking him for the book.

The monks from Cuernavaca have written me to say that they wish to make a foundation in Nicaragua, if I could help them obtain the land. I have written a few letters to Nicaragua, and I am certain that there will be no difficulties in obtaining this; there are many people that would give all kinds of help to this foundation. Besides, what they need is very little. They tell me that they would create this foundation with two Benedictine monks from Martinique—a Father Menard and a Father Munch. I do not know if it is with them that Father Silvano is in hermitage, as you told me. These monks want to found a monastic life of more humility and simplicity, and closer to the true fountains of monastic life: Saint Benedict and the Gospel. Well then, it will be a great thing for Nicaragua to attempt something like this there. In mid-November we will have vacation here (two and a half months), and I think that I will go to Nicaragua during that vacation time, and there I will personally see to it to help realize the Benedictines' projects. With regards to me, I do not have any new projects, only the same one from before, after I complete my studies here. I have just read an article ["*Des homes attentifs a Dieu*"] in June's issue of *Vie Spirituelle*, which seems to me exactly what I want, and for what I believe is my vocation, according to what God has inspired in me through you.

Regarding my headaches, I have been improving more and more and I am almost cured, and I think that I will be completely healed—without taking any medication. I am convinced that this is due to a miraculous intervention by a Salesian nun, Sister María Romero, who lives in Costa Rica. She performs amazing miracles every day—healing of those with cancer, those who are blind from birth, incurable madmen, and multiplying money for the poor and clothes that she distributes to poor children, etc. She is Nicaraguan, and was my mother's schoolmate. My mother went to visit her in Costa Rica and asked her for this cure for me, and Sister Romero made assurances that I would have it, and that I would rise to the priesthood; and as payment in return for this, I was to remember her during Mass. My married sister did not have children, and Sister Romero arranged it so that she could have one last year. She told her that the Virgin Mary (with whom she speaks regularly) had informed her, and my sister conceived on the exact date that Sister Romero had said. Therefore, I cannot attribute my health to anything else but this, because I do not take any medication. Every other treatment before had failed.

I remember you always as the first intention in my prayers, and united always in our union with God, with regards, in Xto.,

Ernesto Cardenal

Letter 33

[No Date, 1962]

Dear Ernesto:

Here are the translations of Alfonso [Cortés] that I have done [see *Emblems of a Season of Fury*]. I think I will probably get them in *New Directions* 8, together with a short biographical introduction [see *The Literary Essays of Thomas Merton*].

I hope you will point out any errors and make any suggestions that occur to you. And let me know if you can use more copies. I will send three or four more copies in any case.

Best regards to everyone, especially Pablo Antonio. I keep you all in my prayers and Masses. The world situation becomes more hazardous at every moment because of the incompetence and the irrationality of all men and the subjection of the powerful to the instruments of their power.

May God have mercy on us.

Always yours in Christ,

Tom Merton

Letter 34

Dear Father Merton:

I just received the translations of Alfonso Cortés, and they are masterful: a perfect delivery of meaning, without being literal, with enough freedom, but at the same time loyal to the same freedom. In other words, the poems are as they would be if he had written them himself in English. There are, however, a few minor details that I want to point out where I think there is some error in the translation:

In "The Flower of the Fruit," the line: "That changes as it comes to be." In Spanish it has another sense: *Que cambia, o inmuta, el porvenir.* In English it could be: "That changes the future," or something similar.

In "Dirty Souls": "Between which the things"; in Spanish it does not exactly say *"entre"* [between], but rather *"detras"* [behind] (there is not much difference in the translation, but perhaps there is some). "To unify the winds": in the original it is more likely that those details of Form, Light, and Accent unify: *"los que unifican . . ."* But perhaps there is also no difference; and once all is said and done, it ends up being the same in English as it is in the original. In the same poem, the two following lines seem to me somewhat different from what the original says: *"Porque bajo, entre y sobre los cielos / da la distancia . . ."* ("between, under, and above the skies, / the distances . . .").

"Organ": "came shrilling through the roses . . ." It seems to me that in the original it says that it is the lovers who go laughing behind the roses, but I am not too sure about this, since I do not have Alfonso's poems here and now with me, and I am doing these corrections by memory—I know all of these poems by memory, but as I told you I am not too sure about this line.

Everything else is stupendous. They are formidable translations. It makes me very happy that they will appear in *New Directions*. James Laughlin has just written a very kind letter to me, informing me that he is going to send me *Breakthrough to Peace*, and asking me if I received *The Behavior of Titans* and *The Wisdom of the Desert*, which he sent before, and that he laments not publishing those poems of mine. I am responding to his letter.

I hope that you have received the letter that I wrote you about a week ago [September 24, 1962] along with a package of a few publications and magazines.

I await those new copies of the Alfonso translations. I will take a copy for him at the asylum when I go to Nicaragua in November.

United always in my prayers,

Ernesto Cardenal

Letter 35

Dear F. Merton:

I received your impressive and tremendous *Breakthrough to Peace*, more impressive during these last days, with "rumors of war," already foretold by Jesus—James Laughlin also sentd me another copy a few days ago. The bellicose tensions have subsided a bit, at least for the moment, but the anguish has been great: my own anguish has been especially great after reading the Cold War Letters and this book, books which have made me more aware of the horror that the world is continually headed toward with ever increasing speed—and too few are conscious of this.

Here in Latin America, the war has not been a preoccupation until now, when war seemed near and inside the same Latin America. Nuclear annihilation is not considered a danger here, perhaps because the first threat felt here by all is Communism. Atomic weapons tend to be regarded as a guarantee against that danger. And besides, all of those who are against communism are instinctively in favor of the USA; they have placed faith in the USA; they are certain that the USA will not make use of those arms in an act of aggression . . . There is some naïveté in this, and also the newspapers that obey orders, as in all places, do not speak of the great dangers that nuclear armament signifies for humanity. The majority tend to have a simplistic mindset, or they have either placed their faith in Russia or in the United States. Furthermore, there also exists the sheer sense of impotence: that the world's destiny is in the hands of the two giants, that the rest of the countries are merely nothing more than spectators who applaud one or the other. Let us hope that *Breakthrough to Peace* is translated into Spanish; it will guide many minds, as will your other writings about this horrible subject.

With this letter, I am sending you a few of the latest publications that have arrived here for me. I leave for Nicaragua the day after tomorrow to spend some vacation time; I will be there until February. Perhaps I will mail these items from Panama (where I will spend a couple of days), since I will be leaving almost directly from the seminary to the airport, and will not have a lot of time available beforehand. My family has insisted that I spend these vacations with them, and for me going to Nicaragua is always pleasant and useful. I always do some apostle work there with friends and interact with the youth, and the literary movements always have so much vitality, and some of them are very valuable. As usual, I will go to Río San Juan with Coronel, probably with Pablo Antonio, and there will spend a few days of very productive intellectual and spiritual retreats.

I am sending you a few articles that I published very recently, that are also part of materials I am collecting for a book. It will be titled, *La Revelación Cósmica [Siguiendo a] Daniélou*: what he says about the cosmic religion of pagan peoples. I am collecting a lot of information about all the primitive religions of the world, and about all the non-Christian peoples, and am reading everything I can find about this subject matter. In this book, I will present a great number of prayers, theological ideas, mysticism, etc. of the primitives, wherein Christian prophecy is always evident—a Christ foretold—as in the great myths also. Those Kogi Indians from Colombia of whom I speak in this article are absolutely interesting, and in this book I will present many singular things from many lands.

Sudamericana has not written to me as of yet. I have no news from them. I suppose that *La torre de Babel* will be published soon.

My address in Nicaragua is: Post Office Box 206—Managua—
Nicaragua

United in Christ, and entrusting you very much in my prayers,

Ernesto Cardenal

[P.S.] Did you finally receive the anthology of *Poesía revolucionaria nicaragüense*, and my own book of *Epigramas*?

Letter 36

Dear Ernesto:

Today your package and letter arrived, and I will carry out my intention to write to you finally. You can imagine I have been more and more swamped by correspondence and affairs, but that does not mean I have forgotten all the things I want to tell you.

To begin at the beginning: I am afraid I cannot find copies of your translations in manuscript of "The Tower of Babel," "Signed Confession [of Crimes against the State]," "Atlas [and the Fatman]," etc. They do not seem to be anywhere in the room here and my theory is that I must have sent them to someone [Sr. Thérèse Lentfoehr] who is making a collection of manuscripts, editions, and whatnot. I will write to her and see. But the trouble is there are several such collections going and I may have sent the texts to another, for instance the one at the University of Kentucky.

Later, she had written to Sudamericana for you to receive half of the rights, so that should be clear.

I know this was censored a long time ago, or at least some of it was censored. "The Tower," I am sure, was censored. I have had a great deal of trouble with censors. There is a Babel of inscrutable censorships and reprobations at work in the Order. I have finally resorted to getting things censored in England when there is any question that they contain anything more than statements like "It is nice to pray. Good morning, Father, have some holy water. We never eat hot dogs on Friday, etc."

Yes I have received your *Epigrams*: they are magnificent. The *Revolutionary Poetry of Nicaragua* [*Poesía revolucionaria*] too I have received: there is much in it that is most deeply moving. I am grateful for your corrections of the translations of Alfonso, and I have put them into the text. The poems are to be published in a New Directions anthology but unfortunately I can see that J. Laughlin is going to waste an enormous amount of time getting down to business with it. I may give them to some magazine, and will draw on your very fine article for a biographical introduction.

Your poems about the Indians have been simply superb. I am sure your whole book [*Literatura indigena americana: Antologia*] will be splendid and look forward to seeing it. You have a very great deal to say and I know it is most important. This is something far deeper than *indigenismo* with a political—or religious—hook inside the bait. This is a profound spiritual witness. Also a reparation, and a deep adoration of the Creator, an act of humility and love which the whole race of the Christian conquerors has been putting off and neglecting for centuries. It reminds me that some day I want to write something about Vasco de Quiroga. I have not forgotten about the Indians and all that they mean to us both.

I also am studying "cosmic revelation" in a slightly different form: the philosophers of the twelfth-century school of Chartres ["News from the School of Chartres"]. Splendid and almost unknown people, they were too far ahead of their time to be received with unmixed applause and strangely some of their attackers were Cistercians. But they have a profound sense of symbolism and myth, together with boldness in rational investigation and a metaphysical sense which makes them more than Platonists, but forerunners of Aquinas and of the most solid and spiritual metaphysics of Being. I hope to do some translations when I can get to the texts, but they are almost unknown, and still in manuscript. The enclosed poem is inspired by one of their glosses on a pagan myth ["Gloss on the Sin of Ixion"]. I will also send you the little book of *Clement of Alexandria* I did, which includes his exploitation of Greek traditions.

I sent the *Merton Reader* to you in Colombia, but I asked the publishers to send one to Pablo Antonio, so it should be there now. Please let me know if it has not arrived and then I will send one myself, by air. What is Coronel [Urtecho's] address? I can send one to him also. I hope you have a wonderful time in Río San Juan. Please give my best wishes to Pablo Antonio and Coronel; I wish I were there to converse with you all. I must stop now. Pray for Louis Massignon, the great Islam scholar, who just died. He was a great organizer of non-violent action in Paris and also did much for Christian–Moslem dialogue.

With all my blessings and cordial friendship in Christ,

Tom

Letter 37

Dear Ernesto:

In my other letter I said nothing about the clippings you sent, except in a general way, the remarks about your poems about Indians being based mostly on other things you had sent before. But now I have read the clippings and I want to add a few things. First of all, the poem about Bartolomé de Las Casas is most moving, and so is the article about the mystical tree, which seems to me to have a deeply prophetic quality. I think you are aware of things that most people are completely oblivious to. I think there may well be a great cataclysm and after it the poorest and humblest people, the Indians, may remain to pray [to] God to pardon and revive the human race, with the Africans. This is only a repetition of what I said in the letter [to Pablo Antonio Cuadra] about Giants, but I say it again.

Your Psalms [*Salmos*] are terrific. Those are the versions we should really be chanting in choir. How few monks think of the real meaning of the Psalms. If priests knew what they were reciting every day. I am sure some of them must realize. Do we have to be in the concentration camp before the truth comes home to us?

Ventana is very alive and appeals to me more than most other "little magazines." Again it has a prophetic quality in it, and a simplicity that is lacking in the more frustrated or the more pretentious publications. I was especially happy to see a new poem of Alfonso Cortés. If that is a madman's poem, then I must be mad, because to me it is one of the most lucid and sane poems I have ever read. And again it has that fabulously direct metaphysical intuition that reaches through surface concepts to the very act of being, the actuality of *ens* [being] breaking through the temporal and through our artificially spiritual concepts to manifest itself in its transcendence. I have translated the poem, and perhaps you will tell me if I have it right.

In Pablo Antonio's little book, *Zoo*, I recognized some of the poems I liked before, as well as new ones. I am very grateful to him and will write soon. Did the letter appear in *El Pez y la Serpiente*? I never saw it. Perhaps it is on the way here, or delayed. I have only two issues of *El Pez y la S*.

By the way, thanks for sending the beautiful volume of Eduardo Carranza. Surely you would like me to return it. Tell me where, and I will send it. He is a very perfect poet and his perfection is a delight. The whole book is a delight.

As to politics and the world situation, a little news comes through sometimes and then long periods of silence. The rumors, then more denials, and silence. Yet I wonder if I really know less than those who get the papers. The question is that the world is full of great criminals with enormous power, and they are in a death struggle with each other. It is a huge gang battle, of supremely well-armed and well-organized gangsters, using well-meaning lawyers and policemen and clergymen as their front, controlling papers, means of communication, and enrolling everybody in their armies. What can come of it? Surely not peace. There will be repeated crises, like the last one in which intellectuals fled from the U.S. to Australia and in which the students of Oxford drank up all the old wine in the Union Club because they thought there would not be any more time for drinking anything. The cataclysm will come without giving anyone time to drink up what may be left. It will not be planned by the cleverness of men. And we must pray and be joyful and simple because we do not after all understand most of it. Behind it are good meanings, which escape us. But let us avoid false optimism, and approved gestures. And seek truth.

I like the issues of *Nivel*, too. I think José Lopez's poem *"Marcan los relojes dolores similares"* is an extraordinarily good poem about peace (in *Ventana*). Now I must stop. Who will civilize North America? That is the big question, and perhaps it is being asked too late.

Let's pray for each other. Please greet all of my good friends. I am happy for all of the good news that I receive from you.

Blessings always, and cordially in Christ,

Tom

Letter 38

Dear F. Merton:

Thank you very much for your two beautiful letters, written on the same day last month. I am happy that you liked the two newspaper articles with information that will form part of my book about *La Revelación Cósmica*. I truly believe that the Holy Spirit is guiding me in this research, placing at my disposal a great amount of very beautiful, extraordinarily revealing material that I did not know existed before. This research that I am doing about primitive peoples—the Africans, Indians in America, and Polynesians, etc. has been a great comfort to me during these dreadful days in our Nuclear Era. Those other eras, Paleolithic, Neolithic, etc. still give me a lot of hope and much faith in humanity. Your "Clement of Alexandria" will also be very useful to me for my book.

A few days ago I sent you the first two volumes of the work, quite large, that Coronel is writing about the history of Nicaragua [*Reflexiones sobre la historia de Nicaragua*]. I think the first volume will be especially interesting to you. I also send you an issue of *La Prensa* with one of my articles about Taoism and your translation of Alfonso Cortes. To me that poem seems masterfully translated, the meaning perfectly conveyed, and it is more clearly understood in its English translation than in the original, which is more difficult. And we have discovered a very curious thing in regards to this poem. He had already written it before with another title ("*La vida*") in 1923, a few years before going crazy, with a different meter (longer verses) and with a few different rhymes. The poem is almost the same, yet it is different. This new one is like a "translation" performed upon itself. And overall this new poem is better than the first one, but the older version helps one understand the new one a great deal. I am certain that this other one was written recently because he never tends to give us old poems, nor does he even like to remember them. As I pointed out in my essay, the modifying of previous poems to create new poems with his own elements is quite common for him. Here now I am sending you the poem from 1923.

Pablo Antonio Cuadra told me that he had sent you *El Pez y la Serpiente* by airmail immediately after it had come out. Since you did not receive it, he sent it again by airmail, and I hope that you have now received it. A new issue of the magazine is coming out, which we will send you immediately as soon as it is out. The magazine has been coming out on a very limited basis because Pablo Antonio Cuadra has a lot of other work to do with the newspaper and he practically runs the magazine by himself. After Christmas we shall go to Río [San Juan] to reunite with Coronel. How much we wish that you could also be here with us! The address for Coronel is: José Coronel Urtecho—Las Brisas—Los Chiles (frontera norte)—Costa Rica. His ranch is situated on Costa Rican territory, on the border with Nicaragua.

A few days ago I went with Father Ángel Martínez to San José de Costa Rica. There we visited the Nicaraguan nun, about whom I have spoken to you before, Sor María Romero, who is performing great miracles almost on a daily basis like the ones of Father Pio. She is a great miracle worker. I spoke with her at length; she is a very simple and natural woman, and what most impresses me is the natural way that she speaks of the extraordinary. She showed me the records of her latest healings—matter of factly—and the places where clothes and food multiply for her to give to the poor, etc. She made a prayer pact with me, and I also asked her to pray a lot for you. Father Ángel Martínez will go in February or March to the United States and is thinking of going to Gethsemani to see you.

You can return Eduardo Carranza's book to me in Colombia, when you no longer need it. He will be very pleased to know that you liked it. He is currently the best poet in Colombia, a Catholic poet, very religious, and a very good friend of mine.

I am sending you this newspaper clipping about Lanza del Vasto, which perhaps you have not seen. I am very interested in that experiment that he is conducting, and I am currently reading his book, *Las cuatro plagas*, which is very good.

Pablo Antonio Cuadra (PAC) sends his regards. We hope that you will send us the address for Henry Miller and Father Berrigan, so that we can get in touch with them.

Remembering you in my daily prayers, and wishing you a Merry Christmas in our Father, with greetings in Christ.

Ernesto Cardenal

Letter 39

FEBRUARY 25, 1963

Dear Ernesto:

First of all, I want to say that I have translated a few selections from your *Gethsemani, KY* and "Three Epigrams" and I am asking Laughlin to include them in a book of my poems with some other translations. I think he will, and the translations will make the book better. I will also have some of (the same ones of) Pablo Antonio, Carrera Andrade, Vallejo, Alfonso Cortés, and Raïssa Maritain. The rest of the book will include my own new poems, "Hagia Sophia" and the "Letter to Pablo Antonio." So you see you will all be involved in a book that will almost be a collaboration. I hope it will turn out very well. The title is *Emblems of a Season of Fury*. The Cortés translations will also be printed by Laughlin, he says, in *ND* 18. But as usual he is very slow about that.

I received two copies of *El Pez y la Serpiente* with the "Letter to Pablo Antonio" and also the more recent issue. Your translations of American poets were very fine. I have also sent some material to your friends at *El Corno Emplumado*.

Yes, I know Lanza del Vasto. There was a Jewish student of mysticism here who had visited the Community of L del V and spoke highly of it. I have also read what I think is his most interesting book, *Le pelerinage aux sources* (i.e. to the sources of the Ganges). He is great friends with Victoria Ocampo. I have read parts of the "4 Plagues" and it is terrific. I have also read fine articles of his in peace publications. Talking of Victoria Ocampo: her friends got up a volume of Testimonios for her, and I was included: they put my name as "Thomas Merton S. J." Speaking of S. J.s, I never received news from any of your Jesuit friends.

Did I ever send you the translations I did from Raïssa Maritain? She has done some very remarkable things (of course she is dead now) and there might be place for some of them in *El Pez*. You could write to Jacques Maritain for her two books of poems; I think he would be glad to send them for translation purposes. He is at Faculté de Theologie, Fraternité, Ave Lacordaire, Toulouse, Hte Garonne, France. He teaches philosophy to the Little Brothers of C[harles] de Foucauld. [He] is happy there, and wrote me a couple of marvelous letters, especially about "Hagia Sophia," which he liked very much. Raïssa has done a journal, or rather she kept one that is to be published, and it is amazing. She was one of the great contemplatives of our time.

I am very interested in knowing about the holy sister of Costa Rica [Sister María Romero]. God does not cease to employ those who are close to Him by the simplicity of their faith. Though I have been quite busy, I see more and more that the dimension of my life that has meaning is the solitary one, which cannot be expressed. There are things that can and must be communicated, but it is an error to attach too much importance to them. I think it is really a waste of time for me to write more books on "the spiritual life" in the usual sense of the word. I have done enough already. And at the same time it seems futile to write about the way the world is going: yet it is true there are times when one must speak. But one must be sure of the necessity. James Baldwin has written several terrific books about the race situation in this country. You can get review or study copies from his editor, Dial Press, 461 Park Ave. South, New York 16. Ask for *The Fire Next Time*. They are going to send me copies of his novels and I'll pass them on to you.

Here are a couple of new poems: and under separate cover I am sending the new, enlarged (mimeographed) edition of Cold War Letters to La Ceja. With that, also a translation of a letter of "Guigo the Carthusian." Did you ever read his meditations? Tremendous.

I have to go now. I think often of you and all my friends in Nicaragua. I hope you have done well with Coronel at the Río San Juan, and all that you tell me about Ometepe sounds stupendous.

With best cordial wishes and blessings, complete friendship, in Christ our Lord,

Tom Merton

Letter 40

Dear Father Merton:

It has been a few days since my return to the seminary, beginning my second year in Theology. I am always very content here, enjoying my little paradise of peace and inner silence, amidst the beauty of the countryside that surrounds us, within these mountains of Antioquia, and with some free time every day for reading and literary work.

I left Nicaragua during a time of elections. There is a new imposed president [René Shick], who is a "puppet" for the Somozas—these were actually *Hitlerian* elections. But the situation has not at all remained calm with this. A breakup between the Somozas and the new president seems very probable, and perhaps much later this will lead to a genuinely free election. In any case, new developments are expected to occur there soon because the Somozas are weakening, despite their efforts to retain power, and opposition against them is very strong.

Notwithstanding the ongoing bad political situation, there is much vitality present in the country and an admirable spiritual fecundity. The country is especially producing many young poets, more than in any other place in America. Coronel, Pablo, and I are creating an apostolate among them and we have been very good for them. Many young people in Nicaragua are becoming Marxists, as in all of Latin America, but the new poets and artists that are emerging—and there are many and [they are] highly valuable—are Christians, and more than one of them, perhaps later, may end up in a contemplative vocation.

These young men have decided to boycott the magazine *Ventana*, where they had been collaborating, because it is controlled by Marxists (from *La Universidad Nacionál*, which is a beacon of Marxism), and they plan to start their own magazine, on which all of us will work together, also helping in the boycott of *Ventana*. A young man, Napoleón Chow, who also collaborated with *Ventana*, told me that he has been corresponding with you. He is truly one of ours who has infiltrated among the Marxists; he has a religious calling to add to that, and is valuable. And I believe that he will not continue collaborating with that magazine.

I hope that you have received my last letter that I wrote to you from Nicaragua, with some newspaper clippings, and a second version of Alfonso's poem. He is now writing very good poems, like the ones from before, very mysterious and very *Alfonsesque*. In the next few days they will be publishing a book of his in Nicaragua [apparently never published before], which I will make certain is sent to you. I think the choices were made without judgment, and that all his work is published there, good and bad, scrambled.

In this letter I am sending you two fragments of my historical long poem about the Conquest, "The Doubtful Strait," which I believe is going to be published in Nicaragua this year. An anthology of Latin American poetry has been published in the USA (*New Voices of Hispanic America* by Darwin J. Flakoll and Claribel Alegría. Boston: Beacon Press, $4.95). They told me that I have been included in it, together with a few others from Nicaragua, but I have not seen it. I think that it should be interesting, and it is about the newest poets.

I received the *Merton Reader*, a magnificent edition. I have been reading, to much avail, pieces that I did not know before. I also very much liked "The Prison Meditations [of Father Delp]," and a professor from the seminary, who was also very interested in these, would like to translate them. Father Voillaume came to the seminary today, the one from the *Hermanitos de Jesus*, and he gave us a talk where he said very good things—some somewhat similar to those in the prologue to "The Prison Meditations."

Guadarrama has never gotten in touch with me about the publishing. I also have not heard anything from Sudamericana.

United always in Christ,

Ernesto Cardenal

Letter 41

MARCH 13, 1963

Dear Father Merton:

I have received your letter and the translations of my poems, which to me seem exquisitely done, and which I appreciate so very much, especially being aware of how difficult it is for you to be able to set aside time, since you have so many things to do, and so little time (just maintaining that correspondence would be enough to prevent one from ever having the time to do anything else, and I think that there is something miraculous in the mere fact that you could do all of this with so little time). So, I appreciate those translations very much, as I do those lines written about me, and I am very pleased that all of this will appear in your book of poems, *Emblems of a Season of Fury* [*Emblemas de una temporada de furia*].

One epigram that has a translation that is not faithful to the original: "No one knows who killed, or was killed" [*Nadie sabe quien mato o fue muerto*]. In reality it is: "Who was killed, or *were* killed" [*a quien o quienes mataron*]. Because perhaps it is one dead, or many dead. The doubt is not about *who* kills them.

In the epigram about the sirens, a line is missing and perhaps it is better like this. Because it is a difficult line to translate, and one that is incorrect in the edition published by the *Universidad de México*. It is: *Como el grito de la cegua en la noche* ("Like the scream of the siren in the night"). They printed *"yegua"* instead of *"cegua"* because they were not familiar with that word (even though it is Nahuatl). She is a female ghost from a popular indigenous myth, who terrorizes during the night, a sort of Lilith-like Nahuatl siren (in Mexico they call her *Cihuanahuatl*). I think it is very good to leave that word out in English, as you did, because it does not make sense.

Very beautiful, the two poems of *Marcario* ["Macarius and the Pony" and "Macarius the Younger"]. I wish to translate them, however the problem is that there is no place to publish them in Latin America. Currently here in Colombia there are no good publishers; there are some in Mexico, albeit a few, and we are too cut off from the southern, deepest reaches of South America. These two poems echo those lives of medieval saints, and I've wanted for a long time to write a few lines like these about a few American saints: Saint Martin de Porres, St. Rose of Lima, etc., along the same lines of the historical narrative poems that I have written before.

And speaking of saints, the Nicaraguan nun who lives in Costa Rica, Sor María, is performing great miracles daily: she is a personal Lourdes. On my way back from Nicaragua, I went to visit her with Pablo Antonio and we spent the entire afternoon with her. She showed us a tree next to the kitchen in the convent, completely full of birds of all colors (a bold occurrence in the tropics, where there is no spring and where there are always birds, but rarely so many ever seen together in one single tree), as if they were inside an invisible cage. She told us with complete natural ease that this was one of the latest miracles performed for her by the Virgin: that she really liked birds, and since she could not see them, because she could not go outside, she had asked the Virgin to bring them here, and there was this tree, every day, filled with birds. She lives surrounded by the extraordinary with such a natural ease, as if it were all so ordinary. She is very cheerful, she is always in a very good mood, and one is frequently laughing with her, as it must have been with St. Teresa. I spoke with her about you and asked her to pray a lot for you and your intentions. I plan to write to her in the next few days and I will remind her. She provides food and clothing to thousands of the poor on a daily basis, and great numbers of people arrive to ask her for healings, and she performs many miracles for them.

The bulletin of [*American*] *Pax* that you sent me was very good. I always hope to receive those kinds of things. They are very useful for my own development and for preaching what needs to preached, whenever the occasion comes up for me. Here in Hispanic America there is also a lot of disorientation regarding this subject. And I have also read the new collection of Cold War Letters with passionate interest. I am certain that those writings of yours are doing much good in the USA, no doubt within a small minority, but soon we shall see its fruits. I wish that you could send that collection of Cold War Letters to Howard Frankl, the American poet whom I took to the baptism in Cuernavaca. He was led to God through strange paths—marijuana was one of those paths—and now he leads a life of self-imposed poverty and prayer in Los Angeles. He has thought about living a life of contemplation later with me in Nicaragua. He will like the Cold War Letters very much, and they will do him much good. His address is: Howard Frankl / 706 ½ W.Z. 7th St. / Los Angeles 7, CA.

I will write to Pablo Antonio and have him ask Jacques Maritain for Raïssa Maritain's poems for the magazine. I would also like us to connect with Henry Miller as you suggested, and with F[ather] Berrigan as well, but we need the addresses for these two.

There is a seminarian that has just arrived here and he told me that he owed his vocation to your books he read in the USA; especially, he told me, that he owed being here in the seminary to the book *Ascent to Truth*, and is very grateful for all the good that you have done for him.

During Holy Easter Week we usually go and assist in service to the parishes, and last year I was in a small town here, in Antioquia. But this year I chose a remote place on the Río Magdalena, a parish in the jungle that is sure to be a beautiful place. On another occasion, I also wish to go to the Amazon, in the Colombian part, where the Capuchins have a mission, but that will be during a longer vacation break. I have great desire for the Amazon.

In Río San Juan, I was only with Coronel. Pablo Antonio could not go. But our time there was very useful; we talked about a lot of important issues, we made some plans about the future in those places where Coronel already lives as a true anchorite, and we also spoke about you very much. All in all, these days were like spiritual exercises.

Always remembering you in my prayers. United in Christ,

Ernesto Cardenal

Letter 42

Dear Ernesto:

Thanks for your last letter with the fine new poems of Alfonso. They seem to me to be among his best, and not the easiest to translate either.

The *Sewanee Review* has taken two of my translations of his poems, and another ("Truth") with my poem about him will be in a new magazine called *Continuum*. In the same issue will be my translations of your Gethsemani and epigrams. I did not have time to make the correction, and am sorry for the error. I will have to do something about it in the book, when it comes at the end of the year.

Jubilee printed my translations of Raïssa Maritain. I hope Jacques has sent you her books. She is a fine poet.

Here are some things that might interest you. The piece on Zen [published as "The Zen Revival" in *Continuum*] will be revised a little, but it is all right as it stands, I think. It can be developed further.

This is only a hasty note. More after Easter.

All my blessings in Christ,

Tom Merton

To the above, Merton added, by way of postscript, the addresses of Fr. Dan Berrigan and Bro. Antoninus (William Everson).

Letter 43

Dear Father Louis:

In your letter of April 8th, you mentioned to me that your poem about Alfonso ["To Alfonso Cortés"] was going to be published. I hope that you will send it to me, since I am still not familiar with it (you have not sent it to me).

My trip to Río Magdalena was very interesting, even though it disappointed me a little. The place was in the midst of the tropics, but the river there was not very beautiful (it was not as beautiful as Nicaragua's Río San Juan, and I thought it would be like that). The waters there are dirty because the river drags a lot of dirt. A lot of civilization has also come in; the misery of civilization: poverty, ugliness, prostitution, bars, unemployment, etc. Many of us seminarians went to help out at the parish in those places during the Holy Week of Easter, and we did help some; in the end, it was a very good pastoral and human experience.

I read your essay about Zen ["The Zen Revival"] with great interest, and it helped me to clarify my understanding of Zen a little more, which I find quite difficult. My understanding of Zen is still not precise, but I think that I already had an experience of a bit of Zen under your spiritual guidance at Gethsemani. I do not know if I am mistaken, but I believe that I received practical instruction in that sense, not with words exactly, but rather with practice through spiritual direction; that spiritual life is not a life separate from the other one. From that moment, I think that my life of union has been a little Zen, somewhat simple and natural like the other vital functions. This has also served me in order to teach something to others, and only give direction to a few who always look to me—thanks to those teachings with you in Gethsemani, which was a huge grace from God. Others have also benefited through me from those teachings.

I do not know if Pablo [Antonio Cuadra] might have already received Raïssa's poems. I hope so.

Sor María Romero, the nun of great miracles in Costa Rica, has written to me that she is including you, with your first and last name, with all her spiritual brethren. She does so with great enthusiasm.

Here goes another fragment of my historical poem about the Mexican conquest, based on Bernal Díaz's account, which MacLeish also drew from. They have just published this fragment in Mexico in a magazine ["Bernal Díaz"].

Our *Antología de la poesía norteamericana* has already been published, and I suppose that you have already received a copy.

United always in prayer, I bid you regards in Christ,
Ernesto Cardenal

Letter 44

Dear Ernesto:

Thank you for your letter and for the excellent new poem ["Bernal Díaz"]: when will all these poems be out in book form? When I have the book, I will perhaps translate a few of them. They are really splendid.

I am enclosing sheets from the magazine *Continuum* with my translations of your other poems, unfortunately not corrected. I was not sure they were going to publish these, so I only corrected the copies I sent to New Directions for the book. The book will be called *Emblems of a Season of Fury*, and it is appearing this fall. I think it will be quite good, and besides all my new poems and translations, it will include the "Letter to Pablo Antonio."

Somebody ought to write an article on the Christian Democrat Movement in South America for *Continuum*. I have asked them to send you copies of the magazine. You may think of someone well qualified to do it. You ought to do an article on contemporary Latin American poetry for them. The editor is Justus G. Lawler . . . Why don't you write to him about this? I think he would be very interested. As to the article on Christian Democrats, maybe Napoleón Chow would know the best one to do this. He wrote to me about his course at Bogotá, and said he had visited you. He spoke of *Ventana*, and thought that perhaps he and a few other Catholic writers ought to stay with it, because if they withdrew, the whole thing might fall completely into the hands of Communists. I think it is important that Catholics, at least some of them, do not adopt a policy of withdrawal. For religious and clergy it is perhaps different. We do have to be circumspect. But at the same time certain of the laity ought to be able to go far in their own sphere. I think one of the weaknesses of the Church that the Cuba situation brought out was the fact that as soon as things got to be a little hot, and the Communists became aggressive, the Catholics became negative, adopted a condemnatory stance, and assumed that all attempts to go on collaborating with Castro were an infidelity as long as he did not openly repudiate Communism. This had the result that the Church became identified with the policy of the U.S. State Department, and the results were fatal.

However that may be, I think that *Continuum* needs someone sending live information from Latin America, and I hope you will get in touch with Lawler.

Your friend in Argentina wrote me a great letter but I still haven't had time to answer it. I am terribly pressured by more and more correspondence, by all kinds of problems and matters. A faculty member of a Protestant theological seminary wants to come here for a retreat and they want me to direct the retreat. Now I have all the novitiate brothers together with the chorus in one novitiate: were are already on the same wing that you know, thank heavens: I wouldn't have wanted to move the brick building in the middle of all of the machines.

A yogi from India stayed here the other day and will come back later for a retreat. Then I'll talk with him and hopefully he'll give a few talks to the novices. He is a very interesting and spiritual person, and I believe we will get along. In regards to Zen, Dom Aelred Graham has written a considerably good book called *Zen Catholicism*. I will ask the editor to send you a copy—I reviewed it for the magazine *America*.

This is really just a hurried note; but please pray for me during Pentecost week; I have received permission to make a retreat at the hermitage and I hope it will not be interrupted, but will be fruitful. I often remember you and all my Latin American friends in Mass. God be with you and bless you, always. Stay well, and walk with God. Cordially as always in Christ,

Tom Merton

Letter 45

LA CEJA

JULY 17, 1963

Dear Father Merton:

I have been in Bogotá spending some twenty days of our vacation time, and I have put myself in touch with all the young writers there. I have brought back a great number of publications that I will send you through regular mail. With this letter are a few newspapers and things for you, and one of my articles about the Uitotos Indians ["*El relato de la creación de los indios uitotos de Colombia*"], part of the book about the religious experiences of the primitives, which is coming very far along now. I have gathered large amounts of facts, stories, poems, etc.; absolutely beautiful things about many primitive peoples, especially the Indians in America and Africans. With all this information I have been gathering, I think this book will be three hundred to four hundred pages long.

I am very happy about the election of our new Pope [Paul VI] whom I believe will be great for the Church, including for our personal destiny here in America, perhaps with new things to do in the future. I hope that he will be a good agent for these things. By the way, one of the first official acts of this new Pope was to make our Father Rector a bishop because he is a very prominent person in the Colombian clergy, and has received a lot of credit for the foundation and the success of this seminary.

Father Ángel Martínez was in the USA and really wanted to go to Gethsemani to see you, but due to his poor health, he could not make the trip—he suffers from acute ulcers and lives only by miracle. He is currently in Nicaragua again, and [he] hosted a retreat for poets and intellectuals, which Pablo, Coronel, and practically all the writers and young poets attended.

I have just received *Zen Catholicism* [by Dom Aelred Graham]. I think this is a very important book, and I will begin reading it immediately. Many thanks.

I have just received *Continuum* and have written to Mr. Lawler about the things you told me. I have also been in touch with Henry Miller about the publication in *El Pez* that you suggested to us, and he said that he would send me the book.

United always in my prayers,

Ernesto

Letter 46

Dear Ernesto:

I think you know Cintio Vitier, in Cuba . . . He is not sure whether our letters are getting through, and neither am I. I have just sent the letter of which the enclosed is a copy. You might drop him a line and ask him if he received it, and if not you can send him the copy. If mail is not getting through directly, I thought we might send things through some other country, for instance Colombia.

Thanks for the *Colombiano literario*, with the translation of the "Letter to Pablo Antonio," and its fabulous presentation. I am very happy about it. Thanks especially for your magnificent essays on the creation narrative of the Huitotos. That is really a wonderful field for you, and I am sure you will continue to find things there that will be of the greatest importance for all of us. Someday America (North, Central, and South) will perhaps be the great living unity that it was meant to be and that it now is not. That will not be possible if it tries to be the rootless culture that it now is: a sort of cancerous orchid transplanted from somewhere else.

This is only a note to let you know about Vitier. I wrote to Pablo Antonio and sent him some things for *El Pez*. I like *El Corno Emplumado*—the Cuban poets in the last edition were very good. Are you going to publish your psalms [*Salmos*] as a book? I hope you'll do that.

God bless and best wishes in Christ,

Tom

Letter 47

SEPTEMBER 15, 1963

Dear Father Louis:

I received your letter of August 1st with the copy of the latter for Cintio [Vitier], which I sent to him. He is a friend of mine and we had been writing to each other beforehand. He has just replied to me, telling me that he had received your letter before receiving the copy that I sent him, and that he was extremely grateful for it. I suppose that he has already responded to you. It seems that they have not personally bothered him yet and he continues at his job, which I think is as the director in a library. However, he has not sided with Castro, and he tells me that he will not collaborate with any official newspaper; since they are all official, he will not collaborate with any of them or publish anything. In any case, his life must be very difficult. When he was in Mexico, he used to tell me that they [did] not impose any religious persecution on adults, but they gave the children an obligatory atheist indoctrination, and this was harder for the Christian parents than if they had been personally persecuted.

He feared much for his small children, and I think that this is what makes him suffer the most on the personal level regarding the current situation in Cuba. In his letters, he has always asked for many prayers, and they reveal a situation of anguish. Naturally, he had been with the revolution at the beginning, but he told me that the current regime in Cuba was actually Soviet and Stalin-like.

I received *The Fire Next Time*, which the editors sent me, and I have not read it yet, but I think that I might write something about the book. I have also been receiving the pro-peace publications that you have been sending me, and I wish that you would continue sending me all these publications, because I plan to write several poems about this subject; I am already starting to do so. Laughlin has also written to me, and [Henry] Miller wrote to me to send *The Wisdom of the Heart.*

Sudamericana has written to me to say that they are now publishing *La torre de Babel.* [They said] that they will pay me $70 for the translation and that the royalties would be divided between the two of us, of which they will send me half of the first payment of 50 dollars. Is this all right? Thank you very much for participating in this. I was hoping to publish the edition of my *Salmos* here in Colombia, but I have to pay for the edition and I did not have the money to do it. I will do so with this [*La torre*], which Sudamericana is sending.

I am discovering very good things regarding the religion of the Indians in America. The book is going to be extensive and with surprising material. It seems to me that the Holy Spirit is helping me in these discoveries. There is a book of prayer and other religious things from the North American Indians that you showed us once at the seminary. Do you remember which one? I remember that it had pictures of Indian Chiefs, among which was one of Sitting Bull, and I think that there was something about Sitting Bull or another chief regarding meditation. I would like to know the title of this book in order to request it if you remember which one it is.

I would also like to know which publisher has published the translation of Dr. Wu's *Tao Te Ching* that you cited in an article. Thank you very much.

United always in prayer,

Ernesto Cardenal

Letter 48

[NO DATE, 1963]

Dear Ernesto:

Your letter of Sept. 15 arrived while I was in the hospital, and more recently the box of magazines has come, for which I am most grateful. I was not in the hospital for anything too serious, just the results of an old spine injury.

Yesterday I received one copy of the new book of mine, from New Directions: *Emblems of a Season of Fury*. It is the one including the translations from your poems, Alfonso, Pablo Antonio, etc. ND will surely be sending you a copy, but if they do not, please let me know. I was distressed to see that somehow that mistake in one of your epigrams had got into the book. I had meant to correct my translation, and was sure I had done so. I am positive that I sent them a correct translation, to replace the earlier incorrect one. But then the mistake got by me in the proofs. I am very sorry.

I am sending you a mimeographed copy without corrections of a manuscript on art, a revision of an older book I believe you have seen (unpublished) ["Art and Worship"]. If you are interested and want to translate it, and place it with someone who is more interested, I will split the rights of author and Spanish translator with you. It would be some help to publish some of your own poems. I suppose that Sudamericana would want it, but in any case they have the moral right of the first choice. I don't hear anything more from that person in Spain [Editorial Guadarrama] to whom, I believe, I sent *The New Man*.

I am sending you John Wu's translation of the *Tao Te Ching*. The same place has published a translation of an important Chinese Zen work, the *Platform Sutra* of Hui Neng, but unfortunately the translation, though probably good in its own right, uses terminology that misses the real Zen meaning and does not correspond to the kind of language used by the best Zen men, like Suzuki. At least there should be some agreement on terms. I have written a long article on Zen, in fact I think I sent you an earlier version, but I have rewritten it for *Continuum* ["The Zen Revival"]. I hope Lawler has been in touch with you. But if not, it is because the magazine turns out to be more political than literary. I told a new magazine [*Charlatan*] edited by a Protestant group at the University of Iowa to get in touch with you; I have sent them some notes on Julien Green ["To Each His Darkness: Notes on a Novel of Julien Green"] and also some abstract sketches of mine. I forget whether I have sent any of these abstractions to Pablo A., but he might like them for *El Pez*.

I received a letter from Cintio and wrote him a longish letter, sending also a packet of poems, in October. I don't know if he received them. I was wondering if perhaps a series of three large envelopes from the U.S. might have caused him trouble. He told me also, guardedly, that things were not as good as they were painted in Cuba and indicated that it is really a Stalinist absolutism they have there. This is a very great shame. It can be said that the future of the world depends in large measure upon the quality of the social reform, let us say revolution, that is effected in Latin America. It is the weakness of very poor and underdeveloped countries to have to swing into a rigid absolutism dominated by force in order to maintain a certain stability in social change, and this defeats itself. Everything depends on education and leadership, and on the capacity of the intellectuals for creative and independent development, and the great danger is that men will be lacking who can measure up to the greatness of the task. I certainly hope and pray that the Church may be able to provide an impetus for creative thinking, but the task is gigantic.

Did the magazine *Ramparts* send you the issue with my long article on the Negro problem here ["The Black Revolution: Letter to a White

Liberal"]? Recently I have played in the novitiate some excellent tape recordings of interviews with the Negro leaders, including Martin Luther King and Malcolm X of the Black Muslims. Their talks were very impressive. How did you like [James] Baldwin?

The [Vatican] Council seems to have been going well. The general impression is that the second session is "not exciting," but I would certainly say that the decision on the collegiality of bishops is one of the most important things done by the Church in the last five hundred years. It can have a tremendous meaning. Also, if lay deacons (even married) are allowed, this can be of tremendous significance, especially in Latin America.

I look forward to seeing your book on Indian religion. I think this is really a very important project, and coming just at the right time it can have a decisive effect, both spiritual and cultural, throughout Latin America. I hope it will do so. The book I showed you here was *The Sacred Pipe* by Black Elk, and I think it was published by the U. of Oklahoma Press. I went looking for it just now but could not locate it anywhere. You know how books disappear here. It was a very fine book, anyway, and I am sure it should not be hard to obtain.

Well, I will put the art ms. ["Art and Worship," unpublished] and several other things in an envelope for you, and hope it will all get there safely. I have been doing a lot of studying on St. Anselm, and Sartre, finding rather surprising affinities between them. This is not what anyone would have expected. I am also reading Nicholas of Cusa, a very great mind and a most original thinker of the fifteenth century, who has been very much underestimated. A mystic and "apophatic" theologian, he also foreshadowed the kind of relativity that we have since [Albert] Einstein, insisting that the universe had no center and no limits: this long before Copernicus and Galileo. He was a Cardinal and no one made any difficulties for him because they did not understand what he was talking about.

I should stop now, but I send you my best wishes and blessings. I will write about the journals once I've dived into them. Did I send you a mimeographed copy of the notes on art and freedom [*"Respuestas sobre arte y libertad"*], which I wrote for Miguel Grinberg?

United in prayer and truth, in Christ,

Tom

Letter 49

November 13, 1963

Dear Father Louis:

We leave on vacation this week, for almost three months, and I am going to spend them in Nicaragua (until February), and my address there is PO Box 206 Managua-Nicaragua. Together with this letter I am sending you those articles about the Cuna Indians that I know will interest you ["*Las Cunas*" and "*El cielo de los indios Cunas*"]. They are an amazing culture. I had been researching all of this in books, but I have just met the tribal chief of the Cunas [Yabilinguina], who has come to Colombia to speak with the president and is lodging at the home of some missionary nuns. I had a very interesting interview with him that will be published in a few days, and I will send it to you. You will see just what beautiful things the Cacique told me. He spoke of peace for most of the time, and how they do not fight because when God made them, he told them that this earth was not for fighting. I have made friends with him and I will take advantage of this trip to stop by and visit the Cuna tribe, in the archipelago of San Blas, which lies in front of Panama in the Caribbean. I will make the trip on bus from here to the Panamanian border, and there I will take a little boat to the archipelago. I will stay there among the Cunas for a few days, and then head to Nicaragua. Every day I become more interested in Indian-related things and am learning more from them. This, I believe, will also become like a kind of vocation for the rest of my life. And by the way, I owe you for my ability to begin to understand and love the Indians, and most of all for being able to see in them the religious and spiritual values that I did not see before. And that almost no one here in Latin America ever sees. The things that I discuss in these articles about the Cunas have surprised many because they were unknown.

Yours in Christ and united always in prayer,

Ernesto

Letter 50

Dear Ernesto:

Your letter arrived just after I had sent one to you at La Ceja. Perhaps it will be forwarded to Nicaragua, perhaps not. It does not really matter. I am very happy to hear of your visit to the Cuna Indians on San Blas Islands. I remember my friend Dona Eaton used to talk about them: she came from Panama. I don't remember much of what she said, but the name "San Blas Islands" made a lasting impression. Your two articles were superb. I am sure the interview will be most important, and your visit even more so. The more time you spend with them the better. I think indeed that this is really an important aspect of your vocation, and that rather than becoming purely and simply a conventional priest, you should think in terms of this strange kind of mission in which you will bring to the Church knowledge of these peoples and spiritualities she has so far never understood. This has been a factor in the lives of the greatest missionaries, however: to enter into the thought of primitive peoples and to live that thought and spirit as Christians, thus bringing the spirituality of these peoples into the light of Christ where, indeed, it was from the start without anyone realizing the fact.

In my letter I mentioned I was sending a manuscript of my book on sacred art ["Art and Worship"]: it's an uncorrected mimeographed copy, just to give you an idea of the book. My idea is that, if you have time in La Ceja, you might be able to prepare an edition in Spanish and act as agent for it; if you can, we will split the rights in half: it's not a long book, and if you would like to, you can pick your own illustrations for the Spanish edition. Anyway, I'm not sure how they will illustrate it here.

The Abbot General [Dom Gabriel Sortais] died last week, and now [President John F.] Kennedy has been killed. It was a shock to hear the news yesterday, and we are not quite clear what happened or who was behind it. But in any case, it was, like all such things, purely senseless and pointless. Kennedy was a good man and a competent president. He was not able to carry out his best ideas, but he still tried to move in the right direction, though sometimes he found himself going the wrong way perhaps. But I am very sorry over this senseless act, so pointless and purposeless, and so needlessly cruel.

I hope to hear more from you about the indigineous tribes. Give my regards to Pablo Antonio and Coronel, and to everyone in Managua, etc. I'm going to send a copy of my book of poems with the translations [*Emblems of a Season of Fury*] there. This was the other thing I mentioned in my letter. Out of equivocation, they printed an incorrect version of my translation of one of your epigrams. I'm sorry, I thought I sent them the correct version, I'm sure I did this. But then I myself should have seen the error in the proofs.

Best wishes for you always. Very cordially in Christ,

F. M. Louis

Letter 51

Dear Father Louis:

Thank you very much for your letter from November 23rd, which I received here in Nicaragua. My visit to the Cuna Indians was something stupendous. These are very beautiful islands, and contact with their culture was an impressive experience. I had previously interviewed the main tribal chief [Yabilinguina] in Medillin, who, despite not being baptized, is a saint and a wise statesman, and spoke to me all the while about peace and of non-violence (I am sending you the interview with this letter). I was not able to see him again in San Blas, since the chief was still in Colombia, but I was still very well received by the Indians. They lodged me in the hut belonging to the Congress, where they hold their general assemblies, and there they gathered to hear what I came there to do. I explained that I admired their culture and traditions and that I had written about them, and that I wanted to get to know their culture and traditions better in order to write more about them and make sure that they would be better known in America and better appreciated. This pleased them and they allowed me to attend their Congress, and I tape-recorded a few discussions in Spanish and Cuna, as well as chanting, etc. The social order is as I had described it in my articles: they live a kind of Christian Communism. And they speak of God all the time. The island where I stayed was itself an entire village of very beautiful straw huts, with very clean and very narrow roads of almost one meter wide. I was only on one island, but there are many more and there are missions on some of them (Catholics and Protestants). On some other occasion, I hope to spend a longer time [there] to be able to visit more islands and make a truer connection with that culture. I hope to do this next year; this time, I was not prepared for anything else other than a quick visit to the island where the chief had invited me. But now I have friends there, and I hope to make more contacts through the Catholic missionaries.

I am very encouraged by what you tell me regarding this aspect of my vocation. That is how I see it. I now see it clearly that I should continue to write about these subjects all my life (about the Indians). In America, they are completely unknown. And I will be a defender of those spiritualities. Especially I plan to dedicate myself to the Cunas; I can do a lot of good for them, spiritually and materially, making America see the value that is in them—what we in our pride have ignored. I will send you other writings about these subjects later, as I continue publishing.

I will not see the letter that you wrote to me at Le Ceja until I return there in Februrary. The same goes for the book about sacred art ["Art and Worship"]. I think that I will have time to translate it. I am very interested in doing it and I really appreciate your offer of splitting the author's rights in half, as you mentioned. Pablo Antonio suggests that the book be published with Guadarrama. I will write to the publisher to propose it.

Carrera Andrade has just arrived in Nicaragua as an ambassador. I have not seen him yet, but we will see each other in a few days, and I think that we will be good friends; we have spoken on the phone and he asked about you. Pablo has already spoken with him (he has just arrived in the country), and we are very happy to have Carrera here. His presence is going to be very good for all of us, and he will also find company that will please him.

I do not know if I will go visit Coronal in [Río San Juan]. Either way, he will come to Managua before my return to Colombia, so we will all get together here with him.

Odilie Pallais has charged me with sending her regards to you, and to tell you that she always prays for you.

United with you also in my prayers, I wish you Merry Christmas, in Christ.

Ernesto

Letter 52

Dear Father Louis:

Upon my arrival at the seminary, I found a copy of the book about sacred art ["Art and Worship"] that you sent me, and I am very interested in translating it, so I hope that you will send me the definitive copy that will be published. I think that we can easily find a publisher, and I think that Guadarrama would be good for this; they are coming out with magnificent publications. I already wrote to a friend of mine who is in Spain, so he can propose it to Guadarrama. I also think that this publisher is now interested in publishing the other book that you had once planned with them—this friend has told me so—and I am hoping that they will also let me know about this soon. Regarding *La torre de Babel* at Sudamericana, I have not had any news. It has been months since they said that they were going to send a contract, and they have not done so.

When I was recently in Nicaragua, I went to visit Coronel Urtecho in Río San Juan, as I have done so in previous years, and there he proposed that we should translate one of your books, both of us: it would be a kind of Merton Reader [*Antología de Merton*] for Latin American readers. Coronel is very interested in this project and it also seems very good to me. There we will select the texts that would be of most interest to Latin Americans, and the ones that can do the most good for people, including older books, as well as the latest essays about current themes, the Cold War, etc., and poems too. Coronel wanted to begin quickly, translating a few chapters from *New Seeds of Contemplation*, and for this he would like a copy, since he does not have the book; his address is: José Coronel Urtecho. Las Brisas. Los Chiles (Frontera Norte). Costa Rica.

Emblems of a Season of Fury is a very beautiful book, and it is a great honor for me to be included in the company of such good poems. There are a few new ones in there, like the one of Averroes, "Song for the Death of Averroes," and the one about the Chartres school, "News from the School at Chartres," which I did not know and liked very much. Thank you for the book and the inclusion of my poems.

I have received Laughlin's letter and also another one from Lax, all the way from Greece, and in both of these they tell me that you have been ill, although they do not give me more details. I hope that the illness was not serious, and that it has passed and that you are well. Either way, I have been entrusting you to my prayers more often, and have been a bit worried. Are you all right?

Thank you very much for Dr. Wu's *Lao Tzu*; it is a very beautiful edition and it will be absolutely useful for my studies (I also have many other translations).

United also in prayer, and wishing you safe keeping with God,

Ernesto

Letter 53

MARCH 10, 1964

Dear Ernesto:

I was glad to get your letter and your new piece, the "Letter to a Paéz Indian," which is simply magnificent, most moving. I liked very much too your splendid interview with Yabilinguina and in fact I gave a résumé of it to the novices here and they were all very much moved. In fact many of the young professed brothers were present also, as I have them now in conferences too. The pictures of the San Blas people are fine, most beautiful.

Miguel Grinberg is here, and I am very happy to meet him. His meeting in Mexico sounds like a very great thing; certainly the Spirit is moving through South America and Latin America generally, and this movement of poets and artists toward a new spiritual consciousness is certainly the most hopeful thing that I have seen in the world lately: and God knows there is not much that offers any real hope apart from charismatic things like this. We simply cannot look to the established powers and structures at the moment for any kind of constructive and living activity. It is all dead, ossified, corrupt, stinking, full of lies and hypocrisy, and even when a few people seriously mean well they are so deep in the corruption and inertia that are everywhere that they can accomplish nothing that does not stink of dishonesty and death. All of it is rooted in the cynical greed for power and money, which invades everything and corrupts everything. But Miguel and the poets have shown a genuine integrity and love which are sane and hopeful in the extreme, particularly because the same longing for life and truth is manifesting itself everywhere at the same time and independently. I hope that the great awakening of South America is at last about to begin, for the future belongs to South America, Africa, and Asia: but above all I think to South America. If only the great sense of love and solidarity and human strength can totally take roots, and the masses of the people, particularly the indigenous people, may attain full consciousness of the meaning and strength of their presence. You will have a very significant part in this, and I hope that at least by my prayers I will also. I was touched that you mentioned me in your letter.

I say the future belongs to South America: and I believe it. It will belong to North America too, but only on one condition: that the United States becomes able to learn from South and Latin America and listen to the voice that has so long been ignored (a voice which even ignores itself and which must awaken to its own significance), which is a voice of the Andes and of the Amazon (not the voice of the cities, which alone is heard, and is comparatively raucous and false). There is much to be done and much to pray for.

I am happy that you and Coronel [Urtecho] want to do a special anthology, and I enclose a copy of the letter I sent to Sudamericana about rights to the material in their books. This may be difficult if they refuse, but if they publish the book themselves there should be no difficulty, but you should keep after them.

On the other hand, there is a vast amount of things Sudamericana has *not* pubslished. For example:

All of the books of poems and the essays, including some included in the books of poems.

The Behavior of Titans, The New Man, Spiritual Direction and Meditation, "Art and Worship," and other unpublished books which are finished now.

In addition, many articles, etc. But it's better to not use the articles on nuclear war because they have silenced me on this point. However, the selection of *New Seeds [of Contemplation]* on this material is available.

I will send Coronel *New Seeds* and other things that might be of use to him, and I will put in an envelope some new things of mine for you. I still do not have the good copy of "Art and Worship" back from the censors, but I will send it as soon as I can.

My health is fairly good; I have a permanent injury to one of the vertebrae of my neck, but with care I can avoid too much trouble with it.

I do not want to have to have an operation, which might do more harm than good. I think I can live with it all right.

It has been good to have Grinberg here and to hear about the new poets everywhere. I am going to try to keep more in touch with these things, for it is here that one finds, I think, some of the most authentic and honest spiritual life in the world of our time. In the monasteries there is still simplicity and joy among some of the monks but the structure is so false and artificial that one has a hard time keeping serious about it, and it is often very discouraging.

Best wishes to you and God bless. I will be saying Masses for Latin America soon and I keep you especially in mind, together with my good friends, Pablo Antonio and Coronel, etc. etc. and also Morales, all the poets and people of San Blas, and all of the indigenous.

With all the best in Christ,

F. M. Louis

Letter 54

Dear Ernesto:

A letter from Coronel tells me that you and he are getting down to the project of translations for a kind of reader. I sent him a lot of material, perhaps too much, and my own feeling is that the book should not be too long. On the other hand as it quite probably will be done by Guadarrama, I suppose it should be representative. A lot of the books have not come to be known in Spain. I leave that all to your judgment and his. For my own part I like the recent works best. Here is an article on Gandhi that might be interesting. It is terribly important now to keep the concept of non-violence alive. What is happening is that in the race movement in the U.S. the non-violent tactics are being discredited because the gains that were made have been taken back and nullified. Restaurants have quietly segregated themselves again, etc. Token concessions were made, and then everything went back as before. This is a very serious situation because now violence is going to begin, slowly, sporadically, but the situation will get definitively rotten, and I see no alternative. Perhaps in the long run this is the only way that the realities can be brought out and kept in full view. People do not want to see them. This is a very unrealistic country.

The fact remains that a non-violent political ethic is terribly important everywhere. I read "*Colombia macheteada*" ("Macheted Colombia," by Eduardo Perilla) in *El Corno*. If we cannot get things organized it is going to be something like that everywhere. And it is totally senseless. But the senselessness of physical violence is necessary, perhaps, to manifest the senselessness of economic and cultural violence. And the basic violence of a life without God, without silence, without prayer, without thought.

New Directions will do a small book on Gandhi, consisting of selections I made and a long introduction ["Gandhi and the One-Eyed Giant"]. If it gets by the censors it ought to be fairly useful. I hope it will.

I have been a little ill with a bad back resulting from old injuries, but it is nothing serious, simply a nuisance that I have to live with. Father Sylvanus was living for a long time as a hermit in Martinique and is now in Texas. Dom Jacques Winandy O.S.B. is starting a small community of hermits there [Martinique]. I haven't heard anything of S[ylvanus] in some time. I get a lot of time in the hermitage that is now on the hill behind the sheep barn, and am planning to write less, perhaps. There have been meetings of Protestants here often, but I do not want to overdo this. A group of Hiba-kusha, or survivors of the atomic attack on Hiroshima, will stop here next week. They are touring the world on a peace mission. I think the outlook for world peace is better at the moment, at least as regards nuclear war with Russia. On the other hand, affairs like that in Vietnam are very bad indeed, and the mentality of the military people and industrialists in this country remains very unhealthy and dangerous. If tensions are less, it is not due to anyone in particular here, though [President Lyndon B.] Johnson seems good in this regard and Kennedy made a serious attempt to follow up Pope John [XXIII]'s encyclical [*Pacem in terris*]. I think that the split between Russia and China has done a lot temporarily to make things better, but in the long run who can say whether this will turn out better or worse?

Did I write you that Miguel Grinberg was here? Maybe I did. By the way, Sudamericana wrote again concerning *The Tower of Babel* and they said that they didn't know where you were and for that reason didn't send the contract. I gave them your address a while back. But it would be better if you wrote them. If they don't follow through soon we'll have to think of something. I think that they will if you write them. On the other hand we can simply publish the translation somewhere else.

All the best to you and God bless. By the way, I forgot if I finally sent you the complete text on "Art and Worship." Please let me know. The complete text contains some ten pages on the constitution of the [Vatican II] Council and its legislations on sacred art. This wasn't mimeographed and was done by machine. It also has a new preface.

May God be with you. Let us trust Him and He will not fail us, nor will He fail mankind, which belongs to Him.

In the charity of Christ,

Tom Merton

Letter 55

Dear Father Louis:

Thank you for your last and very good letter, which I just received. Coronel also wrote me, and is very enthusiastic about the material that you sent him and the reader that we are planning. It seems very good to me that Guadarrama would be the one to publish this book, because it is a very good publisher, but if Sudamericana can publish it, I think it would be better, because they are the ones with greater distribution in Latin America; but perhaps this is a problem that does not need to be considered yet.

I really liked the article about Gandhi ["Gandhi and the One-Eyed Giant"] and I have a great desire to know the selection from Gandhi that you will publish in New Directions [*Gandhi On Non-Violence*]. I am actually preparing a poem, perhaps somewhat extensive, about Gandhi, made primarily by using his own writings and teachings.

I still have not received *El Corno* [*The Plumed Horn*], where "*Colombia Macheteada*" appears. Also, I did not know that they had published it there, but I am very pleased that they did. This poem was written by a young seminarian, a colleague and a very good friend of mine in this seminary [La Ceja]—his name is Eduardo Perilla—and he wrote it under my direction, or rather, with my help, since he has only just started writing and learning the techniques; but I think that he can go on to become a good poet because he knows how to capture experience very well. This seminarian wishes to join me later in the contemplative life in Nicaragua, and I sincerely believe that he has the contemplative vocation.

During this Holy Week, he accompanied me on a brief expedition that we made to the Cuna Indian tribe, on the Caribbean coast of Colombia near Panama. I sent an article with an account of this trip to a newspaper in Bogotá, and I hope that it will be published soon, and I will send it to you when it is published. Especially beautiful is what the Cacique told us about the injustices that they are suffering, and there [in the article] I reproduced the entire discussion. They are real *gandhianos* and practice non-violence. A priest had never entered their midst before, but we were very well received. I promised to help them in regards to the injustices and the pillaging that they are suffering at the hands of the whites, and in the next few days, I hope to have an interview with the governor of Antioquia to intercede for them and ask that they be protected.

Miguel Grinberg writes me frequently and I see that his visit to Gethsemani impressed him very profoundly. He plans to stop by to visit me here in the seminary on his return back to Argentina.

I received the new copy of "Art and Worship" [*Arte y culto*] and I will begin to do the translation soon. I do not really like the literal Spanish translation of your title: *Notas sobre arte y culto*. I do not like it very much. *Notas sobre arte sagrado* sounds better, and better yet, I think, would be to simply use *Arte sagrado*. Let me know which one seems best to you.

I have just written to Sudamericana again regarding *La torre de Babel*.

I hope that your health has improved. I have been very sorry that you have been suffering these things, and I am increasing my prayers for you. Next year is my ordination; afterward I will go to Nicaragua, but I also wish to visit you in Gethsemani to talk about the life that I will lead in Nicaragua.

Embracing you united in Christ,

Ernesto

Letter 56

July 12, 1964

Dear Ernesto:

It is a long time since I have written and I do not remember whether I answered yours of May 16th. Perhaps not. I have been reading wonderful things of yours, and surely I received the copies of *Pájaro Cascabel* and *Américas* [containing sections of "Message to Poets"]. *Américas* is really coming be excellent. I liked Rafael Squirru's little book on the New Man [*The Challenge of the New Man*]. Have you seen it? It is very right. The usual thing we have all been thinking, but which is not yet known or understood enough. The need for admitting to hearing the voice of the new man who is rooted in the American earth (not just in the American machinery), especially the earth of South America. It is first of all important to listen to the silence of the Indian and to admit to hearing all that has not been said for five hundred years. The salvation of our lives depends on it. The things you wrote about the San Blas Indians were marvelous. There is no doubt that you have a providential task in this work of understanding and love, a profound work of spiritual reconciliation, of atonement. It is wonderful to realize the full dimension of our priestly calling in the hemisphere. Not the ridiculous and confused activities based on meaningless presuppositions, but the activity of true atonement, a redemptive and healing work, that begins with *hearing*. We begin already to heal those to whom we listen. The confusion, hatred, violence, misinformation, blindness of whole populations come from having no one to hear them. Hence they speak with knives, as the Negroes are now doing, for all that has been heard about them is still not them.

Alfonso Callejas was here. He offered us again a hacienda at Chinandega, but I told him it was impossible. Fr. Abbot [Dom James Fox] was not here. I am convinced that a foundation on the usual Gethsemani pattern would be impossible. Spencer's foundation in Argentina is miserable. A whole monastery has been built; everything is there except monks. They have about seven I think. If I made a "foundation," it would be without foundations and almost without a roof, but with enough of silence and aloneness to think and pray. The great problem would be avoiding publicity and yet being in contact with those who should know and come. But it is really no problem.

He made other proposals which I thought were very intelligent and with which I could not but agree. I wonder if they will come to anything. Perhaps he will discuss them with you. He seems a practical person. What he tells me of your own ideas seems sound. You should not get involved in too much activity but leave yourself time to write, and that remains a problem. However, I am thankful that I have as much time here as I have. Things are going well with me, and the hermitage is a real blessing for which I am most grateful. Since I have had it I have been able to give up worrying about the deficiencies and limits of monasticism and simply live with God in my own way. After all, that is the basis of monasticism anyway.

Anyway, let's move forward with Gudarrama. I wrote to Pablo Antonio about this.

The best wishes and blessings always in Christ,

Tom

Letter 57

Dear Father Louis:

Now during this month we have been having a mid-semester break and I took advantage of it for a trip to the Amazon, something that I have wanted to do ever since I arrived here. It was an airplane ride from Bogotá to the small port that Colombia has in the Amazon, on the border with Peru and Brazil. An unforgettable trip, unfortunately too brief since I was only there for one week, and more was not possible; but at least I was able to see the great jungles, the beautiful scenery of the river, and sail a bit through it up to the first settlement in Brazil. The river in that region is still not so immensely wide, as it becomes later, but it is already a grand river anyway, the greatest I have ever seen. Nature there is similar to the outlying regions of Río San Juan, although much more wild and dangerous, and also everything is much more vast. I visited the Indians of the riverbanks, very primitive and extremely poor, although it seems to me that they are very content and tranquil amidst that extreme destitution. I spent time with the Capuchin missionaries, who are in charge of the Colombian Amazon region. And that was a great experience, albeit brief, and I give thanks to God for bestowing this upon me—the passage was granted to me by the Colombian Air Force. I hope to write something about this, at least a poem.

Upon my return, I was met with a letter from Pablo Antonio, who has just returned from Europe, and he tells me that he was going to write to you about the issues he discussed with the director of Guadarrama publishing. I am guessing that he has already written to you. According to him, Guadarrama is eager to purchase your publishing rights from Sudamericana, and it seems to me that if Sudamericana is not upholding the contract well, this change of publisher would be a very good thing. Guadarrama is truly becoming a very good publisher, and its distribution in Latin America is improving every year. And I believe that it is a much more responsible publisher than Sudamericana. The translations from Sudamericana are absolutely terrible; the one for *The Seven Storey Mountain* is especially very bad, detestable, and it looks like they have refused to make the corrections that we sent them from Gethsemani. I think that it is necessary to make sure that this book is published with those corrections, whether it is a publication by Sudamericana or Guadarrama. The translation that they [Sudamericana] published is so bad that it seems to me that this alone is enough to request an annulment of the contract.

Pablo Antonio has also let me know that Guadarrama is going to publish my book of brief religious meditations, of which I have spoken to you on other occasions, titled *Vida en el amor.* It was composed mostly from notes, thoughts, and meditations from those days at Gethsemani, and also from ideas that I heard and learned from you. I am happy that it will finally be able to be published at Guadarrama because there it will have more widespread distribution and the ability to do some good for some readers; many who have read it have told me that it has done them much good.

I wrote Sudamericana, asking them about *The Tower of Babel*, and they told me that they had sent me the contract last December, already signed by Gethsemani. I never received it, and I told them to send it again, because if they did send it, it must have gotten lost. I am awaiting a response. I received *Américas* with your message to the reunion of poets in Mexico ["Message to Poets"]. It was very good.

United always in prayer,

Ernesto

Letter 58

Dear Ernesto:

James Anderson, editor of *Charlatan*, wants me to relay to you the information that he is accepting "En el monasterio trapense" for number 2 or 3, and that he has lost your address. I am glad he has taken something of yours. I hope many others in Latin America will send him things. Did you see the first issue? Some good things [are] in it, but [it is] mixed. I had some drawings (abstract) along with an article on Julien Green ["To Each His Darkness: Notes on a Novel of Julien Green"]. Did I ever send you this? Tell me, and I will do so if I did not. The poem that I attached will be in *Blackfriars*, but also in *New York Review of Books* on the same page as one by Spender.

The abstract drawings I did for *Charlatan* were the beginning of a flood of "abstract calligraphies." I have done scores of them, and in fact some are being framed and will be exhibited in Louisville this fall, perhaps also elsewhere. I sent a few to Pablo Antonio, and Coronel mentioned having seen them. You saw some that were not very good in *El Corno*. By the way, how are you all doing? I haven't seen an issue in quite a while. Those are also inconsistent. I liked Miguel Grinberg. I suppose he didn't get to see you, but he was in Managua.

I haven't heard from Guadarrama, but I am anxious to hear from them. Sudamericana is done as far as I'm concerned. I don't know if they seriously plan to continue on with *The Tower of Babel*, but if not, it could appear in the anthology, or somewhere else. But the matter of writing is becoming so complicated that it's a disgrace, that is, the aspect of business.

It doesn't bother me what pertains to writing. In effect, I'm going to try as much as possible to simplify the business side and leave it to the editors. Laughlin knows what has to be done.

Have been reading [Fernando] Pessoa, in Spanish and Portuguese (thanks for sending the [Octavio] Paz translations) and he is a real discovery. I like him very much and may attempt some translations for New Directions. I think I told you I had read some Pessoa to Suzuki and he was delighted with it.

Here everything is as usual except there is some hope of progress toward a serious eremitical colony annexed to the monastery in the lonely hills several miles away. I am very anxious for this, and pray for it ardently. You know how much it could mean: do please keep it in your prayers too. When is your ordination? I think of you often and ask God to bless you and your days to come, as a priest.

The best wishes always. I will send you some of the latest mimeographed works, etc. The novitiate is very peaceful and I am satisfied with it.

In all friendship, in Christ,

F. M. Louis

Letter 59

Dear Father Louis:

I have received your letter from September 26 with the beautiful poem of the little girl from Alabama with her doll ["Picture of a Black Child with a White Doll"], a very beautiful and moving poem. I do not know about the magazine *Charlatan*, and I would like to receive it. I am glad that they would want to publish something of mine.

Pablo Antonio wrote me that he was going to dedicate a page to you in the library supplement of *La Prensa* with some of your abstract drawings and some of our translations. I wrote a small essay for that edition about your writings regarding the nuclear question, but I think that my article did not arrive there in time, since I only just sent it, and they have just written me from my home in Nicaragua to say that this edition has already come out. Anyway, I will publish that essay in *La Prensa* and in some parts of *Américas*. Very interesting that you are now painting. I would like to have one of those drawings, if you have one left over, and one that you have not sent to the exposition.

My ordination is next year, possibly at midyear (in August). I have not wanted to receive any orders or tonsure yet, because I still did not wish to commit myself to incardination, since I first want to make sure that they will allow my plans for a contemplative life. Now, during my upcoming vacation, I am going to Nicaragua, and plan to be incardinated myself there finally. I think that I will be able to obtain an arrangement that would allow me this; either way, I will be incardinated, and later we shall see what God disposes. What you tell me about the colony being annexed to the monastery makes me very happy, and I expect much from this, and I will entrust this to God in my prayers.

My vacation begins on November 14th, and my address in Nicaragua will always be the same: Post Office Box 206—Managua—Nicaragua. I have received an invitation from Cuba to participate in the jury of a literary contest [for *Casa de las Américas*] which they hold there annually for all Latin America. They have always invited foreign personalities to make up this jury and also non-Marxist people. The trip would be in January, so it is while I am on vacation, and can make it. I have written to accept, and it seems to me that I have done well. Is your opinion that I should go? It seems to me that you would think "yes," but I wish to know your opinion on this matter.

I think that I would be able to establish good personal connections with the poets and intellectuals on a purely cultural and personal level, regardless of ideologies and political systems. And also [to establish] contact with Catholics like Cintio, who are not sympathizers to the regime, but have not wanted to leave Cuba.

Not long ago, I also received an invitation to visit the Soviet Union, and I have also written to accept and give thanks. A Costa Rican legislative official from the Left, a friend of mine, had been invited recently and he suggested to them that I be invited so that I could be in touch with the young Russian poets. The trip is less likely because I can no longer make it this year, and in the coming year, if I am already an ordained priest, it is possible that they will no longer wish to invite me; and likewise, the [Church] hierarchy would not allow me to go. Also, in the letter they do not mention paying for my trip to Russia; they only tell me that they will pay for all the expenses during my stay in the Soviet Union. For now, the trip to Cuba is of greater interest to me than Russia, because in Russia I will not be able to speak unless it is through interpreters, and personal contact would be difficult and perhaps not very authentic.

Grinberg was not able to pass through Colombia this time, and from Nicaragua he left for Argentina, but says that soon he plans to come here.

El Corno is certainly very inconsistent and full of all things useless and bad, but the magazine's fundamental attitude is good, and together with the other groups and new magazines in Latin America they are creating an interesting continental movement that only just a few years ago did not exist; and where we have a job to perform, and a mission bestowed by God. I consider this to be the field of action for my apostolate, which no other cleric in Latin America is going [to do], and probably would not be able to do.

Your essay about crusade and pilgrim ["From Pilgrimage to Crusade"] is so beautiful, is almost a poem, and it seems to me truly inspired by the Holy Spirit. The one about Father Perrin ["A Priest and his Mission"] was also very good.

Together in Christ and always praying for you with embraces,

Ernesto

P.S. I beg you to have them send me three calendars from Gethsemani to the seminary, and also send one to Coronel, who is always happy to have one (he likes to have many calendars at his *finca*, and the one from Gethsemani is the one that he prizes the most).

Letter 60

[Handwritten note, without date on a postcard ("The Holy Trinity," Russian, 18th Century, Ikon Museum, Recklinhausen, Germany)]

Dear Ernesto:

Many thanks for your letter. The marvelous volume with the articles by Pablo Antonio and Coronel in *La Prensa Literaria* surprised and moved me. I will write soon to thank them—We have just had a great gathering of Abbots and I have been very busy.

I believe the trip to Cuba seems a good idea and I hope that you go. Also, to Russia—it would be a good experience. But only if you can do it without any problems.

My best wishes and blessings, always.

In Christ,

Father Mary Louis

[P.S.] Here are some drawings for you. More disconcerting than the ones I sent to Pablo Antonio.

Letter 61

[Handwritten note on a half page without a date]

Dear Father Louis:

Many thanks for the beautiful drawings I received; they say so many things, if one contemplates them with stillness and silence. It is a painting entirely spiritual and simple and poor. It seems to me that it is contemplative painting and perhaps also a little Zen.

Tomorrow I leave for Nicaragua. The trip to Cuba depends on what the nuncio in Havana decides. If he approves the trip, I will be able to make it, since this way there would be no danger of ecclesiastic conflicts of any kind—and I think that he will probably approve it, since I know that he is in favor of progressive and transparent politics. We shall see.

United in Christ,

Ernesto

Letter 62

Dear Ernesto:

It is Christmas eve, and I don't know when I will have time to do anything after Christmas, so I want to write you this note now to say that in case you come to America next year, I have received permission from Rev. Father to get together with you, if you are here, for a day. You may of course stay longer but he has restricted his permission to one day, as far as my talking with you is concerned. I hope you come. There are a lot of things to talk over, especially the matters with Guadarrama. I never know with them, and I suppose that I have to deal with them directly myself. I will. It seems definitely certain that the contract with Sudamericana is broken. They have rejected many books when they were committed to receive them all, and they are dragging their feet with *The Tower of Babel*, so I see no reason to keep going with them and they wouldn't be able to object if I go with Guadarrama. But there is also the matter of the anthology [prepared by Coronel], and I will send some new material soon.

José Coronel wrote a good letter, which I hope to answer early after Christmas if I can.

This fall I exhibited some of those abstract drawings in Louisville and it was quite successful. The exhibition will go to New Orleans in January, I think, and perhaps to other cities also. It will be in Catholic colleges mostly, as far as I know. It might be an idea to put a few in the anthology. They are black-and-white and would reproduce very easily and cheaply.

Things are quite quiet in the monastery. There are only eleven novices altogether, choir and brothers, and I have them both. Last year one hundred and nine were interviewed but out of these only three were accepted and came. One of these left. Some others might be coming later though; they have been delayed. Prospects of a South American foundation are almost nil, but there might eventually be one in Norway, as we now have a Cistercian bishop in Oslo.

I hope you will be able to get to Cuba. I think it would be a very good thing. If you go, please tell Cintio Vitier that I got the poems he and Roberto Friol sent and [that I] wrote back, but he must not have got my answer. I wrote to him again the other day, just a note. I would be interested to know if he got it. The new book [*Seeds of Destruction*] is out and I am sending a copy to you. As I may have told you, I managed to get most of the better material on peace into it after all.

The ending of the Council session was very ambiguous and as a result the Protestants in this country have become once again quite dubious about the Church. They see that many bishops want more openness and liberty but they feel that the Pope [Paul VI] is on the side of an entrenched minority, and I wonder if this is not perhaps quite true. The Pope does some very encouraging things, but one finds that he later tends to cancel them out and neutralize them by other acts or statements that are very conservative. Hence I suppose that we must be patient with a period of transition in which everything will still tend to be quite equivocal. The Church badly needs the prayers of all of us. My best wishes and blessings to all my friends in Nicaragua, especially Pablo Antonio and José. Cordially and warmly in the Lord,

Tom

Letter 63

Dear Father Louis:

Many thanks for your letter that you wrote during Christmas to me in Nicaragua. Soon I will return to Colombia, since I need to be there February 6th to begin the quarter term in theology. My trip to Nicaragua has been very productive in more ways than one. I have spoken with Alfonso Callejas, who told me about the interesting things that he is planning in regards to the question of ecumenism, and is following your instructions with optimism; and let us hope that he will have success in his project if God wants it this way. In regards to my projects for after my ordination, things are very good. I have been at Coronel's ranch, and I have already chosen the place where I will establish myself toward the end of this year. It is an island in the archipelago of Solentiname, in Lake Nicaragua. This archipelago is made up of forty-some islands facing the little port of San Carlos on the Lake, and in front of Río San Juan. Coronel's ranch is very close to this place I have chosen, about two hours by boat. The bishop of this diocese has already approved the whole plan that I have laid out for him, and he is the one who will give me Holy Orders. The nuncio has also approved it, and they regard my project with enthusiasm. Many friends here in Nicaragua have offered all the financial help needed to purchase the property there, as well as for the initial agricultural projects and the rest of the expenses. Many young men in Nicaragua wish to join me in this foundation, especially some young poets, and in the seminary in Colombia there are also a few more who wish to do the same, therefore I think that at the very least I will have enough to begin.

My ordination to the priesthood will probably be in August, and I think that I will come and do it here, in Nicaragua, to please my family who want to be present for it. I would come here for two weeks, since I think that the seminary would allow me, and afterward I would have to return to Colombia to finish up the year before coming back to Nicaragua on a permanent basis in November, which is when the course will end. Coronel is absolutely happy with the development of these events, as well as Pablo Antonio, since this project is also very dear to them, and they wish to share in this life just as soon as it is made possible for them. Pablo Antonio, Coronel (who was here in Managua for a while), and I had a spiritual retreat, along with a group of young poets, and it fell upon me to give the talks (I am sending you a newspaper clipping about it). This has been like a rehearsal for the retreats that we will need to have in Solentiname, once I am there conducting that life.

The trip to Cuba could not be realized, unfortunately, since the nuncio in La Habana, with whom I consulted about the trip, suggested that it was not convenient given the current political situation there. I think that Miguel Grinberg has gone in my place to participate as a judge in that literary contest to which I had been invited.

I suppose that Coronel has been writing to you about the anthology. We have been talking about it a lot, when I was there with him in Río [San Juan] and also later when he was here in Managua, and we have already been making the selections of the material that will be included. Coronel is very enthusiastic about this anthology. He is now leading a full life of prayer, an authentic mystical life, and I am certain that he will have great influence over the youngest ones during this new phase that he has entered in his life, as he once before influenced the new literary generations. It is becoming increasingly clear to me that Nicaraguan poetry has a special ministry in Latin America, and this is how Coronel and Pablo

Antonio also see it. It is a literary movement that has not risen at random, but rather a work designed by God's providence, I am certain.

United with you always in prayer,

Ernesto

[A typewritten note without date on a separate card, marked "La Ceja"]

I wrote this letter in Nicaragua about twenty days ago, and I thought that I had sent it to you. I have now returned to Colombia and have discovered it among my papers; I now realize that I did not send it. It is quite likely that instead of mailing you my letter, I sent back the letter that you wrote me, which I was responding to. As such, I would like it if you could send back that letter of yours the next time you write me. I have nothing new to add at this time; everything is coming along well here in the seminary, where I am now beginning my last year.

Ernesto

Letter 64

Dear Ernesto:

The other day I was very happy to get a letter from you, but when I looked inside I found my own letter to you, which you must have put in the envelope by mistake. Presumably you were answering me about your trip here, and when to expect you. But I have not received the information, so please write me about it again. Meanwhile I suppose you may be in Cuba. I hope you are, and that you are seeing Cintio and giving him my regards. I am sure you can do a great deal of good simply by being present among so many other poets.

It is true that not all the "progressive" thought and action in the Catholic world makes perfect sense at the moment. There has been a kind of spring thaw and all the rivers are running mightily, but some of them are just carrying away good ground, and trees, and things that need to stay where they are. I think we have to have the courage to distinguish and to use a certain amount of prudence and above all not simply make a virtue out of condemning everything in sight, while putting nothing of any value in its place. And all that is new is not necessarily an improvement. However, I do think that a great deal that is going on is most salutary and what the Council has done so far is excellent. I do not say all this in reference to your going to Cuba. I think that perhaps there has not been enough in this direction of dialogue with the left, which can and should be at the same time quite serious, perfectly clear in its definition as Catholic (without useless and foolish compromises) and yet a valid human communication.

The piece about the *ejercicios* was very encouraging and I was happy with it, happy to see the picture of so many friends, and you looking happy in the middle of it. I also very much like Coronel's translation of my poem on solitude ["*Vida solitaria*"].

God bless you, and be well,

Cordial best wishes in the Lord,

Tom Merton

[Handwritten P.S.] I recently sent Coronel a copy of my new book [*Emblems of a Season of Fury* or *Life and Holiness*] and many new essays.

Letter 65

In early March, Merton wrote to Pablo Antonio Cuadra, expressing concern "that Rome is making inquiries about Ernesto and that these might possibly affect his ordination." [See Merton's letter to Cuadra, dated March 2, 1965, in The Courage for Truth*]*

APRIL 24, 1965

Dear Ernesto:

Thanks for your letter. I am relieved that there is nothing behind that inquiry from the Sacred Congregation. I am surprised that no such request had come in before this, in my ten years as novice master. There must surely have been other former novices ordained somewhere. But perhaps they were handled without reference to me. At the same time, I think it is possible that you might expect some time or other to be criticized for your work, especially on the Indians. Perhaps I am wrong, but I know from experience that one cannot write anything alive without being attacked, and sometimes quite fiercely, by members of the Church. Certainly the most virulent attacks on any work of mine have come from priests and [the] religious, though for the time being they seem to have calmed down and accepted me as an inevitable phenomenon.

I think I owe José Coronel a letter, but I am sure that the book [*Reader*] is coming along well. I was most touched by the letter he last wrote about it, saying how much he had entered into the material and how much it meant to him. I send you some more material, some of the newer things that you probably have not seen.

Actually I am living most of the time in the hermitage in the woods, sometimes eighteen hours out of the twenty-four, only coming down to the monastery for strict necessities and work in the novitiate. It is a wonderful life. Actually it has transformed me, and I am now at last convinced that I have found what I have always been looking for. Provided that it goes on this way.

I have been in contact with Ludovico Silva. The poets in Caracas impress me, and there seem to be some lively publishers there. I wrote a preface to Ludovico's poem on the bomb ["Prólogo" to *BOOM!!!: Poema*]: I very much liked your "Apocalipsis", *in illo tempore*, in *El Corno*. Your pieces on the San Blas Indians have been great, too. F. Martínez sent me an admirable book (in manuscript) [*Sonetos irreparables*]. It is a shame that you haven't been able to get here this winter, but I hope to see you one of these days. Meanwhile, as we approach your ordination, I will keep you more and more in my prayers and Masses. I have to go for now because someone whom I am directing is coming and I want to put some things in this envelope.

God bless you, and best wishes always,

F. M. Louis

Letter 66

Dear Father Louis:

Thank you for your letter, which I have just received, from April 24th. I have also just received a letter from my bishop with the authorization for Orders, since he has now received the dispensation from Rome. The report that they had requested from Gethsemani had therefore been only in regards to that dispensation. It is probable that this is an unnecessary procedure, but here in the seminary they tend to abide by it (I think that in Rome they do not require it for someone who has only been a novice, but they do recommend it). Either way, I have already received the authorization and next week I will receive tonsure and afterward Minor Orders. I think that the ordination of priesthood will still be in August.

During these days I am submitting the book of poems about the Trappists, *Gethsemani, KY*, to print at Medellín because the previous edition, which had been in very limited release, is now sold out. On the dust jacket I wish to have a photo of a monk, as it also appeared on the first edition. However, that previous photo was not a good one, since it was copied from a calendar. I now wish to copy this other one from a calendar too—which I am now mailing to you with this letter—and hope that someone can do me the favor of sending me the original photo so that I may copy it because this one from the calendar cannot be reproduced well. I beg you to ask the monks in charge of this to give you the photo soon, because the edition of the book will be coming out soon. I have decided to use as a prologue what you wrote ["Ernesto Cardenal"] before about those poems when you translated them, and I assume that there will be no difficulties in reprinting this.

Soon I will also send you another collection of poems that they are publishing for me at Medellín, *Oración por Marilyn Monroe y otras poemas*.

My articles about the Indians have been very well received by everyone up to now, and approved by the priests who have read them. I know that I should maintain a great deal of prudence, despite everything, even though I will not be able to keep silent when my duty is to say something on certain occasions. The bishop, who has accepted me, seems very understanding; he is Franciscan Italian, and I do not think that he is a revolutionary, but I do not think that he will object to these writings. In any case, we know that we must always have the prudence of the serpent, while at the same time act like the dove.

The photocopied materials that you sent me seem extremely interesting and very important for my future plans, and I will begin to read them very intently. There are several in this seminary who wish to go with me. Two of them wish to leave with me by the end of the year, abandoning their sacerdotal careers because they feel a stronger calling toward a contemplative life. Two or three more wish to leave later, once they are ordained as priests. This material that you sent me regarding issues of monastic life will also be very important to all of them.

My trip to Gethsemani was not scheduled for this last vacation, but rather for after I leave the seminary, around January. I will try to see if some North American institution would pay for my trip to the United States in order to conduct some library research about the indigenous peoples, and to visit a few Indians. This way I can also take the opportunity of visiting you in Gethsemani. I think that this trip is possible.

Ludovico Silva is extremely happy with the prologue [to Merton's poem regarding the bomb]. He writes me often and I can see that he is a very fine young man. The first time that he wrote me he told me that he was an atheist, and perhaps a communist (his brother is one and runs a very good magazine over there), but later in his letters I have seen that he has grown a lot closer to God, and the contact with us has influenced him, while the same is happening with many others in Latin America. They are good, while the atheism or communism of a few them is false, and in some sense understandable, given the circumstances of many of these countries and the falsified religion that they have come to know. And they are very receptive to a true religiousness if they are presented with it. This is the nature of our mission here.

Thank you for your prayers; you may also count on mine.

Together in Christ,

Ernesto

Letter 67

Dear Ernesto:

Thanks for your letter. I was able to get the photograph without trouble or delay and I hope it reaches you safely. I was especially glad to hear the good news, and I will keep you in my prayers as your ordination approaches. I think in fact that this is a great grace for you and for the Church in Latin America and I am especially glad to know that your work is appreciated. I am afraid that I myself come in contact with so many retarded and suspicious types, especially within the Order, which is French and rigid, that I am prepared to see danger for everyone else. But certainly I for my own part have an immense amount of trouble trying to say anything at all that diverges from what is absolutely familiar. I think my higher superiors would not be content unless I confined myself to the statements made in the Catechism, copying them verbatim. Then all would be "safe"; as a matter of fact, what I am doing now is availing myself of a clause in the censorship statute of the Order that says that short pieces published in "small magazines" do not need to be censored. They do not say how small the magazine has to be, but the tendency of the chief American censor is to treat most magazines of a literary character as "small," which in fact they usually are. Thus I am able to breathe a little more freely and say some of the things I think need to be said, without having to go through an auto-da-fé each time.

There is no question that you have a very clear vocation to understand and interpret the religious riches of pre-Columbian America and of the traditions that have still survived from that hidden past. You are perfectly equipped for it and will do immense good. I also think that your foundation will be something quite providential and will be greatly blessed. Would that some day I might be able to see it, but as long as Dom James is abbot this will be impossible as he has a veritable phobia about my being out of the monastery for any reason, except to see the doctor in Louisville. He is now away at the General Chapter and will also go to Norway, where he will probably make a foundation. I have personally little interest in this foundation and know he will not even think of sending me. In addition, I ask myself if it is appropriate at this moment. But it could be a good idea.

However, with the monumental stupidity of Johnson's foreign policies and the crass ignorance of the State Department, I would just as soon not be a member of an American Trappist group in a foreign country at the moment. In our life there are enough troubles without having to try to explain to other people why America continues to exist. Or how. The nonsense in Vietnam is a piece of irreparable folly and even if Johnson gets away with it as he hopes to, he cannot profit by it seriously, and this country has nothing to gain by it except the knowledge of its own iniquity and stupidity. I hope it will gain at least that, but I doubt it.

I have had some kind letters from Doria Olga Elena in Medellín and I like her poems. She sent a picture of the whole family, which is delightful.

In Christ our Lord,

F. M. Louis

Letter 68

Dear Father Louis:

It moves me deeply to let you know that the date of my ordination for the priesthood will be within a week, on August 15th. I have just come out of a weeklong retreat, where I have been meditating a lot over these mysteries of God's mercy. The day after tomorrow I will receive the diaconate here in the seminary, two days afterward I will leave for Nicaragua, and on the day of the Assumption the bishop will ordain me there that afternoon in a pretty chapel belonging to the nuns of the Assumption (who are very pleased to have my ordination precisely on that day). My first Mass will also take place in the chapel on the following day. Naturally, it will also be offered up for you among those other, more special intentions. And later on, I will also be able to celebrate Mass on your behalf, as I also know that I will have your prayers for me during this great date.

The other news that I have for you is that I am staying in Nicaragua. My superiors in the seminary have informed me that since there are only a few class days left to complete the course, and we have already finished up some of the subjects, that they will award me the certificates for completing the course. They tell me that this way I will not have the expense of having to return, and will also be able to quickly commence with the work of our little foundation (which my superiors here have always been aware of). I hope then that soon we will be able to begin this, provided the bishop does not place any difficulties in my way. I am not too sure that he will not; in principle he approved my plan last year, but we shall see if he will also truly accept it now, once in practice. He gives me the impression that matters concerning the contemplative life do not bring him too much enthusiasm, and it could be that he might try to divert our foundation toward a more active apostolate. But some people like Pablo Antonio, Coronel, and Jesuit friends of mine could help so that he will not make any difficulties for our plan. Above all, I am counting on God and the Virgin Mary, and I am certain that their Will shall be done.

I will keep you informed how things are going from Nicaragua, and if I will be able to make the trip to the USA (Gethsemani) as I wish on what date.

My address in Nicaragua is the same one that I have always had, P.O. Box 206—Managua—Nicaragua.

I embrace you in Christ now more than ever,

Ernesto

Letter 69

Dear Ernesto:

Today, the day of your ordination, I am especially thinking of you, and as we concelebrate at the High Mass this morning, I will keep you most especially in my offering. May the Lord truly bless your priesthood and all your priestly work, especially all the splendid inspirations that have come to you. May they all bear fruit. They will certainly not do so without much difficulty, but it is certainly happy that a new spirit of understanding and originality is breathing in the Church, and even some of the most conservative elements are forced to recognize it and adjust to it. I am sure that the coming years will be very creative and that prophetic initiatives may be very evident. I expect there will also be a crisis in certain quarters, particularly where there has been much unenlightened conservatism. In such places the transition will be painful. We are going along fairly well here, fortunately.

I have much important news for you. I broke with Sudamericana, and my French translator and agent, Marie Tadié, is trying to arrange an agreement with Guadarrama. I hope it goes well. However, Sudamericana promised to move forward with *Torre de babel* and they may be in contact with you. I hope they have done that. I am sure that there will be no obstacle in the use of any book or material of mine that has been previously published with Sudamericana, but I have to clarify with them the use of some books.

This week I will finally be able to leave the job in the novitiate. Fr. Baldwin is taking it over, and I have received permission to live entirely in the hermitage, coming down to the monastery only once a day to say Mass and have one meal. This is a great step forward. I have in fact been sleeping there and spending most of my time there since last year, and have in fact had as much solitude as one would ordinarily have, say, in the Camaldolese. I find that it suits me perfectly, as far as my vocation is concerned, though I am not a solitary by nature at all. Only grace can make a real hermit of me, but I feel very strongly the exigency of grace in this matter. It is now an imperative demand that I cannot ignore, and indeed I would fear for my soul if I ignored it. I have no desire to do so in any case. The only slight problem is presented by health, but I trust in your prayers and in those of my friends to enable me to overcome this obstacle. My health should be good enough in any case to enable me to live the life well, but it may be difficult to do some of the manual work and chores that I will have to do, as I have a bad back. But the Lord will provide.

I often think what wonderful things have happened in the six years since you left. Your life has been blessed; your vocation is truly from God in a most evident way. He may let you feel your own limitations, but the might of His Spirit will also be evident in your life. Do not fear, but be like a child in His arms, and you will accomplish much for your country. That God will always be with you, and pray for me. Cordial and best wishes to all. Very brotherly and affectionately in Christ,

Tom

Letter 70

Dear Father Louis:

I am now a priest thanks to the Virgin Mary, who has been leading me by the hand toward ordination. These days have been marvelous, these days of first Masses, and one of these first times—the day of San Bernardo—I celebrated for you. Also tomorrow, for the day of San Luis Rey, I will keep you very much present in the moment. Today's Mass was held at the bedside of the sick-stricken Odilie Pallais, our very own saint, who is almost like one with the stigmata for us (and Coronel and Pablo Antonio attended the Mass). The day after tomorrow we will hold a special Mass for the poets and painters, exclusively for them—with a sermon by me, for them. Anyway, these are days of great joy, savoring daily Mass and immersing myself ever more in the mysteries of this great gift I have received.

Thank you very much for your letter of the 15th—so beautiful, the most beautiful. I have also received your latest writings, and I can see that the topics are of extreme interest; I will begin reading them now.

My arrival in Nicaragua and my ordination have had tremendous public repercussions, even in the newspapers and on the radio, as an event of some national importance, and *La Prensa* has especially given it a lot of importance, naturally, as you will see in the issue that I am sending you. All of which is quite beneficial for my work, or rather for the foundation, which is also becoming a necessity: the bishops are extremely conservative, and I have indications that they are not in my favor, but only my own bishop, who is only *moderately* conservative and has accepted my plan since the beginning (albeit not with too much enthusiasm, perhaps, but enough that he at least accepts it). The nuncio has also accepted it. While the nuncio and my bishop are Italians, and moderates, they are far from being revolutionaries. But at least by the sake of being European they are aware of the necessity for a contemplative life in places where it has never existed. The other elements of the clergy, for the most part, do not understand a priest "wasting time" in those endeavors when there is so much need for the apostolate. Because of all this, it is very good that *La Prensa* emphasized the importance of my ordination. I think that after this publication there will be a lot of appreciation felt by many people throughout the country and a lot of support in every sense (and there will also be more support from my bishop for my work, which is what matters).

The bishop told me that I should [not] start with the foundation until he returns from the [Vatican II] Council. I understand very well that he does not want to leave me to do it alone without his oversight, since he still does not know me very well and I am newly ordained. Also, I am not in such a hurry and the time that I need to wait is also not too much. He told me that while he is attending the Council, I could spend part of the time in Managua and the other part in Río San Juan, and this too seems stupendously fine. In the meanwhile, before he returns from the Council, I think that I will be able to make the trip to the USA and visit you, and discuss all of these things in more detail. I also wish to stop by and visit the Benedictines in Mexico. I think the trip would be around the end of October or November. I will let you know later on.

I am very pleased by what you are telling me about the hermitage, where you are now able to spend all the time, and that is a huge step, as you say.

Next week, Coronel returns to Río [San Juan], which is his hermitage; he only came for my ordination. He is working hard on your translations and is absolutely excited about this. Sudamericana has not committed anything to me in regards to *The Tower of Babel*. I am very happy about the arrangement with Guadarrama.

Farewell for now. I will write to you again at another time to inform you of the news here as it continues to develop. For now, I still continue to count on your prayers for this work, and I am already very grateful to you for keeping me in mind during the Mass on the 15th, as I also will do for you, and will continue to do. Let us not forget Alfonso [Cortéz], who, I trust you have already been informed, has inoperable cancer—soon his life, which has been full of great suffering, will end.

United in Christ,

Ernesto

Letter 71

Dear Ernesto:

Here are the pictures of your crucifix. I think they are likely to make very good reproductions. I am sending them along, though I am not sure whether or not you are yet back in Nicaragua. I wonder how you made out in New Mexico. You must have found some very interesting things there.

Things are going along quietly here, though I am having trouble with my stomach. It is perhaps just worn out. My publisher (Doubleday) is coming down to talk over the book I have finished [*Conjectures of a Guilty Bystander*]. My editor thinks it is one of the best I have written and so, oddly enough, does one of the censors of the Order. That is a good sign. It is the long notebook, the big book, of which a part was in *New Blackfriars*.

Things are curiously disturbing in the peace movement here. I wonder if there is any real communication between the two opposing sides in this country. Things will continue to be difficult and obscure. All day long I hear the guns of Fort Knox. In some quarters there is a real war fever, a desire for war, in the hope that it will give life more meaning and people more identity. The old illusion. Probably this is something incurable and we have to face the fact that we live in a very dangerous world. Faith only is the answer, and we must grow always in the purity of faith, otherwise all will be ever greater confusion.

This is only a note to accompany the pictures. I will write more after I hear from you, and if I can get time to work on the Directory.

With all respect to Pablo Antonio and José Coronel,

Cordially in Christ,

Tom

200 |

Letter 72

[Handwritten]

DECEMBER 15, 1965

Dear Ernesto:

I am writing you this letter from Louisville because I am not sure if we are still fully in communication—have you written to me? I am wondering if Fr. Abbot is stopping your mail as I have received nothing.

Lately I have had a great deal of stomach trouble and a bad attack of dysentery. I have been to see the doctor and his opinion is that it would be unwise for me to go to a tropical climate. However, I do not make this a reason for changing my decision. But I want you to know that if things are as they are now, I will probably not come.

The best thing would be for you to write to James Laughlin in April or May, at New Directions, and I will ask him to come down here in June and I will give him my definite decision then, and he can send it to you.

It seems to me that if my stomach is no better than it is now, I should not come, as this would not work out. I will therefore try to let you know in June at the latest.

I hope everything is going well. I will write the preface and Directory [for Our Lady of Solentiname] early in 1966.

Apart from the stomach everything goes well here.

All the best to all of you.

With all friendship in Christ,

F. M. Louis Merton

Letter 73

Dear Ernesto:

Many thanks for your letter and card. I was impressed by all your good words on Solentiname and I am sure there could be no better place in that part of the world. It is certainly providential and ideal, and as far as I am concerned I think we must go ahead as planned and do everything that is required, leaving all the rest to divine Providence. However there are some things to be taken into account, and because of these I think that probably we should be a little more flexible about the time of the petition to Rome. At present my feeling is that it should be put off until 1967. I will set down the various things that are on my mind.

As to the question of health: I do not know how important it is. Certainly I am much better now and I can hope for further improvement. Certainly, too, if I am completely cured it will be another sign of God's will. Let us then pray for that. But the fact remains that medically my condition is more or less irreversible (though I can live with it) and I am above all very vulnerable to everything like dysentery, and this is much more easy to contract in Central and South America, especially as I am not used to conditions there and would perhaps have difficulty in adapting to some things which you take as a matter of course. However, as I say, that is not the most important thing, and if God wills, it can prove no obstacle.

One great point is that from the point of view of the Church it would be ideal if the Abbot gave his permission. Of course as we know this is hardly to be expected as things are at present. But there is a strong possibility that after the Norway foundation, Dom James will retire and with his successor, whoever he may be, I anticipate no real difficulty. In any case, I think that it would be essential for you, before petitioning Rome, to make a formal request to whoever is Superior here. Then you can say to Rome that you have made this request in due form, it has been refused, etc. But it would be worthwhile to wait and see how the wind blows after the Norway foundation, which I expect in the spring of this year. Naturally it would take a little time for the foundation to get settled, but at least it would be worthwhile seeing what Dom J's ideas for his own future might be. This ought to be taken into consideration. For this I think it would be most practical to wait about a year after the Norway foundation. If this foundation is delayed, then we can reconsider that.

I think also it would be an advantage for you yourself to get off to a good start before I come, and meanwhile we could still freely correspond about the problems and difficulties that presented themselves and this in itself would be a good preparation for the task. I would be able to come with my mind more prepared for what would be there. I would not have to readjust a lot of purely imaginary preconceptions.

Two other things that I have on my mind and that are perhaps not real problems, but I must nevertheless work them out: First there is the ambiguity in the fact that I am a North American. I know that I am not a typical North American and that I disagree with much that is typically U.S. and because of this precisely I would be able to say things that would be welcome to everyone there. But I do not want to be in any sense whatever a kind of occult cultural ambassador for this society, and I cannot help being so in some involuntary sense. Again, this may not be a serious problem, but I must think it out. Finally there is also the difficulty, for me, that you all there have too high an opinion of me, and you have tended to think of me as much more than I am, with too high expectations of me, and I may unconsciously come with a false idea of myself, or try to measure up to expectations I should not think of, and so on. This is something I must think about for myself.

With all this in mind, I believe that it is important for me to have time to truly enter into the life of a hermit that I lead here. I am only beginning, and after five or six months I am seeing the road I have to follow. With a new life here more silent and profound, these questions will slowly take shape and will respond of themselves, and at the same time resolve my health problem. For this reason I believe that we need to give this time to mature. I conclude, then, that maybe it will be better to postpone the petition until some moment in 1967, such as a year after the Norwegian foundation, and the first step would be to write to the superior here asking him leave to go to Nicaragua, with permission for six months, after which I can obtain regular permission from Rome according to the customary routine. If he refuses, then petition the Pope. Meanwhile, we'll see what happens.

I am taking advantage of a visit from Ed Rice to send you this. Laughlin might be here before I expect him. He might come in April. The best would be for you to write before the end of March.

All my blessings. I am happy that your health is under control. I have known that by now the Bishop will have let you go to Solentiname, or that he will soon. I will write more when things unfold.

Pray for me, and I will always keep you and your project in my prayers.

In Christ our Lord,

Tom

Letter 74

Dear Ernesto:

I want to send off this note to you before the retreat begins (this evening). Thanks for your card and message. I like the notebook of Asilia Guillén. Can you send me other reproductions of her work? It speaks eloquently of Nicaragua.

My stomach is much better, but I still have to take care of it. However I am not concerned about it.

I am happy to hear that the situation at Solentiname is so good and I hope you will be able to go ahead with your plans. In fact I hope the bishop has let you start by now. Naturally I keep all this in my prayers and beg God to bless all your hopes. And I am sure He will in good time.

Did you ever find out what happened to the people at Guadarrama in Madrid? I have no news from my agent either. I do not know precisely what will happen to my book in Spanish. Who is publishing your *Vida en el amor*? It is really excellent—in some ways equal to Teilhard de Chardin, even better, since he was only half a poet.

All my blessings and best wishes. Keep me in your prayers during this retreat. I often think of you. May God be always with you.

In Christ our Lord,

F. M. Louis

Letter 75

Dear Ernesto:

First I want to thank you for the coffee, which arrived safely. It is really excellent and I like it better than the Columbian coffee I had. Then I want to send you the preface, which I have finally written. I hope it is not too long and too philosophical. Still I thought it was worthwhile to write something besides a few conventional words of introduction. Also I sent you an article that appeared in Louisville. I will get to work on the little directory I promised to write for Solentiname later on, perhaps during Lent. I want very much to write it but I have had other things to do. As you will see from the article I want to get away from comment on passing events and write something more fundamental and more monastic. As I am also writing a few poems, I enclose them too. It will be a big package and I hope it reaches you safely.

Above all I hope you are now in Solentiname and beginning with your work. However, you must be patient of all delays. God's providence provides these for very special reasons and He wants everything to work out in His own time, which is mysterious to us. When we look back, however, we find that His plan made everything come out much better than it otherwise would have. So I hope that He will indicate His will to you and bring all your plans to perfection in His own way and in His time. I am still eager to be of assistance to you in any way that I can, and, as I say, I will begin by writing the Directory. Meanwhile I am very eager to hear whether you have begun and to learn how things are going. Any news you send will be helpful in considering the kind of advice I can write for the Directory. I have received a letter from José and will write to him soon.

Something I have been wanting to say is that to work with the Spanish editor of the anthology [prepared by Coronel], I would ask you to go through Mme. Marie Tadié, 1 Square Padirac, Paris 16, France, who is now acting on my behalf in questions of rights in Spain and France. I found that I still can't control this business. Finally, do you know of anyone else besides Guadarrama?

There has been much snow here and it is quite cold, but my wood fire keeps everything pretty warm and I am much happier with it than with the steam heat in the community. God bless you and all my friends there, Pablo Antonio, José, and everyone. Very cordially in Christ,

Tom Merton

[Handwritten P.S.] Bishop [Fulton J.] Sheen was here and since he has charge of sending money to the Missions I gave your name and address. He may help you. I hope so.

Letter 76

[Letterhead with *Nuestra Señora de Solentiname*]

FEBRUARY 22, 1966

Dear Father Louis:

We have now been in Solentiname for ten days, marvelous days, a bit uncomfortable and naturally with a lot of work, but it is a happy experience and one that will be unforgettable. For now, we are sleeping in the small church under construction while we build our own home. The two *compañeros* from Colombia and I make up the community right now; within a few days, another *compañero* will arrive, a peasant from here in Nicaragua. When we arrived, the vegetation here was very high and dense throughout all the areas surrounding the little church. A few workers are clearing it out, and we now have the location ready where the house will be. As we begin to remove the vegetation on this part of the island, you can begin to see the lake (which is very close, since this is a narrow peninsula), and gorgeous panoramas begin to emerge that we had not seen before. From one angle there is a bay with many islands. On the opposite side there is another bay. Up further ahead on a small hill—where we will build a small cabin with an observation deck—there is another different landscape view of another small bay with other islands. The lake is always beautiful and has many different hues at different hours throughout the day.

There are egrets at the outer edges and strange ducks that I do not know what to call. Many birds are singing from the very early morning. There are also dangerous spiders, scorpions, very angry ants, etc., and mosquitoes. The main enemy is the *zancudo* (mosquito), but I believe that once we have cleared the surrounding areas, we will no longer have him;

there are many other islands that no longer do. Soon we will dig a well near the lake to have cleaner water than the lake (we can draw it from the well at almost the same cost as from the lake). The weather is pleasant; it is not hot, and it is very healthy, the healthiest. The nights are filled with huge and brilliant stars, like the ones I saw in the desert in New Mexico, at the [monastery] Christ of the Desert, and I have been surprised to see a star-filled sky in these parts like the desert's.

Coronel came to the island on the same day that we landed here, he and his wife, and they helped us out with the work of unloading everything we had brought here. I spoke a lot with Coronel, and he told me that the *Merton Reader* was moving far along, and that he wanted me to help him select a few of the final items needed. In a few days, we will travel to Coronel's estate and stay there for a few days, to work with him on this and also to discuss many other things that I need to speak with him about.

I received the prologue to *Vida en el amor*: it is stupendous; it is a great thing for my little book. Thank you so much for this. I believe it could not be any better and it is more than I deserve. Incidentally: the book is called *Vida en el amor*, not *La Vida en el amor*, as it appears on the title head of the "Preface." From Guadarrama, we still have not heard anything.

Monsignor Fulton J. Sheen has not written to me, but perhaps we will receive news from him later. Thank you very much for giving him my address.

Greetings, united in Christ,

Ernesto

Letter 77

Dear Ernesto:

I am just getting out of the hospital today after a major operation on the back. I think it was completely successful and the Doctors are pleased with their results, and due to the prayers of so many good friends I think the recovery has been very good. It remains to be seen how I will function in the future.

At the monastery things are the same. The Norway foundation is not yet made and I am not sure when it will be. It is publicly known that after the Norway foundation is settled Dom James intends to retire into solitude—but there is no way of telling how long that will be. In any case whoever his successor is, one can expect more liberal ideas. Any universal initiative in regard to Latin America, even with the most exalted recommendations, will probably be impossible as long as Dom James is Abbot. He was at one moment thinking of taking over the Spencer foundation in Chile and he might conceivably decide to do this. I am not sure.

It is stupendous to know that you are in Solentiname, and as always I hold the project in my prayes. When I can write on the machine again I will think seriously about the Directory.

All my blessings and affection in Christ,

F. M. Louis

Letter 78

Dear Father Louis:

Here are some photos of Our Lady of Solentiname. We still have a lot of material work left to do: the economic organization of the estate (the first crops) and construction. We already have a house built that will later be the guesthouse, and for now we are living there. In these next few days, we start with our other house and we are also beginning the reconstruction of the little church. One of my aunts gave us seven thousand dollars and with this we are doing these projects.

Coronel and Pablo Antonio were here for a few days, and they thought that this place was marvelous, the views of the lake and the rest. They also came here with the bishop, who was coming for his pastoral visit, and they have made great friends with the bishop. The bishop is also very pleased with all of this, and it seems to me that he feels proud to have this foundation within his diocese.

One of the two Colombian *compañeros* who came here has returned home. He was very ill and also had some doubts about whether this was his true calling. I think that his illness was due to these doubts. He has gone home to cure his health and also to reflect on his vocation. The other Colombian *compañero*, William Agudelo, the young poet, is happy here, although he still does not know if this will be a vocation for the rest of his life, or merely temporary. There is a peasant with us, too. Well, now our community is of three. As far as future vocations are concerned, I am not worried, since I know that this is God's business. He will provide them, if that is how he wants it.

Hemingway's widow sent us 150 dollars. She found out about Solentiname through an American businessman who has been in Nicaragua and is trying to obtain a boat from the USA for the children of the Archipelago so they can go to school. The Alliance for Progress in Managua has also approved funds for a ferry for the peasants of Solentiname, which I requested. The amount they will give us is five thousand dollars.

Coronel told me that the selection of translations of your work is very far along and I believe that he has been communicating with you a lot in regards to this.

I still do not know anything from Guadarrama.

We depend on your prayers, always. Embracing you, united in Christ.

Ernesto

Letter 79

JULY 3, 1966

Dear Ernesto:

It was fine to get your letter and to see the fine photos of Solentiname. You really have an ideal place for a small community and everything points to the fact that you will do very well indeed. Naturally beginnings are slow but it is quite possible that before long you may have more vocations than you will know what to do with. For that reason it is good to get organized and get your life going well. I certainly like your situation, it looks wonderful, and I am sure your plans will be blessed.

Your circular letter was excellent, and you can certainly use any material of mine you like in it. I will try to get busy and send you some monastic notes for your use there, and they may also be useful for the bulletin. But I still have not got down to all the work I had accumulated since the operation. At this season of the year I have visitors more often and all last week was shot, practically, because I spent the day with people who came. I hope however to get down to writing again and to get these distractions out of the way.

You will be interested in the important news that Gethsemani is taking over the Spencer foundation in Chile. This is important because it now means that Gethsemani is engaged in work in Latin America. Some monks are going down in August and others in October. I do not think I am likely to be sent there but anything may happen. However, I do not expect to be sent. It is obvious that Dom James believes that my place is here and that he will not consider letting me go elsewhere.

I am glad to hear that you are getting the financial support you need. For a small and poor community like yours, these little gifts are important, whereas for a big Gethsemani foundation that would hardly be a drop in the bucket. You are fortunate in your poverty, which will be blessed.

I shall pray that you may lay down firm foundations for your future monastic life on Solentiname, and tomorrow I will offer Mass for you and your work there. I constantly send you my prayers.

I heard from Pablo Antonio after he had been there and must write to him when I can. As to the anthology, I am glad it is nearly finished. I think it doesn't make sense to consider Guadarrama. Better to be in contact with my agent in Paris, Mme. Marie Tadié, 1 Square Padirac, or it could be that you or José [Coronel] can think of an editor to contact directly. But I think she will be able to handle the business aspects, since it is she who handles my business matters in Spanish (at least concerning books).

It will probably be some time before you go to Rome to get approval. Perhaps it would be worthwhile to come here for a talk about your progress before you do that. In any case, I keep you in my prayers. Pray for me as well. I will send you some mimeographs soon.

Warm brotherly regards in Christ,

F. M. Louis

Letter 80

Dear Ernesto:

I received your letter only the other day, so it took an unusually long time to reach me. I want to reply as soon as I can so as not to let it go, because if I put it aside I may not get to it again for many weeks. I am having a hard time keeping up with letters—as you too probably are.

The news of your progress in building etc. sounds very good indeed. From the way you describe it, your little place is exactly what is needed and will be certainly blessed, indeed already is. The fact that there are only two of you means nothing: on the contrary it will be very good to go for some time without others so that you can cement a firm foundation for the future between you. I shall certainly keep praying.

In such a small community as Solentiname, I mean as regards to the *campesinos* [peasants], I think there is very little danger for you in accepting the office of pastor. The bishop understands fully the nature of your vocation and of your situation and he is not imposing on you something that he intends to be contrary to it. You can certainly carry out the minimal functions of pastor without threat to your monastic charisma, but combining the two. But of course it must be purely spiritual: a question of sharing in the Word of God and the Eucharist, baptizing and helping the dying, but not any of the bureaucratic routines of parish organization—except of course the essential records. I think that if you accept this in simplicity and let the people understand what you are doing, you could have a very beautiful community of the poor around the monastery and in a sort of spiritual relationship with it, which would be much more fruitful than an ordinary parish, and could really develop into something in the future. In other words it is a chance to experiment. I would say that the remoteness and simplicity of the place would make this safe and fruitful. I would dare to have great hopes: as long as a spurious activism does not get mixed up in it. Later on when the community grows, someone else could have the work of administering the sacraments to the people and teaching them.

The only problem would, as I see it, arise when the next bishop comes in. Then he would have you in his grasp and might decide to impose a whole new concept of your duties upon you. That is the only problem, and I would talk to your bishop about it and maybe get some kind of agreement on paper.

I have been going on as usual. Lately there have been a few visitors, including Jacques Maritain last week. He was very happy to be here and I was in my turn very happy to have some good talks with him. Fr. Dan Berrigan was also here. Still active in the peace movement but there is a sort of despair everywhere since it is obvious that Johnson knows he is now in a position of dictatorial power and refuses to listen to anyone who does not agree with his war policy. The situation is extremely bad and the prospects of a very large war in Asia are not unreal at all. Here is where prayers are urgently needed. I know the U.S. will get little or no support anywhere else in the world, and it is a great folly for Johnson to ignore the opinions of the best minds and most civilized people that are still left around, the Pope first of all. Thank you for your prayers and Masses for me. They are much needed. I hope you receive the mimeographed copy that we sent you. I think they stopped them before we sent them.

With all my warm wishes for José and Pablo Antonio and everyone else. I like the poems by William [Agudelo], but I still haven't read them carefully. At first glance, they look great. Concerning Marie Tadié, we are making a new arrangement with respect to an agent in Spain, and it could be that we let her go. I hope so because she has been a burden more than a help. I recommend that you send a copy [of the Merton anthology prepared by Coronel] to [José María] Valverde, who is in contact with an editor and is doing other books of mine. If it is a matter of whether there will be an agent later, then we can leave the official contract and all else to that person. I hope we can get rid of Tadié and then we won't have any problems.

 Warm well wishes and united in prayers in Christ our Lord,
Tom Merton

Letter 81

Dear Father Louis:

Many thanks for your very charming letter, very lovely and very enlightening regarding the purpose of my life as a parish priest in Solentiname. I see things exactly as you do, and actually I cannot find any conflict between a contemplative life and offering the services of a parish priest in this place. The truth is that this place has few inhabitants, and the administering of sacraments is a very simple matter, without any hassles for someone like me, who is searching for a life of quietude and retreat. I also think that the ideal would be to have a priest with a more active vocation, so that he can develop some missionary activity not only on the islands, but also in the neighboring area, which is a completely abandoned zone. And it seems to me that it would be easy to find a priest in the future with this vocation (or a mixed vocation, as a semi-missionary and semi-contemplative).

I think it is a good thing to obtain a written agreement of some kind from the bishop, so just in case he is not around in the future we will not have any difficulties with another bishop. It is not necessary to ask him for this, in fact I do not think there is anything to fear in this respect because it just so happens that this diocese is a prelature given to Franciscan missionaries (Italian), and any other bishop must be Franciscan, from the same community that currently reigns over the diocese. This is a small community and the friars are all good people, and all of them are very pleased with the Solentiname experiment; they think like their bishop, and I do not think that they would change anything that we are doing. Although, as I mentioned to you, it would be worthwhile to have some written document for greater precaution (once all of this becomes more established with some community).

When the trip to Rome becomes necessary, I will stop by the U.S. as you suggest, so that we can talk. It pleases me very much that Maritain was able to be with you in Gethsemani. That encounter must have been very joyous for you, as it was for him.

As you have told us, we will arrange the publishing of the book [*Antología de Merton*] with Valverde. The main problem we are facing is publishing, because there are few publishers in Spanish, and if they are successful editors, they tend to be more commercial than in other countries, or if they are good, they are from poor publishing firms, with limited distribution. A publisher in Chile [*Editorial Santiago*] has offered to edit all of my poems, and I am sending these to them. It is a new publisher and I do not know how good they are.

William [Agudelo] had a very good and extensive selection [of poems] published in *El Corno*; in that same volume, there is also something from Eduardo Perilla, our other *compañero* from the seminary in La Ceja who wrote "*Colombia Macheteada*" and who also plans to come here in the future.

Always remembering you in our prayers and our holy Mass. United always, in Christ.

Ernesto

[Handwritten in the left-hand margin, vertically]

I am still continuing to receive the typed written essays and articles, and they are often my best spiritual readings. Coronel also receives them.

Letter 82

Dear Ernesto:

I have been thinking a lot about you and Solentiname. I am sure that the beginning is slow, but your determination is confirmed, more and more each day, despite all the difficulties. I am glad that they reprinted your letter in *Papeles*. I still have intentions to write something short, *a modo de directorio*, at least. But I have so many other things to do, first—including a preface to Raïssa Maritain's diary, which is an important mystical document; Jacques Maritain was here, and we had a very good time together in October. He's a great old man, and now also lives, more or less, as a hermit.

This is a good opportunity to talk openly about my possibilities of going to Solentiname. They are worse now, than before, now that Gethsemani has taken charge of the monastery founded by Spencer, in Chile [La Dehesa]. It can never be said that Gethsemani has not done anything for Latin America. To the contrary, Dom James goes around everywhere, declaring great interest in Latin America. Unfortunately, his interest is of the kind that places him on the side of the Americans and the rich, and he really does not understand the problems of poverty and their causes, even though he deplores it.

I am convinced that it would be useless to appeal directly to Rome. Dom James is now fully confirmed in his maximum powers and can even appose Rome, and Rome would abide with his decision. The Pope could, of course, ask him, but he will not do it in such forceful terms that it would make a difference. The only realistic thing is to wait until Dom James retires. He has expressed a desire to do this within the next two years, and even though I don't believe that he will be able to let go of power, there is a possibility that he could be speaking seriously. Under the new superior, whoever it may be, I think we would be able to proceed with more ease in a regular fashion, obtaining a normal leave of absence to go, and there would be no real problem. I think this is the only thing we can do, and as such, I suggest we wait.

We are doing a lot of reconstruction here: the church is being completely remodeled, and it no longer has water. But many are still leaving and the community is becoming smaller. Dom James does not seem to understand that this kind of large, rich community has no future. I ask myself what will be in ten more years. Even so, there are good men here and they have a serious desire for a good monastic life. This place is a challenge and a problem, and actually, I feel that I have a huge responsibility with Gethsemani.

Let's hear some news from you. I want to write to Pablo Antonio very soon and send him something for his journal. Does the magazine *El Pez y La Serpiente* still come out?

My warmest wishes always, and a cordial embrace, in Christ, with all my prayers for your health, and for the success in Solentiname.

In our Lord,

Tom Merton

Letter 83

JANUARY 2, 1967

Dear Ernesto:

Happy New Year. What is new? I am sending a couple of things you might be interested in. I just got a note from Alfonso Cortés's sister who imagines that I might be there for the [Rubén] Dario centenary but naturally this is totally out of the question. I have had some interesting visits here, including Jacques Maritain in the fall. Joan Baez the folksinger was here. She is running an institute for the study of non-violence in California, which in a way is quite "monastic." She is a fine person. If she comes down your way I shall make sure that she comes to see you.

You probably know that Suzuki died last summer. I forget if I sent you the little piece I wrote about him ["D. T. Suzuki: The Man and His Work"]. I have done several articles on Camus ["Seven Essays on Albert Camus"], but I think they must have been sent to you. Napoleón Chow was here also, about Thanksgiving. I fully intend to write to Pablo Antonio and to send him some articles when I have time. I will also send you the *New Directions Annual*. I was glad to see your translations of Laughlin in the little magazine from Venezuela. He brought Nicanor Parra here last May; we had a very good visit. I hear occasionally from Cintio Vitier in Cuba.

There is not much news: I continue to live happily and fairly quietly in the woods. Did you receive the two new books that appeared in 1966, *Raids on the Unspeakable* and *Conjectures of a Guilty Bystander*? I think I sent the first but probably not the second. Please let me know and you shall have them.

I have been doing some work on Faulkner, and his novella "The Bear" has a lot of interesting symbolic material that can be used to illustrate the ascent of the spiritual life, and I have given some conferences on it here, in that sense. Perhaps I will write something about it if I get time.

My health is fair enough, though I have a bad arm that requires occasional treatment, but the back is holding up fairly well. Some monks from here went to Chile to take over the Spencer foundation. The monasteries of the Order in this country are not in such good shape as they were ten years ago and there is some likelihood that some of them will close. Gethsemani is still a fairly large community, but I wonder what it will be like ten years from now? The Church is now being entirely remodeled. But the community will not fill it any more.

It is strange to think that it is almost ten years since you came here! Time has certainly gone very quickly. Please send my best regards to José Coronel. We are having a great quantity of problems with my agent, Marie Tadié, and I believe the best thing to do with the anthology is to send it directly to Pomaire (who is now publishing my stuff, and I believe who is publishing yours as well) and they can deal with her [Tadié] later if necessary. It is better if none of us have anything to do with her directly. And what about your book, *Vida en el amor*?

You have all my best wishes and prayers for the New Year. Pray for me. I hope you will gradually get a few more to help you there and to share your peace.

Warm well wishes in the Lord,
Tom Merton

Letter 84

MARCH 11, 1967

Dear Ernesto:

Already some time has gone by since I received your letter. I have had to go to the hospital again, this time only for a minor operation, but on returning I can no longer find your letter to answer it in detail. But I remember its contents and am disturbed. The news you send is not good: but then news everywhere is bad today when things are in such crisis everywhere, and everywhere violence threatens.

Basically our first duty today is to human truth in its existential reality, and this sooner or later brings us into confrontation with system and power, which seek to overwhelm truth for the sake of particular interests, perhaps rationalized as ideals. Sooner or later this human duty presents itself in a form of crisis that cannot be evaded. At such a time it is very good, almost essential, to have at one's side others with a similar determination, and one can then be guided by a common inspiration and a communion in truth. Here true strength can be found. A completely isolated witness is much more difficult and dangerous. In the end that too may become necessary. But in any case we know that our only ultimate strength is in the Lord and in His Spirit, and faith must make us depend entirely on His will and providence. One must then truly be detached and free in order not to be held and impeded by anything secondary or irrelevant. Which is another way of saying that poverty also is our strength.

The coffee has arrived and it is much appreciated. Unfortunately the letter that came with it is lost. I would like to have the address of the firm and the people who sent it, so that I may thank them personally.

Everything goes quite well here, though I have a lot of minor diffi-culties on all sides. But they do not matter. It may become impossible to send out mimeographed texts since I am almost entirely unable to get secretarial help here. I translated a poem of [Rafael] Alberti's on Rome ["Roman Nocturne"] (will send a copy) and the pious little monk who mimeographed it said it was immoral, and showed great reluctance to help me with more work. All this is amusing. I may perhaps write a book on Camus, and I would appreciate prayers for help in this undertaking. I hope you have received the articles I sent on him ["Seven Essays on Albert Camus"].

Let us be united in prayer and confidence. More and more I see that there is no hope whatever but in God. Everything else fails us completely. Certainly I will pray much for you and will soon offer Mass for all of your interests and for our friends when I have a good chance.

Always with my warmest, best wishes, in Christ our Lord,

Tom Merton

Letter 85

Dear Father Merton:

Many thanks for your excellent letter from March 11th. Above all else, I really appreciate your letters because I am aware of the immense amount of correspondence that you must maintain, and the vast number of letters you must also keep from answering. Beautiful also was the newsletter 67 for Lent for all our friends.

William Agudelo, my *compañero* throughout this whole year, has already left for Colombia. After thinking it over a lot here, he has become convinced that his vocation is as a layman, despite having been very happy here (he felt that these days had been the happiest of his life). But at his core, God's voice was not asking him for this life—he felt very sure about this—but instead for one as a Christian in the world and a Christian poet. He also felt that marriage was his vocation; he has a girlfriend in Colombia, to whom he was more or less engaged—willing to leave her if God asked him—but now he is once more going to Colombia resolved to marry because he feels that God is not asking him to let go of this love. Well then, his departure is not any kind of failure, and nothing that I think should be lamented. The only thing that to me is personally lamentable is his absence, because during these long months of Solentiname, we had developed a great friendship and mutual understanding. But this is not important if his departure is God's will, as I suspect that it is. Besides, with God's union we are never alone. And perhaps He wants me to have a bit more human solitude now in order to have a greater union with Him.

Either way, may it be God's will. One thing that I can be happy about is that William took great advantage of his stay here: in his spiritual life, in prayer, his communion with God, *letting go*, etc. (where he made much progress), as he did in his literary work, where he has also made great advances, and I think that he will be among the great poets of Colombia, perhaps the greatest.

There is currently a young Nicaraguan poet with me [Beltrán Morales], not seeking a life of contemplation, since he is more or less an atheist, but only looking for a place to stay because he has many problems of various degrees and he has felt good here. I think there is no harm in having him stay here while he needs lodging, and especially because at this moment this "foundation" is without anyone else. There is no other vocation secured at the moment, only a few slightly possible ones, but I am not impatient since the vocations will come when God wishes it. Two candidates have come, one from the USA and the other from Mexico, but they were both psychologically perturbed cases and I had to send them away. There are always economic hardships, but Providence never eases to help at the precise moment. Last year's crops were bad, and this is why there have been these problems (and the expenses of managing the farm and the construction of the house, etc.). We are now beginning the construction of the church. I will send you photos when I have a guest with a photo camera—I do not have a camera.

I will send you a few books separately, books by a Colombian writer who died about two years ago at a very old age. I did not get to meet him personally and I am very sorry. Only after his death did I come to know his books and discover his great value. A few in Colombia had learned of his worth, but only a few. There was a conspiracy of silence against him and there is one still. He continues to be the Great Unknown, not only in Colombia, but also throughout Latin America, where practically no one knows about him. Coronel, who has now been reading him together with me, tells me that he thinks he is as valuable as Vallejo and

Borges, in certain ways more valuable. This writer's name is Fernando González. He was a mystic and, in his later years, a saint. A mystic and saint, but very original, as you will see in the books that I am sending you. The two books that I am now sending you I had brought here from Colombia (where they are very difficult to find because the copies have been sold out), and it was Coronel who suggested that I send these books to you. We are planning to create an edition of *El Pez y la Serpiente* (which unfortunately has not come out in a long time because of Pablo Antonio's activities) that will be completely dedicated to this writer, Fernando González: his texts, and a few of our reviews about him, etc. And Coronel was saying to me that perhaps you would be interested in writing something about him, and also [asked] if you thought that it would be worth the effort to introduce him to some publishing house in the United States (perhaps New Directions). Above all, Coronel would like to find out your personal opinion about him, especially in regards to the mystical aspect. (This is actually the aspect of his work that is of interest, because he is a mystic before anything else). These books are novels, but in reality the novel is only a pretext for him; these are mystical novels, and he is perhaps the only Catholic writer to have written these kinds of novels. Anyway, you will see for yourself, and later tell us your opinion.

I have seen Coronel a few times and he tells me that he continues reworking the translations and that he is almost finished with the book [*Antología de Merton*]. In my previous letter, which you did not find upon returning from the hospital [because it was lost], I asked you to tell me about that publisher that you had mentioned to me, Pomaire, because I was not familiar with it, and I wished to get in touch [with them]. Perhaps you could write to them about publishing the *Merton Reader* in Spanish. I would also like to publish my *Vida en el amor* with your prologue, since it is yet to be published, due to Guadarrama, which may never again show signs of life.

In that letter I had also mentioned that I have not received—and would very much like to receive—the books: *Conjectures of a Guilty Bystander* and *Raids on the Unspeakable*.

I hope that you have recovered well from your last operation and that you do not continue to have so many operations. I interrupted this letter halfway through in order to go and celebrate Mass, and I have celebrated it on your behalf. Moreover, you already know that I keep you in mind at every Mass. And this solitary foundation of Solentiname needs your prayers too.

United in Christ always,

Ernesto

P.S. The address where you can write to give thanks for the shipment of coffee is Mr. Roberto Stadtagen. Fabrica de Café Presto, Managua (Nicaragua).

Letter 86

Dear Ernesto:

Yesterday's copy of the German edition of your Psalms [English translation, *The Psalms of Struggle and Liberation*, published in 1971] came in, and reminded me that it is a very long time since I wrote to you. The translation seems to me very good and I liked the "Postface," which I thought was understanding and will do you a lot of good with German readers. I wanted previously to interest Hans Urs von Balthasar in your work, and [I] sent him [Stefan] Baciu's article about you in German, but don't know what he thought about it.

I also owe Pablo Antonio a letter of thanks for the big article of N. Chow in *La Prensa*. But I guess we are all in the same boat with correspondence: it is simply impossible to keep up, and the business of long complicated letters gets to be more and more absurd.

One thing you asked me about: the address of Editorial Pomaire. I don't have it here, but Valverde can certainly give you it. Write to him, because he's constantly in contact with them and translates for them. We have had many problems with Marie Tadié, who was acting as agent for me not only in French, but also in Spanish. She became so difficult that I didn't try with her, and the Abbot mediates with her through a lawyer. I hope there is no problem with her in relation to the anthology by Coronel. I suggest sending it directly to Pomaire, and if we have to deal with Tadié later about the contract, so be it.

I am still living in the hermitage and like it better and better all the time. It is quiet enough. Sometimes I get too many visitors, but I think it is necessary to keep up contacts, especially on the ecumenical level, and some interesting people have been here. I am glad not to be too much involved in what goes on in the community. Many changes have been made and I do not know whether or not they are improvements. I am not convinced that big-institution monasticism such as we have here has a real future. I do not say that it is bad, but it is just confused, too big, lacks real cohesion and spirit, and leaves a lot of individuals just hopelessly running around looking for something—they don't know what. The superiors meanwhile are desperately trying to come up with a magic answer that will ensure survival. Many people have left and few are coming. I think that the atmosphere of great uncertainty and questioning (which is necessary now) makes things too unstable for people to settle down in a monastery. They need to feel they are in possession of something solid and permanent, in order to commit themselves to it. There are of course other kinds of monastic commitment, a sort of readiness for change and movement: but in that case one cannot expect to keep up much of an institution. One must be free. That is your advantage. You may or may not have companions, but if you have no one it does not really matter. In due time Solentiname will be something very definite in monasticism: but until then it may be very small and perhaps almost nothing. That is not bad at all. But for Gethsemani—that would be a disaster. Hence one must not build institutions that invite disaster so easily!

I am sending you some new writings that you maybe haven't seen yet. You can pass them along to Pablo Antonio or to Coronel, but I want to send them some later, even though I don't have copies of all these things. Pablo Antonio might be able to use the text on Teilhard ["Teilhard's Gamble: Betting on the Whole Human Species"].

Keep me in your good prayers. I pray for you and at some point soon I will offer Mass for Solentiname and for all of my friends in Nicaragua. My best and warmest wishes, in Jesus the Lord, always,

Tom Merton

Letter 87

OUR LADY OF SOLENTINAME

AUGUST 14, 1967

Dear Father Louis:

I am very pleased to receive your letter from the 26th, and I agree with you that for now it is not important whether or not I have companions. I am alone for now, but I am very happy in this solitude, and I am in no hurry to have vocations. I will welcome them when God sends them, as God wills it. There are some who have expressed the wish to come here, but these vocations are not for certain. I have always had visitors every once in a while, especially young poets or writers. The other day a British poet, who is now in New York, passed through here, and I think that his visit here did him some good. The bishop has been here twice. I think that this week some Franciscans will also come to stay for a few days. Many young poets from Latin America write to me to tell me that one day they will come visit me; as it is all ready, this place naturally seems very attractive to them.

William Agudelo, the young Colombian poet, left in April. He had discovered that his vocation was marriage, and he left to get married to the girlfriend that he had in Colombia whom he felt he loved very much. But he also loved this place very much, was very happy here, and he accomplished a lot within this kind of life. Here he learned to love poverty, the solitude and simplicity of life, and abhor the futility of affluent life in the cities. His plan is to come to Solentiname as a married man, to live on a very small islet that is very close by (it can be seen from the window of our house) in order to lead a poor and simple life, a true

Christian contemplative-matrimonial life. I think the plan is stupendous, a truly prophetic plan, and it could become a good example. This couple could provide this place with a great Christian testimonial. The girl he is marrying is a graduate teacher, and our plan is for her to have a school here for the poor children on these islands. The girl is beginning to understand the "vocation" of that marriage of theirs in Solentiname. And I am beginning to understand that it is possible for the monastic community to have a few married couples in the neighboring areas to help within the peasant community and in the liturgy, while [they] at the same time are benefitting from our neighborhood (church, spiritual guidance, etc.). There are a few young married couples in Managua who have expressed the desire to lead a Christian life here, "away from the world." This is why I think that William Agudelo's plan could be very important. Perhaps later on other married couples will be able to settle nearby and work a communal farm modeled after the ones from the *Catholic Worker*.

In this sense, William's departure has not hurt me, [for] it seems to me that his arrival here, as well as his plan for an upcoming marriage, and his liking the place so much, all of this obeys a certain mysterious plan of God. Besides, William is a very good poet, one of the best young poets in America, and now he has been gaining many admirers among the youth with the things he has published in *El Corno* and other journals. He is a curious case of beatnik and hippie, at once very pure and very holy.

I have received a letter from a Benedictine Catalan from the Montserrat monastery, who is now in Louisville. He spoke with you recently and you gave him my address since he wants a contemplative community, not institutional, a simple and primitive life like this one. He wrote asking me for details about this place and I wrote to tell him in simple terms about what is here and what I intend to do. I told him that it would be very good if he came, at least for a time, to test life here. I understand that he is an artist because he was chair of the art department in Montserrat, and it just so happens that he was the one who—according to his letter—sent me the beautiful and rustic chalice that I had ordered from Montserrat for my ordination: it is a rugged chalice with red enamel, in the shape of a Greek cup, and it is the one that we use here for Mass in Solentiname.

I see Coronel frequently. Most recently, he told me that the next time he writes you, he will let you know that he is still working on the *Reader*, and that he is almost finished, and also that he has finished translating the *Chuang Tzu*, and is sending you a copy, if you would like one, in case you wish to make corrections on the translation, or modify anything for the Spanish edition, or write a special prologue for the Spanish edition, etc. I just wrote to Valverde, asking him for the address to Pomaire for the book.

I assume that you have been receiving the *Boletin de Solentiname*. The idea for this bulletin was mostly to publish in Spanish and in mimeograph some of your essays that you have sent us in English. And we think that at least half these bulletins will consist of your essays, and the rest, some news about Solentiname or other miscellany. In addition, Coronel has come up with an original idea: the creation of a Merton Reading Club in Managua. This club, which we are organizing with Pablo Antonio and other friends and sponsors of Solentiname, is comprised of a select group of English readers to whom we will be sending one monthly Merton article in English, mimeographed from Solentiname, which will be selected by Coronel and me based on what we think could be of special interest to them. From now on, we would like two copies of every mimeographed article that you send to me in Solentiname, instead of one. That other copy is the one that we would send to the Merton Reading Club in Managua. That copy will be passed around from hand to hand to all the members of the club (which will be a select group of about twenty people). It is not necessary or practical to send a copy to each individual, for they will be sent one copy to be circulated hand to hand and lent to each other.

My Jesuit brother [Fernando] is being ordained as a priest on September 23rd in Mexico, and my family is giving me the trip fare so that

I can go to the ordination. I was hoping not to move from here, not even to go to Mexico, or to any place else, but the special circumstances have mandated this trip, like a duty to charity that trumps my desire for solitude and isolation, and I have to comply. I shall go to Mexico for about ten days. I will see some old friends and the trip might be advantageous on many levels. I assume that you already know about [Dom Gregorio] Lemercier, who secularized himself along with his entire monastery. He was left with no other choice because in Rome they had forbidden him that essay about psychoanalysis. But I do not expect too much from that essay; it seems to me that his admiration for psychoanalysis has gone too far.

Thank you for all the Masses. I offer many on your behalf. I do not receive any stipends for my Masses and my intentions are always free, so I can celebrate many on behalf of my friends. The day before yesterday it was on your behalf.

Do not worry if you do not have time to write too often.

United always in Christ,

Ernesto

Letter 88

Dear Father Merton:

It has been a long time since I last wrote to you, and I have not received a letter from you. I do not know if it is because of the amount of correspondence that is always accumulating for you, or because my letter did not arrive. Father Romano has written to me from Chile, letting me know that he is there in a hermitage and that he would like to come here and continue with this life. I responded that it would please me very much if he came, and he told me that he would discuss it with his superior and the he would think about it, and within three months he would resolve whether to stay in Chile or come here. Father Romano was telling me about the resignation of Dom James [Fox] and the lection of Father Flavian Burns. I suppose that this is absolutely favorable and what has been anticipated in order to realize the Gethsemani-Nicaragua project. I wish to know what has been going on with all of this. Meanwhile, my prayers are always for this (precisely today, my Mass was on your behalf).

I have here a very nice Nicaraguan *compañero* who is trying out this life and it could possibly be his calling: this is how he is feeling. There is also a young painter [Róger Pérez de la Rocha] who is highly esteemed; he is a Marxist (mostly in the emotional sense) and was an atheist when he arrived, but now he has been undergoing a positive evolution. He is here as a long-term guest (for about one year) and his presence is beneficial for him and for us. He is eighteen years old, but I believe that he is going to be one of the greatest artists in Nicaragua and Latin America; already he is beginning to open up interesting new paths in painting, much more than the others, and I think that his stay in Solentiname will be significant in his life.

A young Cuban monk from Mount Saviour, whom I met at Christ of the Desert, has also written to me and he wishes to lend his help here in the foundation; he believes that the chapter of his monastery will have no difficulty in giving him permission, and I think that he will be of much help here, even if he comes for a time, or stays indefinitely afterward. But anyway, let us leave God to make his own plans.

Coronel has already finished the translation of *Chuang Tzu*, and in the next few days he will send it to Pomaire. Meanwhile, he continues working on the *Reader*. It looks like the German translation of my *Psalms* has had widespread exposure because the edition sold out in six months, and now they are putting out another and preparing translations in Dutch, Swedish, and Polish. They also edited an anthology of my work in Cuba [*Poemas de Ernesto Cardenal*] and they let me know that it sold out in five days. Even though these accomplishments are trivial and have no value and do not even mean that the poetry in it is very good, nevertheless it pleases me to be able to have influence, especially over the youth in Latin America, within a certain medium that the Church has neglected; and if God permits it, then this is a vocation that needs to be pursued. May it be His will, if we do not like it, or even if we like it.

I have always wanted to receive your last two books: *Raids on the Unspeakable* and *Conjectures of a Guilty Bystander*, where, according to what you have said to me before, you mention me on several occasions in one of your books.

William Agudelo is due to marry within the next few days in Colombia, and was to arrive here immediately afterward with his wife to attempt to realize his plan for an evangelical married life of simplicity and poverty in Solentiname—or some place on these islands. I think they will come in a few days and I trust that it is God's plan.

United with Him, I embrace you,

Ernesto

Letter 89

Dear Ernesto:

Many thanks for your letter of the 5th. I think there must be something wrong with the mail. I am sure I sent you those two books. However, I will send other copies, and the new one also, *Cables to the Ace*. I am also running a magazine [*Monks Pond*] temporarily—four or five issues only. A copy will be on the way to you. I want to translate some of your "Psalms." I can't find a copy here, though I know there must be one around. Do you have an extra one? Please send me one if you have one available. I will use a few "Psalms" in the magazine before it closes down. [None of Cardenal's "Psalms" appeared in *Monks Pond.*]

Yes, we have a new Abbot [Flavian Burns]. But if you mean by Gethsemani-Nicaragua project a new foundation, I think that is completely out of the question. I do not think there will be any more Gethsemani foundations. As you know we took over the Spencer foundation in Chile. I asked to be sent there in order to be in Latin America, but the permission was refused. However, I do think it will be possible for Fr. Flavian to let me come to visit you for a time and to study the situation. Not right away, because since Dom James is still living here, as a hermit, Fr. Flavian has to take him into account and is a little afraid of him. Please write and tell me what is the best time to come. When is the dry season? If possible, I might come at the end of this year and spend at least a few weeks with you. There are very many reasons why I want to leave this country, and yet for those same reasons I think I ought to stay. It seems wrong to escape the immense rottenness, the evil, the judgment, that are inevitable here. Do you know that some fanatical Catholics in Louisville have burned my books, declaring me an atheist because I am opposed to the Vietnam War? It is completely incredible. This country is mad with hatred, frustration, stupidity, confusion. That there should be such ignorance and stupidity in a civilized land is just incomprehensible.

On the other hand, I would be ashamed to be in a Latin American country and to be known as a North American.

But in any case, apart from all these ideas one way or the other, it is necessary to see whether or not God really wants me there. In so many ways this seems to be the place for me, here. But I want to come to Solentiname and see what it is like, see if it seems to be where God wants me, though I rather doubt it. For one thing, I believe I would be a kind of tourist attraction, and would have to be seeing people all the time. It is bad enough here. But there is some protection.

If I were to leave here, I would want to disappear completely and go where I was not known at all, and cease to have any kind of public existence whatever.

I think the idea of William Agudelo [Colombian poet] living there with his wife is just tremendous. I think that the whole future of monasticism depends on some broadening of perspectives like this.

I often pray for you and think about Solentiname. I don't believe, however, that it will be the right place for F. Romanus [Father Romano]. The best, always, in Christ,

T. M.

Letter 90

Dear Ernesto:

I have been meaning for a long time to write you a decent letter. There are several reasons for the delay. The chief of these is that much is happening here and I have many plans for the end of the year. But nothing is fully certain yet. I am going to Japan and then to Thailand, where there is a meeting of Asian Catholic Abbots. I also have to preach a retreat at the Cistercian monastery in Java. After that I am not sure what I will be able to do. If I can get the money and the contacts I hope by some miracle to get to Nepal in the Himalayas—and then see what happens. Burma also is another possibility—but again a quasi miracle will be required.

If these do not work out it is possible that I may get to Nicaragua for a few weeks with you. In any case, wherever I go, I want to have a hidden and quiet time of retreat after the traveling. One thing is certain, that I need real solitude and I need to get away from the constant pressure of visitors and more or less superficial demands in the matter of work; articles, commentary, prefaces, etc. Where I am here at Gethsemani, I am too well known and too accessible.

Fr. Flavian our new abbot is very fine. He has spontaneously suggested that I form a small hermit colony in California or somewhere hidden (it would be in an isolated part of the Northern California coast). Much depends on his finding the place, and on it remaining really hidden!! I wonder if Northern California is really likely to fill the requirements. But I also wonder about Nicaragua: I am too well known there also. But in any case, if I do not go further into Asia I think I will spend a few weeks at least with you, if God grants it. But I make no firm promise. I do hope very much to go to Nepal. It would be marvelous.

But also in any event I hope to come to Solentiname. I will keep in touch with you and let you know. I should go to Japan early in November and if I do not go to Nepal or Burma, should fly back early in January. Though something else might happen to delay me—I might stay longer in Indonesia. In any case I do not have to be back at Gethsemani too soon, and my plans are flexible. Please pray that God may guide me.

I have a very definite feeling that a new horizon is opening up and I do not quite know what it is. If it is something in Asia then I will need very special grace. My secret hope is to go to the Himalayas. But I do not insist on any desire of my own. If it is clearly God's will for me to settle in Nicaragua or in California, I ask only to see it clearly and to do it faithfully.

Since my Abbot of his own volition is planning a hermitage in California and wants to entrust it to me, this does take first priority, I think. But we'll see what comes of it. In any event I hope to see you either in Jan. 1969 or the following year.

Your *Mayapán* [long poem] is fine. I am doing some things like that now in a poem. I'll send you bits when they are published. William's latest poems in *El Corno* are magnificent, strong, rugged, impressive, clean.

I very much want to see you all again. I want to get out of this country. The atmosphere is stifling and very sick. Perhaps by a miracle [Eugene] McCarthy might get elected—the people are for him, vested interests and established power against him. If he is not elected I will find it difficult to return here!! This will become a police state in all reality.

I promise faithfully this time to send you some books. Sorry to have been so negligent about that.

Blessings, peace, and love in the Lord,

T. M.

Letter 91

To the Most Rev. Archbishop Paul Philippe

Secretary of the Holy Congregation of the Religious

Most Reverend Archibibishop and Dear Friend:

No one ignores the crucial importance of promoting contemplative life in Latin America today. Further, the Church has urged dioceses and religious houses of the United States to send priests and [the] religious to help in South America. Innumerable requests for foundations have been sent in to Cistercian monasteries of the United States, particularly Gethsemani. It is not possible to say exactly how many such requests have been refused by Gethsemani, but I am sure the refusals number more than twenty, all of them attractive offers of land, etc. At the same time it is understandable that the success of the usual type of Cistercian foundation in Latin America would be problematical. Two foundations made from Spencer are in grave difficulties.

Father Ernesto Cardenal was recently ordained as a secular priest (August 16, 1965) in Nicaragua. He is a former novice of Gethsemani who left for reasons of health. During his novitiate, when he was under my direction, we spoke frequently of the contemplative life in Latin America. He is now beginning a small contemplative foundation, following the Rule of St. Benedict, but not affiliated with any Order, in Nicaragua. Feeling that I am in some way the originator of the idea, and desiring to have the guidance of someone experienced in monastic life, he has approached me and asked if I would consent to accept the charge of Spiritual Father, giving conferences, instruction, and direction while his community is in the process of formation, at least. I have replied that I would certainly consent to undertake this task if I could be loaned by my community to his community, either with a leave of absence or if Your Excellency thought necessary, an exclaustration. The idea would be for me to continue my monastic life in his community while remaining a member of my own Order canonically. However, as this is a suggestion that my own Superiors would regard as novel and unacceptable, it has been thought well to present it directly to Your Excellency for advice and for some indication of God's will in this regard. It is felt that Your Excellency would be able to see the whole project in better perspective.

Speaking personally, I believe that this step would be a greater perfection in my own monastic vocation. It would fit the traditionally monastic idea of exile from one's own country and people, at the same time providing a life of greater solitude on a small island in the Lake of Nicaragua, and with greater poverty and simplicity. It would also be a response to a call of charity from Catholics who are in serious spiritual need. However, I take no personal initiative in this matter and leave the decision entirely to higher Superiors. I would appreciate hearing directly from Your Excellency about your reactions to this project, and will follow whatever you say.

With cordial and filial respect in Christ our Lord,

F. M. Louis Merton

Letter 92

To His Holiness Pope Paul VI

Holy Father:

This letter will be presented to you by a delegation of faithful Catholics from Nicaragua in Central America. These faithful realize in a most urgent manner the great need of the contemplative and monastic life in Latin America today. After repeated, unsuccessful attempts to obtain a foundation from the contemplative monasteries of the United States, especially the Abbey of Gethsemani, they are now beginning to form a contemplative community under the direction of Father Ernesto Cardenal, who was a novice at this monastery under my direction, and who, after leaving Gethsemani for reasons of health, has been ordained as a secular priest and is forming a small community to live a contemplative life and provide a place of retreat for the intellectuals of Nicaragua, for students, writers, and so on.

Since this project was, in part, conceived in conversations with me when Father Cardenal was a novice here, and since I am very interested in the project myself, they have asked me if I would consent to join the community and act as Spiritual Father, giving conferences and direction, and offering guidance that would help the community to understand correctly the Rule of St. Benedict and monastic traditions. The community wishes to follow the Benedictine Rule. I gladly consent to offer this service provided that my Superiors see fit to permit me to be absent from my monastery and continue my monastic life (remaining canonically a member of my own Order) at this new community.

Because this is a very unusual project, and because of the difficulties that present themselves, these petitioners have found it necessary to come to Rome in order to ascertain, from higher Superiors, whether this is not the will of God. It is hoped that higher Superiors will interpret the will of God for all of us in this case. As the situation in Latin America today is so urgent, and as monasteries of the United States have been repeatedly urged to send men to Latin America, it is felt that the Abbey of Gethsemani, which has so far sent no one, could at least spare *one priest* in this very special case, in which the most prominent Catholic intellectuals of an entire nation have joined themselves together to make the petition.

It is felt by all of us that Your Holiness would be in a special position to see, in its full perspective, the meaning of this petition and of the project with which it is concerned. For that reason the matter is being submitted directly to your Holiness at the same time as the secretary of the Sacred Congregation of Religious is being consulted about it. Your Holiness's interest, support, and blessing would indeed be most warmly appreciated. Begging the blessing of Your Holiness, I remain your most humbly devoted son in Christ our Lord,

Thomas Merton

Translator's Afterword

I translated Fr. Ernesto Cardenal's letters from English to Spanish after coming across the 1998 Spanish edition of the correspondence of Cardenal and Thomas Merton, *Del monasterio al mundo*, edited by Santiago Daydi-Tolson, who also translated Thomas Merton's letters— all but one of which were written in English—into Spanish. Thomas Merton could read Spanish, but I have the impression that Cardenal, in writing to him, made some effort to speak directly and plainly, as he was aware that Merton was not a native Spanish speaker. Cardenal's prose in these letters often comes across as somewhat breathless, unpunctuated, and sometimes grammatically circular, or without a definite end in sight, which made the task of catching his tone in English a labor, though a very interesting one.

This work was complicated for me in other ways as well—primarily because my family is Nicaraguan. I was born in Los Angeles, but my parents moved back to Nicaragua when I was two, and we stayed in the country for two and a half years before moving back to the States. And so, after many years of trying to put the tragedies of Nicaragua behind me, I was suddenly back, returned in memory, while working on these letters. As a toddler, I chased chickens and piglets and played hide-and-go-seek with older cousins on various family farms spanning the Nicaraguan countryside, from Chontales to the Somoto—a small town on the northern border. Cardenal's language brought me back to brief, early memories of cows, of sunbathing in the corral, of being lulled to sleep on a hammock by the musky smells of warm glassy black water during nighttime ferry crossings across Lake Nicaragua, and of watching lizards zigzagging with comical urgency up drainpipes while my mother bathed me in an outdoor sink. I was back, and deeper inside, the sensual Central America of Ernesto Cardenal's early poems.

And then there was politics. In those early years of childhood paradise, the security and independence that families like ours had enjoyed for generations, by taking refuge inside our economically self-sustained agrarian way of life—an almost pre–industrial age, colonial model of doing business, where a handshake between land-owning neighbors and town elders could guarantee a loan and allow us to lightly maneuver around party politics, without compromising too much—was suddenly buckling under the weight of a new world order that had been slow-boiling in cruelty since many decades before my birth.

Before the 1980s, political parties like the *Liberales* or *Conservadores* were antiquated nationalistic identity fiefdoms, fronting as political philosophies but mostly organized around old family alliances and loyalties that most Nicaraguans were born into. Our unique social class, as wealthy land-owning peasants with middle-class sensibilities, had positioned our family strategically between the rural *campesinos*, who trusted us, and those in powerful positions, who respected us and therefore facilitated access and social connections in our favor. "My father would let Somoza García hunt on his land; they liked each other," is what my grandfather used to tell us about *"El Viejo, Somoza,"* or the "Old Man, Somoza," and the so-called good old days, when my great-grandfather and Somoza were still young men during the 1920s. "The old man wasn't like his son, that madman," he'd say, referring to Somoza García's son, Anastasio Somoza Debayle. Despite their personal affinities with the first Somoza, or "the old man," my great-grandfather and grandfather had been *Conservadores*, not *Liberales*—which was, in fact, a political party, basically serving as a front operation for the Somoza regime. I am convinced that what kept my family truly safe and alive during all those years before the Sandinista Revolution was their reluctance to vote and to publically endorse any political party. Politics for my grandfather were, at best, only a necessary evil for those who lacked the character and courage to govern themselves or to conduct ethical business relationships without the ever-looming threat of a good public shaming. My family's Christian Catholic faith, not politics, were the teachings that informed their morality, social commitments, and ideas about charity for the sick, poor, and *el projimo*, or their fellow human beings.

The indiscriminate carnage of the civil war in Nicaragua during the late 1970s stripped away the last vestiges of shame, dignity, and propriety that the privileged minority of our country had perceived for centuries as inalienable to their class, by divine right. Divisions and distinctions between politics, religion, and private and public life were exposed as purely superficial aesthetic elitist conceits whose pretense only benefitted those in a position to negotiate access and trade favors between Church hierarchy, the wealthy, and those with political clout—discretely behind the scenes and away from any transparent accountability. In a morbid and brutal turn of events, the civil war freed many Nicaraguans from suffocating class constraints, naive social taboos, and legacies of Spanish and European colonization, which prayed on our anxieties and fears— perhaps we would never be anything more than very polite, well-trained, housebroken monkeys from the banana tropics. Simply put, the war served as shock therapy, rousing the poor and rich alike from decades of self-denial, fantasies, and myths—bringing us up to date with other postcolonial global struggles that had already broken significant ground almost two decades earlier, between the late 1950s and late 1960s.

The letters between Ernesto Cardenal and Thomas Merton between 1958 and 1969 hold great personal significance to me, not only because they are historical documents—offering anecdotes and references about noteworthy literary, artistic, and political figures of this era of great turmoil and resistance and, essentially, a poetic fleshing out of political events, leading up to Nicaragua's Sandinista Revolution—but also because as we read deeper, into each letter, these dates, timelines, names, and grand political ideas slowly give way to the immediate pre-occupations of daily life and the quotidian struggle of finding meaning, purpose, and love. I am currently the same age that Cardenal was while he was writing these letters, and I have just begun to better understand state-sanctioned violence as a very intimate problem of the heart and human psyche that must be solved one person at a time. I say this as someone who cannot reconcile, move forward, and heal from the wounds of Nicaragua's history of struggle without also understanding how these events intersected and disrupted the health and sanctity of my own humanity and that of the individuals in my family. The time period of these letters coincides precisely with my mother's adolescence, when she was coming into her own political awakening and building up her own intellectual resistance to a system she was already recognizing as obscenely unjust. *"Durante la época de mi General"* ("during my General's era") is my mother's dark and humorous way of referring to the Somozista regime—when she copes with her memories of the country she left behind—especially after she's had a few cocktails.

Like many veterans, my mother and father found it almost impossible to talk about or work through most of the physical and emotional trauma they had suffered while in Nicaragua and afterward, as they began to trickle into California as refugees. When my mother speaks of Nicaragua, very clear distinctions are made and disclaimers are loudly announced before she begins any story. In her mind, it is absolutely crucial that you truly understand which Nicaragua she's referring to in her *relatos*—because there are definitely more than a few different versions of our country and people, converging, collapsing, and splitting like the growing earth-skin of our volcanoes. The Nicaragua of her early childhood, during the summer before she was supposed to attend third grade—right before Somoza García was shot, during the fall of 1956, amid a failed coup, and before all the schools in her town were closed for a year—that was the Nicaragua of climbing trees behind the church and getting spankings for ripping her dress and being an incorrigible tomboy, and of staging elaborate Bible-themed pageants with her brothers and sisters at home for her parents and aunts and uncles during those pitch-dark nights at the family farm, to drown out the bellowing of pumas in the mountains.

Like most Nicaraguans from my generation, I was raised to venerate poetry, especially that of our Nicaraguan poets, like Rubén Dario, Pablo Antonio Cuadra, and Ernesto Cardenal. You speak with any Nicaraguan, and they will proudly inform you that we are all poets and that Nicaragua is the land of poets—poetry is our most prized export. Indeed, this is how most *Nicoyas* felt about Ernesto Cardenal when I was kid in the early 1980s. His snow-white hair and black beret made our jungle revolution cool. The magazine covers and propaganda publications his face graced during my teenage years signaled a bohemian Frenchness to me, while also helping shellac a sheen of universal, romanticized militancy over the crude reality of what had truly been a sea of dark indigenous bodies, wading waist-deep in the sweltering mountains of our banana republic jungle during the height of the U.S.-funded Contra campaign against the Sandinistas.

These were some of the complexities for me as I immersed myself in these letters while living in Oakland, California. And during that time, in the fall of 2011, my city and community were in the throes of the Occupy movement, and I was spending my days on the street, helping translate political propaganda—activities that would lead me directly, just a few years later, to Ferguson, Missouri, during the summer of 2014, to join a movement that this street-level uprising ignited against State violence across the country.

I need to thank Professor Robert Hass for continuing to be my teacher, mentor, and friend, more than fifteen years after taking my first poetry class with him at UC Berkeley. I was able to undertake this rich and transformative project only because of his sponsorship, guidance, and support. Also, I am eternally grateful to Fr. Cardenal for giving permission to Counterpoint Press to reprint these letters after I translated them, and also for very generously spending two long afternoons talking to me about those years, which were full of the exhilaration of the revolution for him and full of complicated pain for my family.

A person who cannot go without mention is Lorena Sandoval, my mother, who not only aided me in many of these translations, providing crucial insights about unique Nicaraguan idioms and ecclesiastic terminology in these letters, but who also kept me encouraged, focused, and inspired to continue researching and writing about our own family history.

—Jessie Sandoval

APPENDIX

Chronology and Landscape

It is useful to track the chronologies of Thomas Merton and Ernesto Cardenal alongside the development of liberation theology in Central and South America and alongside the priestly career of Francis I. Among the important figures in this story are Father Camilo Torres Restrepo (1929–1966), a Colombian; Father Gustavo Gutiérrez (b. 1928), a Peruvian; Fr. Leonardo Boff (b. 1938), a Brazilian; and Father Juan Luis Segundo (1925–1996), from Uruguay.

1915	Thomas Merton is born in Prades, France, to a New Zealander father and an American mother, both painters.
1921	Merton's mother, Ruth, dies of stomach cancer, after which Merton lives sometimes with his father, sometimes with his maternal grandparents in New York, sometimes in schools in England and France.
1925	Ernesto Cardenal is born into a wealthy family in Granada, Nicaragua.
1931	Merton's father, Owen, dies of a brain tumor in London.
1933	Dorothy Day founds the Catholic Worker movement in New York City, which combines direct aid to the poor with direct nonviolent action on their behalf.
1933	At Cambridge, Merton drinks, parties, gets a girl pregnant (a matter settled through his guardian by attorneys), and is sent away in 1934: "My attitude was a common Cambridge attitude of total indifference to religion."

1935   Merton begins again at Columbia University.

1936   Jorge Mario Bergoglio, the future Pope Francis, is born in
            Argentina.

1938   Merton, working on a dissertation on Blake, becomes a Catholic.

1939   Merton visits Cuba, which begins his interest in things
            Latin American; he works at Friendship House in Harlem,
            a settlement house associated with Dorothy Day's
            Catholic Action. He is ambivalent about religion and
            social activism.

1941   Merton enters the Abbey of Gethsemani as a novice on
            December 10, a few days after the bombing of Pearl Harbor.

1943   Merton's younger brother, John Paul, an RCAF pilot, dies when
            his plane crashes over the English Channel.

1942–1946   Cardenal studies literature in Mexico City.

1947–1949   Cardenal studies at Columbia University; he edits a volume
            of new Nicaraguan poets and studies Ezra Pound and other
            American poets.

1948   Merton publishes *The Seven Story Mountain*.

1950–1953   Cardenal returns to Nicaragua; he writes poems of Nicaragua's
            colonial history, love poems, and political epigrams, which
            circulate in mimeograph form.

1954   The April Revolution against the Somoza dictatorship in
            Nicaragua fails; several of Cardenal's colleagues are arrested,
            tortured, and killed.

1955   The CELAM Latin American Episcopal Conference in Rio de
            Janeiro is held.

1956	Somoza is assassinated. Cardenal undergoes a conversion experience as he is writing *Zero Hour*; he commits to nonviolence.
1957–1959	Cardenal lives at Gethsemani; he writes *Gethsemani, KY* and the meditation journals that will become *To Live Is to Love*.
1959	The Cuban revolution overthrows the Batista regime.
1959	Cardenal enters a seminary in Cuernavaca, Mexico.
1961	Merton publishes "Original Child Bomb," a prose poem meditating on the bombing of Hiroshima.
1962	Merton writes "Concerning Giants," his essay addressed to Cardenal's uncle Pablo Antonio Cuadra, analyzing the Cold War culture of his time and the future role of Latin America; he calls the piece "an angry tirade."
1962	Pope John XXIII opens the Second Vatican Council.
1964–1965	Bergogilo teaches literature at a high school in Santa Fe, Argentina.
1965	Cardenal is ordained in Granada where he grew up.
1965	Father Juan Luis Segundo establishes a center for the study of religion and society in Montevideo, which the Uruguayan government shuts down in the 1970s.
1966	Cardenal establishes the community at Solentiname, an island in Lake Nicaragua, and offers Mass and readings of scripture to the largely illiterate peasant and fishermen families.
1967	Bergoglio is ordained in Argentina.
1968	The second CELAM conference, in Medellín, Colombia, turns to social justice and the agenda of Vatican II.

1971	Fr. Gustavo Gutiérrez, a Peruvian priest, publishes *A Theology of Liberation*.
1974–1983	The "dirty war" occurs in Argentina. Death squads eliminate 7,000 to 30,000 people—liberals, socialists, union leaders, and revolutionaries. Father Bergoglio is made a very young director of the Jesuit order during this time when the military junta purged left-leaning Catholic priests.
1974	Father Juan Luis Segundo publishes the first volume of a five-volume *Theology for the Artisans of a New Humanity*.
1977	The Trujillo regime raids Solentiname and burns it to the ground.
1977	Fr. Leonardo Boff publishes *The Sacrament of Life*.
1979	The Sandinista revolution overthrows Somoza regime; Cardenal becomes Minister of Culture.
1979	Fr. Gutiérrez is banned from attending the third CELAM Conference in Puebla, Mexico.
1980	Archbishop Oscar Romero is assassinated in El Salvador while he is celebrating Mass in the cathedral at San Salvador.
1983	Pope John Paul II visits Nicaragua and rebukes Cardenal.
1984	Pope John Paul II defrocks Fr. Cardenal.
1985	Father Leonardo Boff is officially silenced by the Roman Curia.
1989	Right-wing death squads commit a massacre of six Jesuit professors and their housekeeper and her daughter at their university quarters in El Salvador.
1992	Boff leaves Franciscans and the Church after being blocked by

his religious superiors from attending an Earth Summit in Rio de Janeiro.

1994   Cardenal resigns from the Sandinista party in protest against the government's authoritarian policies.

1998   Father Bergoglio becomes Archbishop of Buenos Aires.

2013   Bergoglio becomes Pope Francis.

2014   Pope Francis reinstates Cardenal's priesthood.

2015   Oscar Romero is beatified.

From the Spanish of Ernesto Cardenal

SELECTIONS FROM *GETHSEMANI, KY*

(Translated by Thomas Merton)

1

Spring has come with its smell of Nicaragua:
Smell of earth recently rained on, and smell of heat,
Of flowers, of disinterred roots, wet leaves,
(And I have heard the lowing of distant cattle . . .)
Or is it the smell of love? But this love
Is not yours. Love of country, is the Dictator's love
The fat Dictator with his sports clothes and panama hat:
He was the one who loved the country, stole it,
And possessed it. In that earth he lies embalmed:
While love has taken you away to a strange land.

2

Like the flights of ducks
That go over calling
That in the autumn nights go over calling
To lagoons in the south they never saw,
And do not know who takes them, nor where they go,
So we are carried to Thee not knowing where.
Just like the flights of ducks that come from the south
And pass over Kentucky calling in the night.

3

Every evening the L&N
Goes singing through these Kentucky fields
And I seem to hear the little train at home
In Nicaragua, when it borders the Managua Lake
Across from the volcano, just before
Mateare, going around the bend
Across from Bird Island, piping and singing
Its iron song of wheels and rails,
With the first lights of Managua there
Far off, shining in the waters . . .
The L&N goes off
Into the distance with its song.

4

The sound of passing cars, (if a car comes)
On the highway outside the novitiate
Is like sea surf. You hear one begin
To come far off and the sound grows
More and more, the motor roars,
Tires sing on the damp tar
And then it goes away, dies down,
Is no longer heard. Later some other engine
In the distance begins to come again.
Like waves in the sea. And I, like waves
In the sea, once ran along tar roads that go
To no definite place. And still at times
It seems I go by the same roads
And do not stop going and arrive at no place,
That I am not the one in the novitiate
Seeing the cars pass,

But that I have seen the novitiate
Through the window of that car that just went by.

5

When the first signs go on
When they light up the marquees
Of the movie theaters
Here we hear nothing but swallows.
At 7 p.m. the Trappists go to bed
In broad daylight, like noon,
And with a full moon like midnight.
The horses are quiet in the stable.
The trucks sleep in the garage.
The tractors are still
Before the barn.
Above the water tank: the aluminum moon.

6

The long freight train
Wakes me in my cell
I hear it coming from far off
In the night. It passes and passes, whistling,
Seeming that it will never all get past:
Cars and cars and cars bumping along!
I fall asleep again, and it is still passing
Panting in the distance and still whistling,
And between dreams I ask myself
Why they still have trains
And where they take their freight, and what freight,
Where the cars come from
And where they can possibly go.

7

The zinc roofs in the moonlight
And the tin shop, the gas tank
And the water tank, all look like silver.
Like a star, like a cigarette,
Far out, over Nally's hill,
A passenger plane
Passes and flashes in the night.

8

A dog barks far out
Behind the black wood. Further still
Behind another wood, another dog answers.

9

Like empty beer cans, like cigarette butts;
My days have been like that.
Like figures passing on a TV screen
And disappearing, so my life has gone.
Like cars going by fast on the roads
With girls laughing and radios playing.
Beauty got obsolete as fast as car models
And forgotten radio hits.

Nothing is left of those days, nothing,
But empty beer cans, cigarette butts,
Smiles on faded photos, torn tickets
And the sawdust with which, in the mornings,
They swept out the bars.

10

I turned out the light to see the snow,
And I saw snow through the window and a new moon.
But I saw that both snow and moon
Were also a window pane
And that behind that pane you were watching me.

11

I do not know who is out in the snow
All that is seen in the snow is his white habit
And at first I saw no one at all:
Only the plain white sunlit snow.
A novice in the snow is barely visible.
And I feel that there is something more in this snow
Which is neither snow nor novice, and is not seen.

12

That auto horn sounds familiar.
So does this wind in the pines.
This zinc novitiate roof
Reminds me of my house at home.
They are calling me with the auto horn.
But my house, near the road
Where the cars went by all day
Was sold years ago. Strangers live there.
This was no known car. It is gone.
The wind is the same. Only the sighing
Of this rainy autumn evening is well known.

From "A Letter to Pablo Antonio Cuadra Concerning Giants"

by Thomas Merton

The largest, richest, and best-developed single landmass south of the equator is South America. The vast majority of its population is Indian, or of mixed Indian blood. The white minority in South Africa would quite probably disappear. A relic of European stock might survive in Australia and New Zealand. Let us also hopefully assume the partial survival of India and of some Moslem populations in central and northern Africa.

If this should happen it will be an event fraught with a rather extraordinary spiritual significance. It will mean that the more cerebral and mechanistic cultures, those which have tended to live more and more by abstractions and to isolate themselves more and more from the natural world by rationalization, will be succeeded by the sections of the human race that they oppressed and exploited without the slightest appreciation for or understanding for their human reality.

Characteristic of these races is a totally different outlook on life, a spiritual outlook that is not abstract but concrete, not pragmatic but hieratic, intuitive and affective rather than rationalistic and aggressive. The deepest springs of vitality in these races have been sealed up by the Conqueror and Colonizer, where they have not actually been poisoned by him. But if this stone is removed from the spring, perhaps its waters will purify themselves by new life and regain their creative, fructifying power. Neither Gog nor Magog can accomplish this for them.

Let me be quite succinct: the greatest sin of the European-Russian-American complex that we call "the West" (and this sin has spread its own way to China) is not only greed and cruelty, not only moral dishonesty and infidelity to truth, but above all *its unmitigated arrogance toward the rest of the human race.* Western civilization is now in full decline into barbarism (a barbarism that springs *from within itself*) because it has been guilty of a twofold disloyalty: to God and to Man. To a Christian who believes in the mystery of the Incarnation, and who by that belief means something more than a pious theory without real humanistic implications, this is not two disloyalties but one. Since the Word was made Flesh, God in man. God is in *all men.* All men are to be seen and treated as Christ. Failure to do this, the Lord tells us, involves condemnation for disloyalty to the most fundamental of revealed truths. "I was thirsty and you gave me not to drink. I was hungry and you gave me not to eat . . ." (Matthew 25:42). This could be extended in every possible sense: and is meant to be so extended, all over the entire area of human needs, not only for bread, for work, for liberty, for health, but also for truth, for belief, for love, for acceptance, for fellowship and understanding.

One of the great tragedies of the Christian West is the fact that for all the good will of the missionaries and colonizers (they certainly meant well, and behaved humanly, according to their lights, which were somewhat brighter than ours), they could not recognize that *the races they conquered were essentially equal to themselves and in some ways superior.*

It was certainly right that Christian Europe should bring Christ to the Indians of Mexico and the Andes, as well as to the Hindus and the Chinese: but where they failed was in their inability to *encounter Christ* already potentially present in the Indians, the Hindus, and the Chinese.

Christians have too often forgotten the fact that Christianity found its way into Greek and Roman civilization partly by its spontaneous and creative adaptation of the pre-Christian natural values it found in that civilization. The martyrs rejected all the grossness, the cynicism and falsity of the cult of the state-gods, which was simply a cult of secular power, but Clement of Alexandria, Justin, and Origen believed that Herakleitos and Socrates had been precursors of Christ. They thought that while God had manifested himself to the Jews through the Law and the Prophets, he had also spoken to the Gentiles through their philosophers. Christianity made its way in the world of the first century not by imposing Jewish cultural and social standards on the rest of the world, but by abandoning them, getting free of them so as to be "all things to all men." This was the great drama and the supreme lesson of the Apostolic Age. By the end of the Middle Ages, that lesson had been *forgotten*. The preachers of the Gospel to newly discovered continents became preachers and disseminators of European culture and power. They did not enter into dialogue with ancient civilizations: they imposed upon them their own monologue, and in preaching Christ they also preached themselves. The very ardor of their self-sacrifice and of their humility enabled them to do this with a clean conscience. But they had omitted to listen to the voice of Christ in the unfamiliar accents of the Indian, as Clement had listened for it in the Pre-Socratics. And now, today, we have a Christianity of Magog.

It is a Christianity of money, of action, of passive crowds, an electronic Christianity of loudspeakers and parades. Magog is himself without belief, cynically tolerant of the athletic yet sentimental Christ devised by some of his clients, because this Christ is profitable to Magog. He is a progressive Christ who does not protest against Pharisees or money changers in the temple. He protests only against Gog.

It is my belief that we should not be too sure of having found Christ in ourselves until we have found him also in the part of humanity that is most remote from our own. Christ is found not in loud and pompous declarations but in humble and fraternal dialogue. He is found less in a truth that is imposed than in a truth that is shared.

If I insist on giving you my truth, and never stop to receive your truth in return, then there can be no truth between us. Christ is present "where two or three are gathered in my name." But to be gathered in the name of Christ is to be gathered in the name of the Word made Flesh, of God made man. It is therefore to be gathered in the faith that God has become man and can be seen in man, that he can speak in man and that he can enlighten and inspire love in and through any man I meet. It is true that the visible Church alone has the official mission to sanctify and teach all nations, but no man knows that the stranger he meets coming out of the forest in a new country is not already an invisible member of Christ and perhaps one who has some providential or prophetic message to utter.

Whatever India may have had to say to the West, she was forced to remain silent. Whatever China had to say, though some of the first missionaries heard it and understood it, the message was generally ignored as irrelevant. Did anyone pay attention to the voices of the Maya and the Inca, who had deep things to say? By and large their witness was merely suppressed. No one considered that the children of the Sun might, after all, hold in their hearts a spiritual secret. On the contrary, abstract discussions were engaged in to determine whether, in terms of academic philosophy, the Indian was to be considered a rational animal. One shudders at the voice of cerebral Western arrogance even then eviscerated by the rationalism that is ours today, judging the living spiritual mystery of primitive man and condemning it to exclusion from the category on which love, friendship, respect, and communion were made to depend.

God speaks, and God is to be heard, not only on Sinai, not only in my own heart, but in the voice of the stranger. That is why the peoples of the Orient, and all primitive peoples in general, make so much of the mystery of hospitality.

God must be allowed the right to speak unpredictably. The Holy Spirit, the very voice of Divine Liberty, must always be like the wind in "blowing where he pleases" (John 3:8). In the mystery of the Old Testament there was already a tension between the Law and the Prophets. In the New Testament, the Spirit himself is Law, and he is everywhere. He certainly inspires and protects the visible Church, but if we cannot see him unexpectedly in the stranger and the alien, we will not understand him even in the Church. We must find him in our enemy, or we may lose him even in our friend. We must find him in the pagan, or we will lose him in our own selves, substituting for his living presence an empty abstraction. How can we reveal to others what we cannot discover in them ourselves? We must, then, see the truth in the stranger, and the truth we see must be a newly living truth, not just a projection of a dead conventional idea of our own—a projection of our own self upon the stranger.

The desecration, desacralization of the modern world is manifest above all by the fact that the stranger is of no account. As soon as he is "displaced," he is completely unacceptable. He fits into no familiar category; he is unexplained and therefore a threat to complacency. Everything not easy to account for must be wiped out, and mystery must be wiped out with it. An alien presence interferes with the superficial and faked clarity of our own rationalizations.

There is more than one way of morally liquidating the "stranger" and the "alien." It is sufficient to destroy, in some way, that in him which is different and disconcerting. By pressure, persuasion, or force one can impose on him one's own ideas and attitudes toward life. One can indoctrinate him, brainwash him. He is no longer different. He has been reduced to conformity with one's own outlook. Gog, who does nothing if not thoroughly, believes in the thorough liquidation of differences, and the reduction of everyone else to a carbon copy of himself. Magog is somewhat more quixotic: the stranger becomes part of his own screen of fantasies, part of the collective dream life which is manufactured for him on Madison Avenue and in Hollywood. For all practical purposes, the stranger no longer exists. He is not even seen. He is replaced by a fantastic image. What is seen and approved, in a vague, superficial way, is the stereotype that has been created by the travel agency.

This accounts for the spurious cosmopolitanism of the naive tourist and travelling businessman, who wanders everywhere with his camera, his exposure meter, his spectacles, his sun glasses, his binoculars, and though gazing around him in all directions never sees what is there. He is not capable of doing so. He is too docile to his instructors, to those who have told him everything beforehand. He believes the advertisements of the travel agent at whose suggestion he bought the ticket that landed him wherever he may be. He has been told what he was going to see, and he thinks he is seeing it. Or, failing that, he at least wonders why he is not seeing what he has been led to expect. Under no circumstances does it occur to him to become interested in what is actually there. Still less to enter into a fully human rapport with the human beings who are before him. He has not, of course, questioned their status as rational animals, as the scholastically trained colonists of an earlier age might have done. It just does not occur to him that they might have a life, a spirit, a thought, a culture of their own which has its own peculiar individual character.

He does not know why he is travelling in the first place: indeed he is travelling at somebody else's suggestion. Even at home he is alien from himself. He is doubly alienated when he is out of his own atmosphere. He cannot possibly realize that the stranger has something very valuable, something irreplaceable to give him: something that can never be bought with money, never estimated by publicists, never exploited by political agitators: the spiritual understanding of a friend who belongs to a different culture. The tourist lacks nothing except brothers. For him these do not exist.

The tourist never meets anyone, never encounters anyone, never finds the brother in the stranger. This is his tragedy, and it has been the tragedy of Gog and Magog, especially of Magog, in every part of the world.

If only North Americans had realized, after 150 years, that Latin Americans really existed. That they were really people. That they spoke a different language. That they had a culture. That they had more than something to sell! Money has totally corrupted the brotherhood that should have united all the peoples of America. It has destroyed the sense of relationship, the spiritual community that had already begun to flourish in the years of Bolívar. But no! Most North Americans still don't know, and don't care, that Brazil speaks a language other than Spanish, that all Latin Americans do not live for the siesta, that all do not spend their days and nights playing the guitar and making love. They have never awakened to the fact that Latin America is by and large culturally superior to the United States, not only on the level of the wealthy minority, which has absorbed more of the sophistication of Europe, but also among the desperately poor indigenous cultures, some of which are rooted in a past that has never yet been surpassed on this continent.

So the tourist drinks tequila, and thinks it is no good, and waits for the fiesta he has been told to wait for. How should he realize that the Indian who walks down the street, with half a house on his head and a hole in his pants, is Christ? All the tourist thinks is that it is odd for so many Indians to be called Jesus.

So much for the modern scene: I am no prophet—no one is—for now we have learned to get along without prophets. But I would say that if Gog and Magog are to destroy one another, which they seem quite anxious to do, it would be a great pity if the survivors in the "Third World" attempted to reproduce their collective alienation, horror, and insanity, and thus build up another corrupt world to be destroyed by another war. To the whole third world I would say there is one lesson to be learned from the present situation, one lesson of the greatest urgency: be unlike the giants, Gog and Magog. Mark what they do, and act differently. Mark their official pronouncements, their ideologies, and without any difficulty you will find them hollow. Mark their behavior: their bluster, their violence, their blandishments, their hypocrisy: by their fruits you shall know them. In all their boastfulness they have become the victims of their own terror, which is nothing but the emptiness of their own hearts. They claim to be humanists, they claim to know and love man. They have come to liberate man, they say. But they do not know what man is. They are them-selves less human than their fathers were, less articulate, less sensitive, less profound, less capable of genuine concern. They are turning into giant insects. Their societies are becoming anthills, without purpose, without meaning, without spirit and joy.

What is wrong with their humanism? It is a humanism of termites, because without God, man becomes an insect, a worm in the wood, and even if he can fly, so what? There are flying ants. Even if man flies all over the universe, he is still nothing but a flying ant until he recovers a human center and a human spirit in the depth of his own being.

Karl Marx? Yes, he was a humanist, with a humanist's concerns. He understood the roots of alienation, and his understanding even had some-thing spiritual about it. Marx unconsciously built his system on a basically religious pattern, on the Messianism of the Old Testament, and in his own myth Marx was Moses. He understood something of the meaning of liberation, because he had in his bones the typology of Exodus. To say that he built a "scientific" thought on a foundation of religious symbolism is not to say that he was wrong, but to justify what was basically right about his analysis. Marx did not think only with the top of his head, or reason on the surface of his intelligence. He did not simply verbalize or dogmatize as his followers have done. He was still human. And they?

Ultimately there is no humanism without God. Marx thought that humanism had to be atheistic, and this was because he did not under-stand God any better than the self-complacent formalists whom he criti-cized. He thought, as they did, that God was an idea, an abstract essence, forming part of an intellectual superstructure built to justify economic alienation. There is in God nothing abstract. He is not a static entity, an object of thought, a pure essence. The dynamism Marx looked for in history was something that the Bible itself would lead us in some sense to understand and to expect. And liberation from religious alienation was the central theme of the New Testament. But the theme has not been understood. It has too often been forgotten. Yet it is the very heart of the mystery of the Cross.

It is not with resignation that I wait for whatever may come, but with an acceptance and an understanding that cannot be confirmed within the limits of pragmatic realism. However meaningless Gog and Magog may be in themselves, the cataclysm they will undoubtedly let loose is full of meaning, full of light. Out of their negation and terror comes certitude and peace for anyone who can fight his way free of their confusion. The worst they can do is bring death upon us, and death is of little consequence. Destruction of the body cannot touch the deepest center of life.

When will the bombs fall? Who shall say? Perhaps Gog and Magog have yet to perfect their policies and their weapons. Perhaps they want to do a neat and masterly job, dropping "clean" bombs, without fallout. It sounds clinical to the point of humanitarian kindness. It is all a lovely, humane piece of surgery. Prompt, efficacious, sterile, pure. That of course was the ideal of the Nazis who conducted the extermination camps twenty years ago: but of course they had not progressed as far as we have. They devoted themselves dutifully to a disgusting job that could never be performed under perfect clinical conditions. Yet they did their best. Gog and Magog will develop the whole thing to its ultimate refinement. I hear they are working on a bomb that will destroy nothing but life. Men, animals, birds, perhaps also vegetation. But it will leave buildings, factories, railways, natural resources. Only one further step, and the weapon will be one of absolute perfection. It should destroy books, works of art, musical instruments, toys, tools, and gardens, but not destroy flags, weapons, gallows, electric chairs, gas chambers, instruments of torture, or plenty of straitjackets in case someone should accidentally survive. Then the era of love can finally begin. Atheistic humanism can take over.

Notes to the Text

Agudelo, William. Columbian poet, born in 1943. He met Cardenal in the seminary at La Ceja in Antioquia, where both studied in preparation for the priesthood. He was interested in Cardenal's monastic project and joined Cardenal during the initial years of Our Lady of Solentiname. His personal diary, *Our Bed Is of Flowers* (México: Joaquín Moritz, 1970), narrates his juvenile experiences in relation to his religious vocation, including his first stay in Nicaragua. He left Solentiname to get married in Colombia, but he returned with his wife to be part of the religious community. His children were born and raised at Solentiname, **78, 80, 81, 85, 87–89.**

Alberti, Rafael. Merton mainly translated the Spanish-language texts of Latin American poets. "Roman Nocturnes" (*The Collected Poems of Thomas Merton* [New York: New Directions, 1977]: 833–836), a translation of five poems from the Spanish poet Alberti's book *Roma, Danger to Walkers* (México: Joaquín Moritz, 1968), is the exception. Merton also translated a poem by José Hernández (*The Collected Poems*: 958), **84.**

"Alfonso Cortés." Essay by Merton (*Emblems of a Season of Fury*: 141–143): **26, 33**; essay by Cardenal (*Cultura* 24 [1962]: 13–27; and also in *Poems*, by Alfonso Cortés. Selected with an introduction by Ernesto Cardenal (San José de Costa Rica: EDUCA, 1970: 7–19). Cardenal, who considered Cortés one of the major poets of his country, dedicated a chapter of his graduation thesis at the University of Mexico to him, **36.**

American Pax. Journal of the North American pacifist movement, **22, 41.**

Américas. Journal of the Organization of American States, in which Cardenal published some of his works about the spirituality of indigenous American peoples, **57.** See: "cosmic revelation," **56.**

Anthology. Book by Cardenal (Santiago de Chile: Editorial Santiago, 1967), **81.**

Anthology of North American Poetry. Selected and translated by Cardenal and José Coronel Urtecho (Madrid: Aguilar, 1963), **18, 24, 43.**

Antoninus, Brother. Dominic monk who, like Merton, was a poet published by New Directions. In December 1959, he sent Merton his poems, about which the latter wrote in his diary: "'Gnarled' said Rexroth about these [poems]. All of them are stilted, rude, bitter, truly powerful. A medieval English, and on top of that, Puritanical, Anglo-Saxon words, a poet of dense texture, substantial and a complete religious feeling. Sensibility of sin. Reaction, disgust. A healthy struggle against the evil of falsehoods found in all parts." (*A Search for Solitude: Pursuing the Monk's Life*. Edited by Lawrence S. Cunningham [San Francisco: Harper, 1966]: 363]), **42.**

Antonucci, Emil. Friend of poet Robert Lax and illustrator of Lax's book *The Circus of the Sun* and also Merton's *Original Child Bomb*, **19.**

"Apocalipsis." Poem by Cardenal (*The Plumed Horn* 13 [1965]: 7–11), **65.**

"Art and Worship." Study by Merton, unedited manuscript. Both Merton and Cardenal's interests in art grew out of their practices in the plastic artists: Merton was interested in photography and publicly displayed his exercises based on Chinese calligraphy; Cardenal is a sculptor and has exhibited his work since before his entry into the Trappist monastery. See *Cardenal the Sculptor* (Prologue by Julio Valle Castillo, Wuppertal: Peter Hammer Verlag, 1989), **48, 51–55.**

Ascent to Truth, The. Book by Merton (New York: Harcourt, Brace and Company, 1951). *Ascenso a la verdad* (Buenos Aires: Editorial Sudamericana, 1954), **41.**

Ascetic and Mystic. Notes that probably became part of the unedited 1961 essay "Ascetical and Mystical Theology," also titled "Introduction to Christian Mysticism," **26, 32.**

"Atlas and the Fat Man." Article by Merton (*The Behavior of the Titans* 24–48), **32, 36.**

Baciu, Stefan. Literary critic and author of an article about Merton and Latin America, "Latin America and Spain in the Poetic World of Thomas Merton" (*Revue de Littérature Comparée* 41 [Apr–Jun 1967]: 288–300), and another on Cardenal, "Ernesto Cardenal, or the Way from Gethsemani to Solentiname" (*Reformatio* [*Evangelische Zeitschrift für Kultur und Politik*]: 15, no. 5 [1966]), **86.**

Balthasar, Hans Urs von. Swiss theologian who formed part of the Papal Commission on Theology after the Second Vatican Council, **86.**

Bardstown. Small town in Kentucky, the closest to the monastery Our Lady of Gethsemani, **7.**

Bay of Pigs (*Bahía de Cochinos*). The failed invasion of Cuba began in Puerto Cabezas, in the northern zone of Nicaragua's Atlantic coast, from which the invading brigade sailed on the afternoon of April 14, 1961; Luis Somoza came to the dock to send off the troops to the Cubans, calling on them to bring him from Havana a hair from the beard of Fidel Castro (Thumbull Higgins, *The Perfect Failure: Kennedy, Eisenhower, and the CIA at the Bay of Pigs* [New York: W. W. Norton & Co., 1987]: 127), **20, 23.**

Behavior of Titans, The. Essays by Merton (New York: New Directions, 1961), **15, 26, 29, 30, 32, 34, 53.**

"Bernal Díaz." Poem by Cardenal (*Cuadernos Americanos* 125 [1962]: 211–216), **43, 44.**

Berrigan, Father Daniel. An important literary and political figure of the 1960s, this Jesuit priest and poet was brought together with Merton because they shared an interest in the cause of peace and actively opposed the Vietnam War. He wrote an autobiography, *To Dwell in Peace: An Autobiography* (San Francisco: Harper and Row, 1987), **23, 30, 32, 38, 42, 80.**

Black Elk. Medicine man of the Lakota Sioux, who famously remembered his life experiences in *The Sacred Pipe: Black Elk's Account of the Seven Rites of the Oglala Sioux*. Recorded and edited by Joseph Epes Brown (Norman: University of Oklahoma Press, 1953). It is very probable that Cardenal's interest in indigenous cultures, especially those of the Americas, had its origin in his talks with Merton in the novitiate. During his studies in Colombia, this interest became greater, as attested to by his articles on the subject and the edited volume *American Indigenous Literature: An Anthology*. Edited by Ernesto Cardenal and Jorge Montoya Toro (Medellín: Editorial Universidad de Antioquia, undated), **48.**

"Black Revolution, The." Essay by Merton (*Ramparts* 2, 3 [1963]: 4–23), **48.**

Blackfriars. British journal of the Benedictine Order, **58, 71.**

Bluefields. Principal Nicaraguan city on the Atlantic coast, upon whose diocese the Corn Islands depend and which was one of the various places in the Caribbean where Merton considered founding a monastic commu-nity. See: Corn Islands, **8a, 9.**

Boletín de Solentiname. To maintain contact with many friends and bene-factors of the community of Our Lady of Solentiname, Cardenal regularly published a mimeographed bulletin of the community's news. In such bulletins they released various texts by Merton, including some of his circular letters, **79, 87.**

Borges, Jorge Luis. He had no contact with Merton or Cardenal, **19, 20, 24, 85.**

"Boris Pasternak and the People with Watch Chains." Article by Thomas Merton (*Sur* 261 [1959]: 9–17; *Jubilee* 7, 3 [1959]: 19–31; and in *Disputed Questions* 7–24), **1, 4, 27.**

Breakthrough to Peace: Twelve Views on the Threat of Thermonuclear Extermination. Edited by Thomas Merton, with his introduction (New York: New Directions, 1962), **23, 25, 31, 32, 34, 35.**

Burns, Dom Flavian. Elected Abbot of Gethsemani at the beginning of 1968. He was much more inclined than his predecessor, Dom James Fox, to consider the wishes of Merton to leave Gethsemani. He was respon-sible for the trip at the end of 1968 to attend the meeting of Abbots in Bangkok, **88–90.**

Cables to the Ace, or Familiar Liturgies of Misunderstanding. A book of poems by Merton (New York: New Directions, 1968), **89.**

Cáceres, Esther de. Uruguayan poet who exchanged two letters with Merton in 1965 and 1966. With the first letter she sent her study "Intro-duction to Reading Susana Soca," and with her second, her book *Time and the Abyss (Tiempo y abismo)* (1965), **25.**

Callejas, Alfonso. Friend of Cardenal since childhood. He was from a landowning family and was interested in the plans to found a contemplative community in Nicaragua. He visited Merton to offer him support and land to establish such a community, **56, 63.**

"Camus: Journal of the Plague Years." Essay by Merton. Included in the seven essays that Merton wrote about Camus between 1966 and 1968 that can be found in the second part of *The Literary Essays of Thomas Merton* (New York: New Directions, 1985: 181–301), **83, 84.**

Cardenal, Fernando. Brother of Cardenal. Jesuit priest who, like his brothers Ernesto and Gonzalo, was actively opposed to the Somoza dictatorship. With the success of the revolution, he served as a minister in the Sandinista government, **87.**

Cardenal, Gonzalo. Brother of Cardenal. Like Ernesto and Fernando, he was also an active opponent against the Somoza dictatorship, **5, 6.**

Carmelite Monastery of Louisville. Convent of Carmelite nuns whose superior showed great interest in the monastic plans of Merton and supported him with advice and prayers, **8, 9, 11.**

Carranza, Eduardo (1913–1985). There is no evidence that either Merton or Cardenal had any contact with this Colombian poet, but both of them found his work valuable, **37, 38.**

Carrera Andrade, Jorge (1903–1978). Merton translated a number of his poems (*Emblems of a Season of Fury:* 125–134) but did not maintain correspondence with him. Cardenal knew Carrera personally, **6, 21, 39, 51.**

Casa de las Américas. Literary contest. Cardenal did not visit Cuba until 1970, when he went as a judge of this prize. His book *En Cuba* (Buenos Aires: Carlos Lohlé, 1972) resulted from this visit, **59, 63.**

Castro, Fidel, Cuban revolutionary, politician, and prime minister. The Cuban Revolution of 1959 was a chief inspiration for the Sandinista National Liberation Front, which was founded in Nicaragua in 1961 with the aim of overthrowing the Somoza regime, **5, 6, 24, 44, 47.**

Catholic Worker, The. Periodical dedicated to political and social critique from a Catholic perspective, founded in New York by Dorothy Day and Peter Maurin in 1933, **19, 23–25, 87.**

Caussade, Jean Pierre de. The most representative Jesuit of the spirituality of abandonment. He lived in the eighteenth century, but his spiritual writings had a great influence in the nineteenth century, **6.**

Ceja, La. Colombian locale where the seminary for vocations is located, and where Cardenal pursued his studies for the priesthood, **23–25, 39, 40, 50, 51, 55, 63, 66, 68, 81.**

Censure. All of Merton's writings had to pass the supervision of the Order prior to publication. In April 1962, orders given by the Abbot General arrived at Gethsemani prohibiting the publication of books or articles about war and peace. Even though Merton obeyed the orders to not publish anything on the theme, he continued writing articles that he distributed in mimeographed copies to his friends. After the appearance of *Pacem in Terris* by Pope John XXIII, the prohibition lost its force and Merton published articles about peace more freely, **67, 71.**

Chamorro, Pedro Joaquín. Cousin of Cardenal, director of *La Prensa* of Managua, and an active opponent of the Somozas, **2, 5, 9a, 24.**

"Chant to Be Used in Processions Around a Site with Furnaces." Poem by Merton (*Emblems of a Season of Fury*, 43-47), **17–19.**

Chávez de la Mora, Gabriel. Architect and Benedictine monk from Guadalajara, Mexico, who designed and restored many chapels in Mexico. He designed a circular chapel used at Santa María de la Resurreción in Cuernavaca. See: Monastery of Saint Mary of the Resurrection, **2.**

Chinandega. Nicaraguan city to the northeast of León and close to Corinto on the Pacific Ocean, **56.**

Chow, Napoleón. As a student in the University of León in the 1970s, he met Sergio Ramírez and other collaborators on the journal *Ventana*. He is a childhood friend of Cardenal, who influenced Chow's conversion. Much later, he maintained correspondence with Merton. He studied in the United States, where he taught in various universities. Opposed to the Sandinista reforms, in his doctoral thesis, *Liberation Theology in Crisis:*

Religion, Poetry, and Revolution in Nicaragua (Managua: Fondo Editorial, Banco Central de Nicaragua, 1992), he critiqued the manifestations of liberation theology in his country; in the chapter "Poetry and Praxis of Ernesto Cardenal," he levels a staunchly negative critique of the literary work and actions of the poet, **40, 44, 83, 86.**

Christ of the Desert. Benedictine Monastery in New Mexico formed by three monks, including a hermitage. In 1965, while returning from seeing Merton in Gethsemani, Cardenal visited here, **71, 76, 88.**

"Christian Action in World Crisis." Article by Merton (*Blackfriars* 43 [1962]: 256–268), **24, 27.**

"Christian Ethics and Nuclear War." Article by Merton (*Catholic Worker* 28 [March 1962, p. 2; April 1962, p. 2]), **25, 29.**

Clement of Alexandria: Selections from the Protreptikos. An essay and translation by Merton (New York: New Directions, 1962), **19, 23, 36, 38.**

Cold War Letters. A selection of 111 letters written by Merton in 1961 and 1962 to many different people, which were reproduced in mimeograph copies to distribute among friends. Some of these letters are included in *Seeds of Destruction* (New York: Farrar, Straus and Cudahy, 1964); 37 are reproduced in *The Hidden Ground of Love: The Letters of Thomas Merton to New and Old Friends*, selected and edited by Robert E. Daggy (New York: Farrar, Straus and Giroux, 1989). Prepared by Merton on his own in 1962 and expanded in the following year, this selection of mimeographed letters was a form of announcing his ideas in spite of the prohibition to write and publish articles about the Vietnam War. See: Censure, **30, 32, 35, 39, 41.**

Conjectures of a Guilty Bystander. Book by Thomas Merton (Garden City, NY: Doubleday, 1966), **71, 83, 85, 88, 89.**

Corn Islands. Nicaraguan archipelago in the Caribbean Sea that faces Bluefields; one of the places in Nicaragua that Merton considered for establishing his experimental monastic community. In a letter of July 13, 1959, a little bit before Cardenal would leave Gethsemani, Merton asked Pablo Antonio Cuadra for all the information he could share about these islands (*The Courage for Truth*, 185); that same day, Merton wrote a letter to Bishop Matthew A. Niedhammer, OFM, of the Apostolic Vicarage of

Bluefields: "Any information regarding the Corn Islands would be well received. We are grounded on the information given by a novice from Nicaragua who says that the islands are very healthy, agreeable, and very calm. Is there a landing pad there? Is there any danger that they might build a large hotel for tourists?" (*Witness to Freedom*, 201). In his unedited memoirs, Cardenal recounts that while in Gethsemani, Merton "invited me to accompany him in the new community . . . A luxurious book about the Virgin Islands had fallen into his hands, and he had chosen that so that we would live somewhere beautiful and secluded. I told him there was a better island on the Caribbean coast of Nicaragua, without any tourism, and still better an island on the sweet waters of Lake Nicaragua," **3, 6, 9, 23.**

Coronel, José Urtecho. Avant-garde Nicaraguan poet who was a big influence on young writers, especially Ernesto Cardenal, with whom he maintained a close friendship. He collaborated on the study, translation, and editing of North American poets, as well as on an anthology by Merton that did not reach publication. He maintained correspondence with Merton (*The Courage for Truth*, 171–176). He also published a large study about the history of his country, *Reflections on the History of Nicaragua (From Gaínza to Somoza): I. During Independence* (1962), *II. The Civil War of 1824* (1962), and *IIB. Explications and Revisions* (1967), **9a.**

Cortés, Alfonso (1893–1969). Known as the "crazy poet" of Nicaragua and admired for his mysterious metaphysical poetry, his work evoked a world of imagination and dreams. Merton, who knew Cortés's work through Cardenal, considered him a visionary and translated many of his poems. In his brief introduction, he states that Cortés had the same strange and unequivocal certainty as Zen (*Emblems of a Season of Fury*, 141–142). His works include *The Odyssey of the Isthmus: A Poem* (1922), *Poems* (1931), *Golden Afternoons* (1934), *Universal Rhymes* (1964), *The Ordinary Poem and Other Poems* (1967), and *Thirty Poems* (1968), **19–21, 23, 25–27, 30, 33, 34, 36–40, 42, 48, 70, 83.**

Cuadra, Pablo Antonio (1912–2002). Cousin of Cardenal. In addition to being one of the most prominent Nicaraguan poets of his generation, he was the editor of the literary journal *El Pez y la Serpiente*, and coeditor of *La Prensa*. He maintained correspondence with Merton starting in 1958 (*The Courage for Truth*, 178–195). Merton published his translation of some of Cuadra's poems in *New Directions in Prose and Poetry*, edited by James Laughlin (New York: New Directions, 1961: 105–115). His book *The*

Jaguar and the Moon appeared in a translation by Merton many years after the death of the latter (Greensboro, NC: Unicorn Press, 1974), **3, 4, 6, 8, 8a, 9, 12, 14, 16–19, 23–27, 30, 32, 33, 35–41, 43, 45, 46, 48, 50, 51, 53, 56–60, 63, 68, 70, 71, 78–80, 82, 85–87.**

Cuernavaca. See: Monastery of Saint Mary of the Resurrection.

Cunas. Indigenous South American people of the Chibcha language who in the middle of the nineteenth century abandoned the continent to establish themselves in the San Blas Islands, facing the coast of Panama. During the 1970s, when they began to admit visitors, they converted their establishment into a tourist attraction, and their embroidery/needlework is known throughout the world, **49–51, 53, 55, 56.**

"Cunas, The." Article by Ernesto Cardenal (*Cultura* 30 [1963]: 50–65; and *Lotería* 104 [1964]: 79–96), **49, 50.**

Daniélou, Father. Monsignor Jean Danièlou, S.J. (1905–1974). Influential French theologian who was an important participant in the Second Vatican Council. In 1959, Merton decided with his superiors of the Order "that it would be better to have someone with whom to consult about the most important and most apostolic problems," and they decided on Daniélou. He represented for Cardenal an important voice with respect to the interpretation of some pre-Christian religions as pre-figurations of Christianity. See: *Revelación cosmica* (Cosmic Revelation), **9a, 11, 19, 35.**

De la Selva, Salomón (1893–1959). Nicaraguan poet. He lived part of his life in the United States and published his first book in English, influenced by the North American journal *New Poetry*, **19.**

Delgado, Feliciano. Spanish Jesuit priest of whom there is no other evidence of relation with Merton or Cardenal except his article "Thomas Merton: Structure and Analysis" (*Razón y Fe* [1963]: 39–48), **31.**

Directory for Our Lady of Solentiname. Merton never came to write this directory for the use of Cardenal and his community, **71, 72, 75, 77, 82.**
Disputed Questions. Book by Thomas Merton (New York: Farrar, Straus and Cudahy, 1960), (Buenos Aires: Editorial Sudamericana, 1962), **24, 25.**

"Drake in the Southern Sea." Poem by Ernesto Cardenal, translated by Thomas Merton (*New Directions in Poetry and Prose*. Edited by James

Laughlin. New York: New Directions, 1961: 105–115; also in *Emblems of a Season of Fury*, 122–124), **3, 4, 15.**

"D. T. Suzuki: The Man and His Work." (*Eastern Buddhist* [Kyoto]: New Series Issue 2 [1967]: 3–9), **83.**

Eaton, Dona. Friend of Merton and Robert Lax since her years as a student at Columbia University, **50.**

"Elegy for Ernest Hemingway, An." Poem by Thomas Merton (*Emblems of a Season of Fury*, 13–14), **16–18, 19.**

Emblems of a Season of Fury. Book of poems and translations by Thomas Merton. In addition to roughly thirty poetic texts by Merton, and "A Letter to Pablo Antonio Cuadra Concerning Giants," this collection appended translations of different Spanish-language poets (Pablo Antonio Cuadra, Ernesto Cardenal, Jorge Carrera Andrade, César Vallejo, and Alfonso Cortés) and of Raïssa Maritain, **39, 41, 44, 48, 50, 52, 64.**

Epigrams: Poems. Book of poems by Ernesto Cardenal. Prologue by Ernesto Mejía Sánchez (Mexico: National Autonomous University of Mexico, 1961). Contains four hundred and nine original epigrams by Cardenal, thirty-five translations of Catullus, and thirty-nine of Martial, **2, 13, 18, 24, 35, 36, 39, 41, 42, 48, 50.**

Estrecho dudoso, El (The Doubtful Strait). Long poem by Ernesto Cardenal on the history of Central America (Madrid: Ediciones Cultura Hispanica, 1966), **27, 32, 40.**

Eudes Bamberger, Father John. He entered the monastery at Gethsemani in 1951 holding a medical degree. Before the numerous cases of "nervous problems" among the novices, in 1956 it was permitted to leave the monastery to pursue psychiatric studies in Washington, D.C. In this same year, Bamberger traveled with Merton to the Saint John's Abbey in Minnesota to meet with the psychiatrist Gregory Zilboorg, who later said after meeting Merton that the latter suffered from neurosis and that his desire for solitude was pathological. Bamberger advised Cardenal about his health problems—chronic headaches and possible ulcers—which obligated him, by the orders of his superiors, to abandon his idea of being a Trappist monk, **8a, 12, 13, 20.**

Evergreen Review, The. Prominent literary journal of the Beat generation, founded by editor of Grove Press, Barney Rosset. They published some of Merton's work, **21.**

Fox, Dom James. Abbot of Gethsemani starting in 1948. He resigned his post at the end of 1967; on January 13 of the following year, Dom Flavian Burns was chosen as the new abbot, **1, 7, 8–12, 56, 62, 67, 72, 73, 77, 79, 82, 88, 89.**

Franco. Novice in the monastery at Cuernavaca about whom not much is known except for a brief mention of him in the Merton–Cardenal correspondence, **9.**

Frankl, Howard. There is not much material about him other than that given by Cardenal in his letters. Recently he has published a memoir, *God, Sex, Drugs, and Other Things* (Montgomery, AL: New South Books, 2016), with an introduction by Cardenal **20, 21, 24, 41.**

Friol, Roberto. Cuban poet who was not one of Merton and Cardenal's contacts in Cuba, **62.**

"From Pilgrimage to Crusade." Essay by Thomas Merton (*Mystics and Zen Masters* [New York: Farrar, Strauss and Giroux, 1967]), **59.**

"Gandhi on Non-Violence." Article by Merton. Selections with a long introductory study published as "Gandhi and the One-Eyed Giant" (New York: New Directions, 1965), **54, 55.**

Gethsemani, KY. Book of poems by Ernesto Cardenal (Mexico: Ediciones Ecuador, 1960), **5–7, 13, 20–22, 23, 27, 39, 42, 66.**

González, Fernando (1895–1964). Philosopher, religious writer, and novelist from Antioquia, known in part for having written experimental philosophical novels in times when there was a great interest in Colombia for novels of social engagement and of violence. He published various novels in the 1930s, and the Nadaists had him as a teacher. Cardenal was interested in his original approach to mysticism through the novel in very unorthodox and provocative ways, **85.**

González de la Garza, Mauricio. Mexican journalist, writer, and composer who lived for months at the Monastery of Saint Mary of the Resurrection in Cuernavaca. An avid Freudian himself, Garza taught the monks about psychoanalysis and conducted "wild" psychoanalysis on the monks without formal training. Lemericier eventually replaced Garza with formally trained psychoanalysts Gustavo Quevedo and Frida Zmud, and Garza would later go on to write a scathing account of Lemercier and the Monastery at Cuernavaca in his novel *Padre prior* (1971). See: Monastery of Saint Mary of the Resurrection, **9a.**

"Grace's House." Poem by Thomas Merton (*Emblems of a Season of Fury*, 28–29), **30, 32.**

Graham, Dom Aelred. *Zen Catholicism: A Suggestion* (New York: Harcourt, Brace & World, 1963). In his book *The End of Religion: Autobiographical Explorations* (New York: Harcourt Brace Jovanovich, Inc., 1971), Dom Aelred recalls that he published "in *The Atlantic Monthly* a critique of the message exposed in the works of Merton . . . In essence, I wrote that in his period of penitence Merton had reacted in an exaggerated manner against the world and its manifestations, and that his message lost something through its ascetic and quite strident tone. But my own tone left much to desire . . . and soon I regretted the form and also, though not quite completely, the source of my essay. I felt that it needed an *amende honorable* and I invited myself to the abbey at Gethsemani, where the abbot and Father Louis himself—the religious name of Merton—received me hospitably. He and I had long conversations and became good friends. We were in contact for quite a stretch of time in the months before his fatal voyage to the east . . . I was grateful to be able to present to him those who had been so generous to me in both India and Thailand." (p. 62), **44, 45.**

Grinberg, Miguel (b. 1937). Argentine writer and editor who founded the literary journal *Eco Contemporáneo* in 1961, and in 1963 he founded *Acción Interamericana* (Inter-American Action), an organization to promote intercultural exchange. Merton had a brief correspondence with him (*The Courage for Truth*, 195–204), **48, 53–55, 58, 59, 63.**

Grou, Jean Nicolas (1731–1803). Jesuit contemplative and mystic/spiritual writer who followed in the tradition of Louis Lallemant that balances contemplation and action, **6.**

Guadarrama. Spanish publisher that never ended up publishing a work by Merton, **26–32, 40, 48, 51, 52, 54–58, 62, 69, 70, 74, 76, 78, 79, 85.**

Guillén, Asilia. Nicaraguan primitivist embroiderer and painter admired by Cardenal, who encouraged among the peasants of Solentiname the creation of a naïve painting with techniques learned through simple observation and practice, **74.**

Herrero, Father Jacinto. Spanish priest who published *Salmos* by Ernesto Cardenal in Ávila, **5.**

Hora 0, La (Zero Hour). Poem by Ernesto Cardenal that appeared in three numbers of *Revista Mexicana de Literatura* (January–April 1957, April–June 1959, and the only edition of 1960). He didn't publish this work as a complete book until years later (Montevideo: Aquí Poesia, 1966), **2, 6, 13, 24.**

Jaguar and the Moon, The. Book of poems by Pablo Antonio Cuadra. Illustrated by the author (Managua: Editorial Artes Gráficas, 1959). Merton translated this book, and it was published years after his death (1974), **24.** See: Pablo Antonio Cuadra.

John Birch Society. Ultraconservative anti-communist North American organization founded in 1958. It was named in honor of John Birch, a Baptist missionary and intelligence official of the U.S. Army who died in communist China in 1945, and who was considered the first casualty of the Cold War, **23.**

Journal for the Protection of All Beings. Journal edited by Lawrence Ferlinghetti, **17, 18.**

Lallemente. With this name Merton wanted to refer, undoubtedly, to the Jesuit Louis Lallemant, a mystic in the line of infused contemplation whose teachings centered on meditation as a basis for action. Merton considered these teachings valuable for anyone who, like Cardenal, entered the Jesuit order holding contemplative tendencies, **6.**

Lamantia, Phillip. North American poet who was a contemporary of Cardenal, distinguished among his generation for his attachment to the aesthetic discoveries of surrealism, **18–20.**

Lanza del Vasto (Joseph Jean Lanza di Trabia-Branciforte). Disciple of Gandhi, whom he met in his journey to India, who founded in France shortly after World War II the Community of the Ark, based on the principles of nonviolence and on a spirituality that refuses materialism and the mechanism of progress. This experiment of communal semi-monastic living in a religious environment of contemplation and poverty, which included families with children and was self-supported by shared manual labor, could not but interest Merton and Cardenal for what it had in common with their own ideas regarding monastic reform. Among many books by Lanza del Vasto, *Les quatre fléaux* (1959) and *Le pelérinage aux sources* (1944) are the most influential in propagating his Millenarian ideas. Jean-Michel Varenne's *Lanza del Vasto: Le précurseur* (1976) offers a good introduction to the figure and works of Lanza del Vasto, and thus to his commune, **38, 39.**

Larraona, Monsignor Arcadio. Secretary of the Sacred Congregation of Religious in Rome, **7, 10.**

"Las Casas ante el rey" ("Las Casas Before the King"). Poem by Cardenal (*La Palabra y el Hombre* 23 [1962]: 405–408), **37.**

Laughlin, James (1914–1997). North American poet, editor of New Directions, who had a huge influence on the literary career of Thomas Merton and with whom he was an intimate friend and adviser. Merton entrusted Laughlin to look after all of his writings, including unedited drafts. Along with Naomi Burton Stone, literary agent of Thomas Merton, and Tommie O'Calaghan, he formed part of the directory of the Thomas Merton Legacy Trust established by Merton himself, **3, 9a, 10–12, 17, 20–23, 35, 27, 34–36, 39, 47, 52, 58, 72, 73, 83.**

Laurel Anthology of Modern Spanish Language Poetry (Prologue by Xavier Villarrutia, epilogue by Octavio Paz. México: Editorial Séneca, 1941). Selection of Spanish and Latin American texts and lyrics prepared by the exiled Spanish poets Emilio Prados and Juan Gil Albert, and the Mexican poets Xavier Villarrutia and Octavio Paz, **24.**

Lax, Robert. North American poet and friend of Merton since their student years and Columbia University; based in Greece, he stayed in constant epistolary contact with Merton. He was a cofounder, with Ed Rice, of the journal *Jubilee*, for which Merton was an assiduous collaborator.

Cardenal translated his poem *The Circus of the Sun* (New York: Journeyman Books, 1960), which was published in *Revista de la Universidad de México*, **1–4, 15, 19, 23, 52.**

Leclercq, Dom Jean. Benedictine monk and specialist in monastic history. Since 1950 he maintained correspondence with Merton, whom he considered a counselor, **19.**

Lemercier, Dom Gregorio. Founder of Monastery of Saint Mary of the Resurrection in Cuernavaca. When in the late 1960s Rome prohibited the continuation of psychoanalysis as a central aspect of monastic life there, he did not comply with the orders and abandoned the religious life along with some of the other monks. The monastery became a clinic. Merton's reaction in the face of this was to reaffirm his desire to experiment with a new form of monasticism. He wrote in his journal of July 27, 1968: "I cannot personally judge Dom G[regorio]. But it is a shame for monasticism. No matter how you look at it, it signifies an abandonment of a monastic experiment . . . Speaking for myself, I am interested in the *monastic* life and its values. And I am doing something with her and not simply abandoning it." (Cited by Michael Mott, *The Seven Mountains of Thomas Merton* [Boston: Houghton Mifflin Co., 1984]: 532), **1–4, 6–12, 17, 24, 87.**

"Let the Poor Man Speak." Article by Merton (*Jubilee* 8 [1960]: 18–21; also in *Catholic Mind* 60 [1962]: 47–52), **27.**

"Letter to a Páez Indian" (*"Carta a un indio páez"*). Article by Cardenal (*El Corno Emplumado* 11 [1964]: 91–98), **53.**

"Letter to an Innocent Bystander." Article by Merton (*The Behavior of Titans*, 51–64), **32.**

"Letter to Pablo Antonio Cuadra Concerning Giants, A." Article by Merton that was as extensively published in Spanish as it was in English. It was published as "Conquistador, Tourist, and Indian" in *God Work* 25 (1962): 90–94 and in *A Thomas Merton Reader*, 89; *Thomas Merton Collected Poems*, 372–391; and *Blackfriars* (Oxford) 43 (1962): 69–81. In translation by José Coronel Urtecho, "Carta a los gigantes" appeared in *El Pez y la Serpiente* 3 (1962): 9–30, *Cultura* (San Salvador) 26 (1962): 65–74, and *Mensajes* (Buenos Aires: Eco Contemporáneo,

1974). In *Revista* (Caracas) 1 (1964): 2–4, the same translation was printed under the title "Los gigantes." *Sur* 275 (1962) published it as "Carta a Pablo Antonio Cuadra con respeto a los gigantes" in translation by María Raquel Bengolea, **19–25, 27, 37, 39, 44, 46.**

Lima, Alceu Amoroso (1893–1983). In addition to translating works by Merton to Portuguese, he maintained correspondence with him, **25.**

"Macarius and the Pony." Poem by Merton (*Emblems of a Season of Fury*, 15–16), **41.**

"Macarius the Younger." Poem by Merton (*Emblems of a Season of Fury*, 17–19), **41.**

MacLeish, Archibald (1892–1982). North American poet. Cardenal made reference to his book *Conquistador* (1932), a long narrative poem about the conquest of Mexico, **43.**

Mantero, Manuel. Spanish professor based in the United States, a specialist in contemporary Spanish poetry and himself a poet. Cardenal did not respond to Merton's commentaries, neither about Mantero's work nor about good Spanish poets, a silence that confirmed Merton's judgment about the lack of interest for them in Spanish poets of the time. When Cardenal left Spain in January 1950, there were still no signs of a poetry of social and political commitment in Spanish postwar lyric that matched the interests of Merton and Cardenal, **21.**

Martínez, Father Ángel (1899–1971). Nicaraguan Jesuit poet who was a professor of Cardenal at the Central American College in Granada, **2–4, 6, 11, 38, 45, 65.**

Massignon, Louis (1883–1962). French Arabist and specialist in Islamic mysticism. His ecumenism, pacifism, and interest in bringing together Christianity with other world religions is often compared with the similar interests of Merton, **19, 36.**

Mayapán. Book-length poem by Cardenal (Managua: Editorial Alemana, undated), **90.**

"Moslems' Angel of Death, The." Poem by Merton (*Emblems of a Season of Fury*, 5–6), **19.**

Mejía Sánchez, Ernesto. Nicaraguan writer and critic, and a contemporary of Cardenal. He was based in Mexico in 1944, where he was a professor at the National Autonomous University of Mexico, **1–4, 6, 8a, 9, 9a,
10, 12, 13, 24, 25.**

The Mennonite. In all probability, Merton refers to this journal, to whose
editor Margaret Shelley Merton wrote in December 1961 in thanks for
the publication of his poem about the death camps (*Witness to Freedom:
Thomas Merton in Times of Crisis.* Selected and edited by William H.
Shannon [New York: Farrar, Strauss and Giroux, 1994]), **19.**

"Message to Poets." Article by Merton (*Raids on the Unspeakable*, 1985).
Selections of the article appeared in *Américas* 16 (1964), **56.**

Miller, Henry. American writer and painter famous for his combination
of surrealism and mysticism and author of *Wisdom of the Heart* (Norfolk,
CT: New Directions, 1941), a book that Merton read with great appreciation. In the early 1960s, Merton began a correspondence with Miller. Ken
Shapero published a selection of said correspondence with an introduction: "Dear Henry: Love, Thomas: The Thomas Merton–Henry Miller Letters" (*Louisville Today* 5 [1981]), **30, 32, 38, 41, 45, 47.**

Mistral, Gabriela. Among her books, Merton spoke of the edition titled
Poesías completas, edited by Margaret Bates and with a prologue by
Esther de Cáceres, given by Doris Dana, who visited Merton at Gethsemani in 1967. In 1958, Merton wrote in his diary: "I am trying to read
Gabriela Mistral, who interests me greatly—her poem about Mexico and
women" (*Search for Solitude*, 145). It is possible that, coincidentally, Mistral had two books by Merton in her library: *The Seven Storey Mountain*
and *Seeds of Contemplation*. The various underlining and marginalia on
the text of the latter indicate that Mistral read Merton attentively, **25.**

Mito. Bimonthly journal of culture published in Bogotá. It was founded
in 1955 by Jorge Gaitán Durán and Hernando Valencia Goelkel. It was
intimately related with an important group of young poets of Gaitán's
generation, but it had a short prominence due to the premature deaths
of the two principle figures of the group, Gaitán himself (1924–1962) and
Eduardo Cote Lamus (1928–1964), **32.**

Monastery of Saint Mary of the Resurrection (*Monasterio de Santa
María de la Resurrección*). The Benedictine monastery in Cuernavaca was

founded in 1950 by the Belgian reformist monk Dom Gregorio Lemercier, prior of the same. According to Valentín López González, the architecture of the monastery was undoubtedly renovated: "Constructed under the planning and direction of Brother Gabriel, whose worldly name was de la Mora, it is of functional architectural style of touching simplicity. The stone, the wood, the most sensible materials are here represented just as they are, neither painted over nor touched up. Brother Gabriel explains that they have used everything that is the cheapest and most current. However, the result is magnificent: [of a] sobriety and good taste, with the circular altar made of round stones and the ceiling of wood and plastic, which with time has acquired a yellow tone like that of parchment, and through which the light passes in gold tones." **1–6, 8, 8a, 10, 11, 18, 19, 24, 27, 32, 40, 70.**

Monks Pond. Journal of only four issues with which Merton wanted to make known the writings of his friends, **89.**

Montecassino. Location in which Saint Benedict established his monastery after having to leave Subiaco, the location of his first community, **4.**

Morales, Beltrán. Nicaraguan poet and part of the so-called Betrayed Generation of the 1960s, **85.**

Morales, Armando. One of the most internationally well-known Nicaraguan painters, born in Granada in 1927. Already in the 1950s, when he traveled to the United States to study, he had begun to exhibit his work internationally, **2, 3–6, 8a, 9, 10, 12, 13, 15, 23, 53.**

"Mount Athos." Essay by Merton (*Jubilee* 7, 4 [1959]: 8–16), **1, 5.**

Mount Savoiur. Benedictine monastery in Pine City, New York, **88.**

New Seeds of Contemplation. Book by Merton (New York: New Directions, 1962), **23, 24, 52, 53.**

"News from the School of Chartres." Poem by Merton (*Emblems of a Season of Fury,* 54–57) **36, 52.**

Nivel. Colombian literary journal, **36.**

Obras completas de Thomas Merton (Complete Works of Thomas

Merton). Project, which didn't reach completion, of an ongoing series of books by Merton proposed in 1958 by Editorial Sudamericana, **23**.

Ocampo, Victoria. Merton wrote five letters to Ocampo between 1963 and 1968 (*The Courage for Truth*, 208–212), **22, 23, 25, 39**.

Olama and *Mollejones* Movement. Attempt to overthrow Luis Somoza in June 1959. Led by Enrique Lacayo Farfán and Pedro Joaquín Chamorro, this attack from Costa Rica was a failure and did not have the popular support that was hoped for. The National Guard captured almost all of the combatants, and Chamorro along with other leaders were jailed by sentencing of the military court, **2**.

Olga Elena de Medellín. Friend of Cardenal, **67**.

Ometepe. The largest island in Lake Nicaragua and one of the locations in Latin America in which Merton thought of founding his community. In his diary of August 29, 1957, he noted: "A letter from Kinlock, the friend of Brother Lawrence [Cardenal] (who cultivates ipecac root in the forest of Río San Juan in Nicaragua), speaks of the isle of Ometepe in the great Lake Nicaragua as the best place for a Cistercian foundation. Mark Twain saw the isle of Ometepe and compared it to a circus tent with one volcano larger than the other. Brother Lawrence flew over Ometepe in 1954 and saw the volcano in an active eruption. The other volcano is inactive. We could grow coffee and sugar cane and oranges and lemons and papayas and do everything on the inactive side of the volcano." (*A Search for Solitude*, 113), **8a, 9, 23, 24, 26, 39**.

Oración por Marilyn Monroe y otros poemas (Prayer for Marilyn Monroe and Other Poems). Book of poems by Cardenal (Medellín: Ediciones La Tertulia, 1965; Santiago de Chile: Editorial Universitaria, 1971; Lima: Instituto Cultural, 1972), **66**.

Original Child Bomb: Points for Meditation to Be Scratched on the Walls of a Cave. Poem by Merton, published as a separate book and illustrated by Emil Antonucci (New York: New Directions, 1962; Greensboro, NC: Unicorn Press, 1982; *Pax* [1961]: unpaginated), **15–17, 19–21**.

Ox Mountain Parable of Meng Tzu, The. Book by Merton (Lexington, KY: Stamperia del Santuccio, 1960), **14**.

Pacem in terris (1963). Encyclical by Pope John XXIII, **54**.

Pallais, Odilie (Otilia). "There was a great saint in Managua," recalls Ernesto Cardenal in his unedited memoirs, "who was Odilie Pallais. Since she was eighteen years old, she was immobile in bed, after having a grave heart condition since adolescence, and could neither get out of bed nor bathe herself on her own. Her food was very scarce—the only thing she could digest being a few mouthfuls of ground vegetables—and this was the same for years. Nevertheless, I admired that she was always joyful and jubilant. She was the president of the National Apostleship of the Sick, in addition to other activities that she performed from the immobility of her bed; she received visitations from those who wished to consult with her and tell her about their conversions or religious vocations," **9a, 10, 23, 51, 70**.

Parra, Nicanor. He met Merton, with whom he maintained a brief correspondence, during a visit he made to Gethsemani on May 7, 1966, on the invitation of James Laughlin, **83**.

Pasternak, Boris. Merton wrote to Pasternak in 1958 and after this letter they maintained correspondence. See *Boris Pasternak, Thomas Merton: Six Letters* (Lexington, KY: King Library Press, University of Kentucky, 1973). In October 1958 Merton wrote in his diary that he was in closer contact with Pasternak than with the people in Louisville or Bardstown, or even in his own monastery. (*A Search for Solitude*, 225), **1, 2, 4, 27**.

Peace in the Post-Christian Era. Unedited manuscript by Merton, **26**.

Pérez de la Rocha, Róger. Like Cardenal predicted in his letter, Pérez de la Rocha turned out to be one of the major painters of Nicaragua. It was with him that Car-denal initiated the drawing activities among the peasants of Solentiname, giving brushes and paint to a peasant who made beautiful engravings on gourds, **88**.

Perilla, Eduardo. Buddy of Cardenal in the seminary of La Ceja. No more information of him can be found except for Cardenal's mentioning of him in his letters, **54, 55, 81**.

Perrin, Father Henri. French Jesuit who, during the German occupation, had to work as a laborer and discovered his mission among the French workers. After the war, he was part of a movement of worker-priests who worked in the factories and lived as laborers as they tried to attract the masses to Catholicism. The movement did not have the support of the ecclesiastical authorities, and Rome suspended it in 1954. Perrin wrote about his experiences as a worker-priest in *Priest and Worker: Autobiography of Henri Perrin* (New York: Holt, Rinehart and Winston, 1964), **59**.

Pessoa, Fernando. The major modern Portuguese poet. Merton translated some of his poems (*The Collected Poems of Thomas Merton*, 987–96), which are found in Merton's journals along with a brief introductory note that says Pessoa is a kind of anti-poet in his Zen-like immediacy, **58**.

Pez y la Serpiente, El (The Fish and the Serpent). Nicaraguan literary journal, edited by Pablo Antonio Cuadra in the 1960s; both Cardenal and Merton collaborated on this journal, **14, 15, 18, 24, 27, 30, 32, 37–39, 45, 46, 82, 85**.

Plumed Horn, The (El Corno Emplumado). Bilingual literary journal edited in Mexico by the American writer and nationalized Mexican citizen Margaret Randall and her husband, the Mexican poet Sergio Mondragón. Both Merton and Cardenal, who collaborated with her, felt that it was uneven in quality, **27, 39, 46, 54, 55, 58, 59, 65, 87, 90**.
Poemas. Book by Merton and translated by Cardenal. Illustrations by Armando Morales (Mexico: Universidad Autónoma de México, 1961), **2, 4, 6, 9, 10, 12–15**.

Poemas de Ernesto Cardenal. Collection of poems by Cardenal published in Cuba (La Habana: Casa de las Américas, 1967), **88**.
"Poesía nicaragüense de hoy, La" ("Nicaraguan Poetry Today"). Essay by Cardenal (*La Gaceta* 83 [1961]), **19, 23**.

Poesía revolucionaria nicaragüense (Revolutionary Poetry of Nicaragua). Book by Cardenal (México: Costa Amic, 1962), **24, 25, 35, 36**.

Pomaire, Editorial. From 1965 on, the Spanish-language editions of Merton's works, which were until then put out by Sudamericana of Buenos Aires, began to appear in Spain through publishers based in Barcelona, predominately Pomaire, which published many books by Merton in translations by José María Valverde, **83, 85–88**.

Pound, Ezra (1885–1972). North American poet admired by José Coronal

Urtecho. His work exerted a great influence on Cardenal, who held Pound as his model poet, **27.**

"Prayer for Peace, A." Poem by Merton (*The Nonviolent Alternative* [New York: Farrar, Straus and Giroux, 1980]: 268–70), **25, 27, 29.**

Prensa, La (The Press). Periodical of Managua edited by Pedro Joaquín Chamorro, cousin of Cardenal and opposer of Somoza, **18, 24, 27, 29, 38, 59, 60, 70, 86.**

"Primitive Carmelite Ideal, The." Article by Thomas Merton (*Disputed Questions*, 218–263), **24, 25.**

"Prison Meditations of Father Delp, The." Study and introduction by Merton to the book *The Prison Meditations of Father Delp* (New York: Herder and Herder, 1963: VII–XXX); also in *Faith and Violence: Christian Teaching and Christian Practice* (South Bend, IN: University of Notre Dame Press, 1968), **40.**

Prologue by Thomas Merton to *BOOM!!!: A Poem* (1966), by Ludovico Silva (1937–1988), a Venezuelan poet and friend of Cardenal with whom Merton maintained some correspondence (*The Courage for Truth*, 223–232), **65, 66.**

"Prometheus: A Meditation." Poem by Merton (*The Behavior of Titans*, 79–88; *Raids on the Unspeakable*, 79–88), **4, 27, 29.**

Quiroga, Vasco de (1470?–1565). Appointed leader of the Royal Audience of Mexico in 1530, who upon arrival in the New World became interested in the deteriorating social conditions of the indigenous tribes under Spanish rule, and who, in little time, established the pueblo-hospitals of Santa Fe in the region of Mexico and Michoacán—indigenous communities inspired by the lectures of Thomas More. In 1536, at the creation of the Diocese of Michoacán, he was named Bishop of the same and ordained as a priest. His "Rules and Ordinances for the Governance of Hospitals" and "Testament" are important writings related to utopian conceptions of the perfect social organization in the New World, ruled by the new ideas of the Renaissance; Rafael Aguayo Spencer included them and other documents in his book *Don Vasco de Quiroga, Thaumaturge of Social Organization* (México: Ediciones Oasis, 1970). Knowing Merton's interest in the reformation of monastic life, it is understandable that Merton was interested in the figure of Quiroga and his work. It was probably no coincidence that, in the year following his reference to Quiroga in his correspondence, the study by Fintan B. Warren, OFM, was published: *Vasco de Quiroga and His Pueblo-Hospitals of Santa Fe* (Washington, D.C.: Academy of American Franciscan History, 1963), **36**.

Raids on the Unspeakable. Book by Thomas Merton (New York: New Directions, 1966), **83, 85, 88, 89**.

"Relato de la creación de los indios uitotos de Colombia, El" ("Creation Story of the Witoto Indians of Colombia"). Article by Cardenal (*Revista de la Universidad de México* 18, 3[1963]: 28–29), **45, 46**.

"Religion and the Bomb." Article by Merton (see: "Christian Ethics and Nuclear War"), **25–27**.

"Respuestas" ("Answers on Art and Freedom"). Written in response to new questions raised by the readers of *Eco Contemporáneo*, journal edited by Miguel Grinberg in Buenos Aires. Reproduced in English in *Lugano Review* 1 (1965) and *Raids on the Unspeakable*, 165–75, **48**.

Revelación Cósmica (Cosmic Revelation). Cardenal refers to the ideas of Daniélou on pagan religions, which in their recognition of the divine through cosmic manifestations responded to a form of pre-Christian revelation. In the introduction to his book *Les saints païens de l'Ancien Testament* (Paris: Editions de Seuil, 1965), and in various other texts, especially *Le mystère de l'Avent* (1948), *Le anges at leur mission d'après les Pères de l'Eglise* (1952), and *Mythes païens, mystère chrètien* (1966), Daniélou put forward the doctrine of the Church in respect to the salvation of those who, being pagans, did not have knowledge of Christianity. Rejecting the term "natural religion," as used to refer to non-Christian religions that evince a knowledge of God through manifestations of creation, and more specifically of the cosmos, Daniélou preferred the expression "cosmic revelation," which in the case of the figures of the Old Testament before the Abrahamic alliance related to a "cosmic alliance" that preceded the Abrahamic one and prefigured Christian revelation. The interest of Cardenal in this material encompasses a broad portion of his work and is particularly visible both in his poetic texts about indigenous American tribes and in his journalistic essays. It could be argued that this vision was a great influence later on in the poem *Cosmic Canticle* (1989), a work in which Cardenal brings into the text of the poem much of the information that he assembled for a book about "cosmic revelation" that he had planned to write, **35, 36, 38.**

Rice, Ed. Friend of Merton during his student years at Columbia, **23, 73.**

Río San Juan. This river originates to the southeast of Lake Nicaragua, just a few kilometers from the Archipelago of Solentiname in the Port of San Carlos. Part of its course determines the border between Nicaragua and Costa Rica. It flows out into the Caribbean Sea. "Possibly the most beautiful region of Nicaragua is Río San Juan," writes Cardenal in the prologue to *El Río San Juan: Estrecho dudoso en el centro de América* (*The San Juan River: Doubtful Strait in the Center of America*), a selection of tests by Ernesto Cardenal (Managua: Latino Editores, 1993: 9–10). "Much of the most important history of Nicaragua—observed—has also transpired by the same channel of the beautiful waters of the River San Juan." José Coronel Urtecho had his farm estate, *San Francisco del Río*, in this region, where he lived retired from the world, **23, 24, 35, 36, 38, 39, 41, 43, 51, 52, 57, 63, 70.**

Romano, Father. He was Cardenal's deputy teacher of novices at Gethsemani, prior to traveling to Rome to pursue advanced studies. Much later he passed through Chile, to the foundation of La Dehesa, where he wanted to leave his hermitage for Solentiname, **88, 89.**

Romero, Sister María (1902–1977). Nicaraguan nun of the Order of Mary Help of Christians who has a reputation as a saint and to whom is attributed innumerable miracles. She was beatified by Pope John Paul II in 2002. She was a college friend of Cardenal's mother, and he knew her well, **34, 39, 42.**

Saint Meinrad. Benedictine abbey located in Saint Meinrad, Indiana, sixty miles west of Louisville, **5, 6.**

Salmos. Book by Cardenal (Medellín: Ediciones de la Universidad de Antioquia, 1964), **10, 15, 37, 46, 47, 58, 86, 88, 89.**

Second Vatican Council (1962–1965). Key series of councils in Rome that reassessed the relations between the Catholic Church and modern society, **48, 54, 62, 64, 70.**

Seeds of Contemplation. Book by Merton (New York: New Directions, 1949), **24.**

Seeds of Destruction. Book by Merton (New York: Farrar, Straus and Cudahy, 1964), **62.**

Selected Poems of Thomas Merton. Introduction by Mark van Doren (New York: New Directions, 1959), **10.**

Seven Storey Mountain, The. Book by Merton (New York: Harcourt, Brace and Company, 1948). These juvenile memories widely disseminated in the 1950s had a great influence on Cardenal in his decision to enter the Trappist abbey, **57.**

Shick, René. President of Nicaragua from 1963 to 1966. During his government, Anastasio Somoza Debayle, Chief Director of the National Guard, gained more and more power. Upon the unexpected death of Shick in August of 1966, the Minister of the Interior, Lorenzo Guerrero, an unconditional follower of Somoza, took over the presidency. In January of 1967, Somoza was elected president (Richard Millet, *Guardians of the Dynasty* [Maryknoll, NY: Orbis Books, 1977]), **40.**

Sign of Jonas, The. Book by Thomas Merton (New York: Harcourt, Brace and Company, 1953), **8a.**

"Signed Confession of Crimes Against the State, A." Essay by Thomas Merton (*The Behavior of Titans*, 65–71), **4, 32, 36.**

Silvano (Sylvanus), Father. Monk in the community at Gethsemani who shared with Merton the desire to be a hermit. Merton noted in his diary that one day "Father Sylvanus went to the city [probably Bardstown] to the doctor and brought back an article in a journal about a man in the mountains of Kentucky who once was a coal miner and spent thirteen years living as a hermit, with a dog in a miserable house without even a chimney and with an old car seat as a bed, 'because of all these wars.' An authentic desert father, and probably not very sure why." (*Turning Toward the World: The Pivotal Years*, Ed. Victor A. Kramer [San Francisco: Harper, 1996]: 105–106). When during these same days Father Sylvanus began to work in the monastery library, Merton wrote: "Now we truly have good librarians!! (Esp. Father Sylvanus. This explains everything, without a doubt.)" In the following year, Father Sylvanus received letters from the hermits of Martinique, an American and Dom Winandy, the ones he ended up uniting with, **31, 32, 54.**

"Sky of the Cuna Indians, The." Article by Cardenal (*Arco* 60 [1965]: 711–712), **49, 50, 65.**

Solentiname, Archipelago of. Islands at the extreme southeastern end of Lake Nicaragua, close to the port of San Carlos on the San Juan River, **63.**

Solentiname, Our Lady of. Monastic community founded by Cardenal in 1966 on the island of Mancarrón in the Archipelago of Solentiname, and destroyed by Somoza in 1977. Formed at the outstart by Cardenal and two Colombian comrades, it soon included some of the peasants of the region. Inspired by Cardenal, many peasants of the Archipelago created a true school of naïve painting, a movement of spontaneous poetry, and even a popular theology. The latter developed in part due to the commentaries on the Gospels that the same peasants made during communal ceremonies and which Cardenal made known in his book *El evangelio en Solentiname* (*The Gospel in Solentiname*) (Salamanca: Ediciones Sígueme, 1975). In *Nostalgia del future* (*Nostalgia for the Future*) (Managua: Editorial Nueva Nicaragua, 1982), Cardenal offered a good selection of paintings from Solentiname and texts that gave an idea of what Our Lady of Solentiname signified for him as a religious, poetic, and political work. In "I Have Always Wanted to Know Solentiname," prologue of *Tu paz es mi paz* (*Your Peace is My Peace*) by Ursula Schulz (Managua: Editorial Nueva Nicaragua, 1982), Cardenal recalls that in "a tiny boat I went directly to a place where they were selling a piece of land, which was on the tip of the biggest island. Upon arriving, to my surprise I encountered that in this place there was a little church of Solentiname, a humble peasant church that the population began constructing twenty years ago, left unfinished and full of bats. The little church was there as if waiting for me, silent, in that wild place." Jaime Quezada, one of the many visitors to the community, left a testimony in *Un viaje por Solentiname* (*A Trip to Solentiname*) (Santiago de Chile: Editorial Sin Fronteras, 1987) of his stay in the archipelago. Everything written by Julio Cortázar in relation to Solentiname and his Nicaraguan experiences can be found in his book *Nicaragua tan violentamente dulce* (*Nicaragua, So Violently Sweet*) (Managua: Editorial Nueva Nicaragua, 1983), **73–82, 85–89.**

"Solitary Life." Poem by Merton (*The Collected Poems of Thomas Merton*, 808–809). Probably written in 1963, but not included in any of Merton's books of poetry, **64.**

"Song for the Death of Averroes." Poem by Merton (*Emblems of a Season of Fury*, 23–27), **52**.

Spencer, Foundation of. Trappist monastery in Argentina, **56**; in Chile, **77, 79, 82, 83, 89**.

"Spiritual Direction and Meditation." Article by Merton (Collegeville, MN: Liturgical Press, 1960), **53**.

Squirru, Rafael (1925–2016). Poet, essayist, and critic of Argentine art, and author of more than fifty books, the majority about Latin American art. Founder and director of the Museum of Modern Art in Buenos Aires, he was the director of cultural affairs of the Argentine Foreign Ministry from 1960 to 1961, and he directed the Department of Cultural Affairs of the Organization of American States between 1963 and 1970. In 1957 he created the *Ediciones del Hombre Nuevo*. His book, *The Challenge of the New Man* (Washington, D.C.: Pan American Union, 1964), is one that was quite of interest to Merton, **56**.

St. John's Abbey, Minnesota. See: Zilboorg, Gregory.

Subiaco. Region close to Rome where Saint Benedict retired to live a hermetic life and where he eventually began his monastic work, **4**.

Sudamericana, Editorial. First publisher to publish works by Merton in Spanish, **15, 26, 27, 29, 30–32, 35, 36, 40, 47, 48, 52–55, 57, 58, 62, 69, 70**.
Sur. Argentine literary magazine run by Victoria Ocampo, **1, 4, 22, 23, 25**.

Suzuki, Daisetz Teitaro. Japanese writer, intellectual, and popularizer of Buddhism in the West, **8, 15, 21, 23, 48, 58, 83**.

Szilard, Leo (1898–1964). American physicist and biologist born in Hungary. He contributed to the development of the atomic bomb and much later was concerned to expose the grave danger that atomic arms signified, **26**.

"Teilhard's Gamble: Betting on the Whole Human Species." Article by Merton (*The Commonweal* 87 [October 27, 1967]: 109–111), **86**.

"There Has to Be a Jail for Ladies" Poem by Merton (*Emblems of a Season of Fury*), **25, 27, 28**.

Thomas Merton Reader, A. Edited by Thomas P. McDonnell (New York: Harcourt, Brace and World, 1962), **31, 36, 40.**

"To Alfonso Cortés." Poem by Thomas Merton (*Emblems of a Season of Fury*, 53–54), **25–27, 30, 43.**

"To Each His Darkness: Notes on a Novel of Julien Green." Article by Thomas Merton (*The Literary Essays of Thomas Merton* [New York: New Directions, 1985]: 124–127), **48, 58.**

"To the Friends of Victoria Ocampo." Article by Thomas Merton (*Seeds of Destruction*, 283–284), **25.**

Toranzo Montero, General Carlos Severo. General-in-chief of the Argentine Army between 1959 and 1961. He was a declared anti-Peronist incarcerated and exiled during the Peron era, and in the following regimes he continued participating in the interventions of the army into politics. Contrary to President Frondizi, he went in the direction of the army's interventionist faction, maintaining a politics of total vigilance against the government that threatened coup d'états. Even though he seized to take power in 1961, he had to renounce his post due to lack of support from the army, in which the legalist line predominated, contrary to his politics of intransigent warfare, **5.**

"Tower of Babel." There are two works by Merton with the title "Tower of Babel: The Political Speech" and *The Tower of Babel*, a moral drama in two acts included in the book of poems *The Stranger Islands* (New York: New Directions, 1957); the letters refer undoubtedly to the latter. Sudamericana did not publish any of these works, **4, 15, 23, 31, 36, 39, 47, 52, 54, 55, 57, 58, 62, 69, 70.**

Universidad Iberoamericana (Ibero-American University, Mexico City). Founded by the Jesuits in 1943. Father Ángel Martínez was a professor there when Cardenal, who was Martínez's high school student in Nicaragua, arrived in Mexico City after his departure from Gethsemani, **1, 2, 9a, 10, 11.**

Vallejo, César. Merton translated and published four of Vallejo's poems, prefaced by a brief introductory note (*Emblems of a Season of Fury*, 136–139). "I cannot read one of his poems," noted Merton in his diary, "without feeling the desire to translate it, out of love for the difficult sufferings and the nobility of the discourse. Greater than Picasso in painting" (*Turning Toward the World*, 335), **1, 30, 39, 85.**

Valverde, José María (1926–1996). Spanish poet, professor, and critic with whom Cardenal made friends during the latter's stay in Madrid in 1949. Translator of various books by Merton for Editorial Pomaire of Barcelona, **29, 80, 81, 86, 87.**

Ventana. Publicación de Arte y Letras de los Estudiantes de la Universidad Nacional Autónoma de Nicaragua (Window: A Publication of Art and Letters by the Students of the National Autonomous University of Nicaragua). Facsimile edition (Managua: Editorial Nueva Nicaragua, 1990). Literary journal of the Left published between 1960 and 1964 in León by Sergio Ramirez and Fernando Gordillo, **37, 40, 44.**

Vida en al amor (Life in Love). Book of meditations by Cardenal, written in Gethsemani and presented with a prologue by Merton (Buenos Aires: Carlos Lohlé, 1970), **23, 24, 29, 57, 72, 74, 76, 83.**

Vie Spirituelle. Catholic journal of progressive and reformist ideas in the line of Jacques Maritain and François Mauriac, published by the Dominicans. Cardenal certainly refers to the article "Des homes attentifs à Dieu," by Hélène Lubienska de Lenval, appearing in issue 484 (1962). The article summarizes an anonymous pamphlet, *The Brothers of Breamore* (Capricorn Press, 1960), which describes a monastic community of lay people established on a remote island in northern Scotland by ex-soldiers of the British Navy who fought in World War II. The description of this community, with its peculiar return to the Rule of St. Benedict, is without a doubt what Cardenal wanted to imitate on his Central American island, **9a, 32.**

Vitier, Cintio. Catholic Cuban writer who, like various other Latin American writers, maintained correspondence with Merton (*The Courage for Truth*, 235–241). He met Cardenal in Mexico, and when Cardenal visited Cuba, Vitier welcomed him at the airport and attended to him during his stay. In his book about the visit, *En Cuba* (Buenos Aires: Carlos Lohlé, 1972), Cardenal dedicated various commentaries to him: "I knew that Cintio did not want to be for the Revolution. Nor did he want to be against it. He wanted to stay at the margin. As a Catholic, he had his reservations. When we spoke in Mexico at the first stages of the Revolution, he confided with me about his fears, because atheistic education was about to start and he had two young boys. But he had seen that it was his duty not to leave Cuba" (11). To this commentary, which coincides with what he wrote in his letters to Merton, Cardenal later on added this about Vitier's own evolution in the years following the death of the Trappist: "After a long lunch, I was alone with Cintio in my hotel room and he told me that now he was totally with the Revolution. Three things had influenced him: the lawsuits by Fidel against the Soviet Union had convinced him that this was a Cuban thing, and not a replication of Soviet communism ... The example of Camilo Torres, who made him see that the Christian could collaborate closely with the communists. Finally, the way of cutting sugar cane; before he had not gone [to the fields]—but this was the last thing that made him identify completely with the people and with the Revolution. Now he has made himself a militant. Now he has been accepted as a member of the jury of the Casa de las Américas, signed all the manifestoes, and is fully integrated into the Revolution" (12–13), **46–48, 59, 62, 64, 83.**

Voillaume, Father René. Prior of the Hermits of Jesus and author of a preface to the English translation of the diaries of Raïssa Maritain, *Raïssa's Journals* (Albany, NY: Magi Books, 1975), **40.**

"We Have to Make Ourselves Heard." Article by Merton (*Catholic Worker* [May and June 1962]), **25.**

Winandy, O.S.B., Dom Jacques. Hermit in Martinique. See: Father Silvano, **54.**

Wisdom of the Desert, The. Book by Merton (New York: New Directions, 1960), **8, 15, 32, 34.**

"Wisdom in Emptiness, A Dialogue: D. T. Suzuki and Thomas Merton." Article by Merton (*New Directions* 17: 65–101) and also in *Zen and Birds of Appetite* (New York: New Directions, 1968), 99–138, **15, 21, 23.**

Wu, John, C. H. (John Chin Hsung). Chinese scholar, jurisconsult, diplomat, and author. Merton, interested in deepening his knowledge of Chinese spirituality, wrote to him in 1961; since then he maintained correspondence with him. The letters of Merton to Wu are reproduced in *The Hidden Ground of Love: The Letters of Thomas Merton on Religious Experience and Social Concerns* (1985, pages 611–635), **19, 47, 48, 52.**

Yabilinguina, Cacique. Chief of the Cuna people in the San Blas archipelago during Cardenal's visit to the region, **49, 51, 53.**

Zilboorg, Gregory. Psychoanalyst of Russian origin who had garnered great prestige in the postwar years among the Washington politicians, writers, and artists; he treated, among others, Ernest Hemingway. He converted to Catholicism and generated great interest among circles of the Church. Merton met him in 1956 at a conference at Saint John's Abbey in Collegeville, Minnesota. Upon this brief meeting with Merton, Zilboorg concluded that the monk manifested a neurosis in his need to always be right, and that his search for solitude was pathological. In a letter to his literary agent Merton admitted a little after the meeting with Zilboorg that, with respect to his personal problems, the psychoanalyst "is clearly the first who has shown in conclusive form that he knows exactly what is going on inside of me. Something is going on with me, although it could not be that serious, but serious enough to cause a huge mess with my work and vocation if it becomes worse" (*Witness to Freedom*, 139), **12.**

Zoo. Book of poems by Pablo Antonio Cuadra (San Salvador: Dirección General de Publicaciones del Ministerio de Educación, 1962), **37.**

Index

"4 Plagues" (Vasto), 127

Abbey of Gethsemani, vii, viii–ix, xiv, xvi, xix, xx, xxi, xxiv, xxv, 9, 10, 11, 12, 13, 14, 17, 19–20, 21, 24, 27, 28, 31, 35, 36, 38, 39, 40, 41, 44, 52, 62, 83, 87, 90, 92, 100, 125, 138, 139, 142, 167, 169, 171, 176, 179–80, 189, 194, 213, 214, 219, 220–21, 223, 230–31, 236, 238, 240, 241, 242, 244, 245
Africa, 121, 124, 142, 161, 267
African Americans, 148–49, 168
Agudelo, William, 211, 216, 219, 226–27, 232–33, 237, 239, 241
Alberti, Rafael, 225; "Roman Nocturne," 225
Albuquerque, New Mexico, 31, 32
Alegría, Claribel: *New Voices of Hispanic America*, 131
Alliance for Progress, Managua, 212
Alvarez, Zuleta, 104
America (magazine), 141
American Christian Peace Movement, 80
American Pax bulletin, 135
Américas (magazine), 168, 171, 174
Anderson, James, 172
anti-nuclear movement, xxvii, 84–85, 92, 93, 174
Antioquia, Colombia, 87, 130, 135, 167
Antología de la poesía norteamericana, 139
Antología de Merton (Merton), 158, 219, 228
Antología Laurel, 90
Antonucci, Emil, 73

"Apocalipsis" (Cardenal), 187
Apocalypse, and Other Poems (Cardenal), xxviii
Apostolic Age, 269
Argentina, viii, xxviii, 25, 90, 93, 99, 104, 107, 141, 167, 169
"Art and Worship" (Merton), 147, 149, 153, 156, 158, 161, 162, 165, 167
Ascent to Truth, The (Merton), xxii, 135
Asia, viii, 161, 216, 240, 241
atheism, xi, 76, 145, 189, 190, 227, 236, 239
"Atlas and the Fat Man" (Merton), 109, 118
Auschwitz, xxii, 68
Australia, 122, 267
Aziz, Abdul, 73

Baciu, Stefan, 230
Baez, Joan, 222
Baldwin, James, 128, 149; *The Fire Next Time*, 128, 145
Balthasar, Hans Urs von, 230
Bamberger, Father John Eudes, 38, 54, 59, 76
Bangkok, Thailand, viii
Bardstown, Kentucky, 31, 32
"Bear, The" (Faulkner), 223
Beat movement, xviii, 70, 89, 99
Behavior of Titans, The (Merton), 65, 96, 103, 105, 109, 114, 161
Benedictines, 17, 20, 89, 100, 111, 198, 233, 244
Bergoglio, Jorge Mario. *See* Pope Francis
"Bernal Díaz" (Cardenal), 139, 140

Berrigan, Father Daniel, 85, 105, 110, 126, 135, 137, 216
Berry, Wendell, viii
Bible: New Testament, vii
Birmingham, Alabama, xxvii
Black Elk, 149; *The Sacred Pipe*, 149
Black Muslims, 149
"Black Revolution, The: Letter to a White Liberal" (Merton), 148–49
Blake, William, xiii, 95
Bluefields. *See* Niedhammer, Bishop Matthew A.
Bogotá, Colombia, 96, 98, 99, 103, 105, 109, 140, 142, 167, 170
Boletin de Solentiname, 234
"BOOM!!!: Poema" (Silva), 187, 189
Borges, Jorge Luis, 73, 75, 90, 228
"Boris Pasternak and the People with Watch Chains" (Merton), 22, 100
Brazil, 91, 170
Bread in the Wilderness (Merton), xxii
Breakthrough to Peace (anthology), 82, 92, 108, 110, 114, 115–16
Brother Antoninus. *See* Everson, William
Brown Hotel, Louisville, 52
Buchenwald, xxii
Buddhism, viii, xxii; Zen, viii, xxii, xxvii, 87, 137, 138, 141, 147–48, 178
Buenos Aires, Argentina, 85
Burma, 240, 241
Burns, Father Flavian, 236, 238, 240, 241

Cables to the Ace (Merton), 238
Cáceres, Esther de, 92
California, 39, 72, 222, 240, 241
Callejas, Alfonso, 169, 181
Camaldolese, 196
Cambridge University, x
Camus, Albert, 222, 225
Canto General (Neruda), xviii
Capuchins, 135, 170
Caracas, Venezuela, 187
Cardenal, Ernesto: "Apocalipsis," 187; *Apocalypse, and Other Poems*, xxviii; "Bernal Díaz," 139, 140; "Coplas on the Death of Merton," xxviii; *The*

Doubtful Strait, 99, 110, 131; "Drake in the Southern Sea," 17, 23; "El cielo de los indios Cunas," 151; "El relato de la creación de los indios uitotos de Colombia," 142; "En el monasterio trapense," 172; *Epigramas*, 13, 69, 90, 92, 117, 118, 127; *Gethsemani, KY*, xxiii, 24, 28, 33, 59, 76, 80, 92, 99, 127, 188, 261–65; *La Revelación Cósmica Siguiendo a Daniélou* (collection), 116; "Las Cunas," 151; "Letter to a Paéz Indian," 160; *Mayapán*, 241; *Oración por Marilyn Monroe y otras poemas*, 189; *Poemas de Ernesto Cardenal*, 237; *Poesía revolucionaria nicaragüense*, 90, 117, 118–19; *The Psalms of Struggle and Liberation*, 230, 237, 238; "Raleigh," xvii; *Salmos*, 121, 144, 146; *Selected Poems*, 48; "Telescope in the Dark Night," xx; "Trip to New York," xxix; *Vida en el amor*, xxiii, 81, 90, 104, 171, 205, 209, 223, 228; "With Walker in Nicaragua," xvii; *Zero Hour*, 13, 58, 90; "Zero Hour," xviii–xix
Cardenal, Gonzalo, 25
Cardenal, Luis, 47
Carmelite Monastery of Louisville, 34
Carmelites, 34, 40, 42, 53, 88, 91
Carranza, Eduardo, 122, 126
Carrera Andrade, Jorge, 29, 78, 127, 156
Carthusians, 40
Casa de las Américas, 175
Casas, Bartolomé de las, 121
Castro, Fidel, 25, 29, 89, 145
Catholic Church, xiv, xv, xvi, xviii, xxv, xxvi, 22, 46, 54, 55, 83, 84–85, 92, 100, 110, 140–41, 142, 148, 149, 153, 155, 175, 180, 184, 186, 191, 195, 202, 223, 237, 242, 243
Catholic Worker, 72, 85, 89, 92, 233
Catholic Worker Movement, xiv
Caussade, Jean Pierre de, 28
Central America, 79, 93, 99, 110, 202, 244
Challenge of the New Man, The (Squirru), 168

Chamorro, Pedro Joaquin, 14, 25, 47, 89
"Chant to Be Used In Processions around a Site With Furnaces" (Merton), xxvii, 68, 69, 72
Charlatan (magazine), 148, 172, 174
Chile, xviii, xxix, 13, 210, 219, 220, 223, 236, 238
China, 164, 267, 268
Chow, Napoleón, 131, 140, 222, 230
"Christian Action in World Crisis" (Merton), 88, 98
Christian Democrat Movement, 140
"Christian Ethics" (Merton), 104
Christianity, viii–ix, xiv, xxii, xxvi, 84, 88, 89, 116, 120, 130, 155, 226, 268–269
Christ in the Desert (monastery), 209, 237
Chuang Tzu, 73, 234, 237
CIA, xxviii
Circus of the Sun, The (Lax), 17, 64, 73, 76
Cistercians. *See* Trappists
civil disobedience, xxvii
civil rights movement, xxi–xxii, xxvi, 148–49
Clement of Alexandria, 73, 268, 269
Clement of Alexandria (Merton), 73, 85, 119, 124
Cold War, xxvii, 110, 158
Cold War Letter 98 to The Honorable Shinzo Hamai (Merton), 106
Cold War Letters (Merton), 82, 115, 128, 135
Collegeville, Minnesota, 54
Collins, Mother Angela, 40
Colombia, vii, xxvi, 81, 87, 91, 104, 108, 109, 116, 119, 126, 134, 135, 142, 144, 146, 151, 156, 167, 170, 175, 181, 182, 183, 208, 226, 228, 232, 237
"Colombia machetada" (Perilla), 163, 166, 219
Colombiano literario (journal), 144
Columbia Review, xiii
Columbia University, x, xiii, xvii
Communism, x, 14, 25, 30, 75–76, 110, 115, 140–41, 155
Congregation of the Religious, 48, 242

Conjectures of a Guilty Bystander (Merton), 200, 222, 229, 237
Continuum (journal), 137, 140, 141, 143, 148
Copernicus, 149
"Coplas on the Death of Merton" (Cardenal), xxviii
Corn Island, Nicaragua, 29, 37, 40
Coronel Urtecho, José, 45, 49, 69, 88, 89, 97, 100, 104, 116, 120, 124, 125, 129, 130, 136, 143, 154, 156, 158, 159, 161, 162, 163, 166, 172, 176, 177, 179, 180, 181, 182, 185, 186, 194, 197, 198, 200, 207, 209, 211, 214, 216, 223, 227–28, 230, 231, 234, 237; *Reflexiones Sobre la Historia de Nicaragua*, 100, 124
Cortés, Alfonso, 73, 76, 79, 83, 93, 95, 97, 98, 105, 107, 112, 113–14, 119, 121, 124–25, 127, 131, 137, 138, 147, 199, 222; "Dirty Souls," 113; "The Flower of the Fruit," 113; "Organ," 113
Costa Rica, 111, 125, 128, 139, 175
Courage for Truth, The (Merton), 63, 186
Cuadra, Pablo Antonio, xxvii, 17, 18, 22, 29, 35, 36, 37, 40, 42, 55, 61, 67, 69, 72, 73, 74, 75, 78, 79, 86, 88, 89, 90, 94, 97, 99, 100, 105, 110, 112, 116, 119, 120, 121, 122, 125, 126, 127, 130, 134, 135, 136, 139, 143, 144, 147, 148, 154, 156, 162, 169, 170–71, 172, 174, 177, 180, 182–83, 186, 194, 197, 200, 207, 211, 214, 216, 221, 222, 228, 230, 231, 234; *Jaguar y la Luna*, 90; *Zoo*, 122
Cuba, xiv, xvi, 75, 83, 144, 145, 148, 175, 177, 178, 180, 182, 184, 222, 237
Cuernavaca, Mexico, vii, xxv, 10, 11, 17, 19, 21, 26, 28, 35, 37, 43, 46, 48, 53, 87, 89, 101, 110, 135
Cuna Indians. *See* indigenous peoples

Daniélou, Father Jean, 43, 47, 53, 74
Darío, Rubén, xvi, 222
Day, Dorothy, 85
Daydi-Tolson, Santiago, xxix; *Del monasterio al mundo*, xxix
Delgado, Father Feliciano, 108

Del monasterio al mundo (Daydi-Tolson, ed.), xxix
Dial Press, 128
Díaz del Castillo, Bernal, 139
"Dirty Souls" (Cortés), 113
Disputed Questions (Merton), 88, 89, 91
Dominicans, 72
Doubleday (publisher), 200
Doubtful Strait, The (Cardenal), 99, 110, 131
"Drake in the Southern Sea" (Cardenal), 17, 23
"D. T. Suzuki: The Man and His Work" (Merton), 222

Eaton, Dona, 153
ecology, xxiii–xxiv
Ecuador, 78, 108
Editorial Guadarrama (publisher), 96, 99, 100, 102, 103, 105, 107, 109, 132, 147, 156, 158, 163, 166, 169, 170–71, 172, 179, 195, 199, 205, 207, 209, 212, 214, 228
Editorial Pomaire (publisher), 223, 228, 230, 234, 236
Editorial Santiago (publisher), 219
Einstein, Albert, 149
Eisenhower, Dwight, xxi
"El cielo de los indios Cunas" (Cardenal), 151
El Corno Emplumado (journal), 127, 144, 163, 166, 172, 176, 187, 219, 233, 241
"Elegy for Ernest Hemingway, An" (Merton), 67, 68, 71
Elena, Doria Olga, 192
El Espíritu Primitivo del Carmelo (Merton), 88
El Pez y la Serpiente (journal), 61, 64, 65, 69, 88, 99, 100, 105, 110, 122, 125, 127, 128, 143, 144, 148, 221, 228
"El relato de la creación de los indios uitotos de Colombia" (Cardenal), 142
El Salvador, viii, xxviii, 20
Emblems of a Season of Fury (Merton), xxvii, 112, 127, 133, 140, 147, 154, 159, 185
Ends and Means (Huxley), xiii

"En el monasterio trapense" (Cardenal), 172
England, x, xiii, xiv, 118
Epigramas (Cardenal), 13, 69, 90, 92, 117, 118, 127
Europe, viii, xiv, 100, 170, 198, 249, 267, 268
Evergreen Review, 76, 78
Everson, William, 137

Farrar, Straus and Giroux (publisher), x
Faulkner, William, 223; "The Bear," 222
Felipe, Leon, 22
Ferlinghetti, Lawrence, 68, 69, 72
Fire Next Time, The (Baldwin), 128, 145
Flakoll, Darwin J.: *New Voices of Hispanic America*, 131
Florit, Eugenio, 104
"Flower of the Fruit, The" (Cortés), 113
Fox, Dom James, xxv, 9, 31, 33, 34, 52, 54–55, 56, 57, 63, 169, 192, 202–3, 210, 213, 220–21, 236, 238
France, viii, ix, 9, 47, 207
Franciscans, 189, 218
Franco, Francisco, 22
Frankl, Howard, 76, 77, 78, 89, 135
Freud, Sigmund, 54
Friol, Robert, 180
Fromm, Erich, 46, 92
"From Pilgrimage to Crusade" (Merton), 176

Galileo, 149
Gandhi, Mahatma, xxii, xxvi–xxvii, xxviii, 163, 164, 166; *Gandhi On Non-Violence*, 166
"Gandhi and the One-Eyed Giant" (Merton), 164, 166
"General Dance, The" (Merton), 83
Germany, 91
Gethsemani, KY (Cardenal), xxiii, 24, 28, 33, 59, 76, 80, 92, 99, 127, 188, 261–65
Gilson, Étienne, xi; *The Spirit of Medieval Philosophy*, xi–xiii
Ginsberg, Allen, xvii

Giroux, Robert, x, xv
"Gloss on the Sin of Ixion" (Merton), 119
González, Fernando, 227–28
"Grace's House" (Merton), 106, 110
Graham, Dom Aelred, 141; *Zen Catholicism*, 141, 143
Granada, Nicaragua, xvi
Great Depression, x
Green, Julien, 148, 172
Grinberg, Miguel, 150, 160, 162, 164, 167, 172, 175, 182
Grou, Jean Nicolas, 28
Guatemala, xviii
"Guigo the Carthusian" (Merton), 128
Guillén, Asilia, 205
Gutiérrez, Father Gustavo, xxviii; *A Theology of Liberation*, xxviii

"Hagia Sophia" (Merton), 110, 127, 128
Harcourt Brace (publisher), xv
Harvard University, xxv
Havana, Cuba, xiv, 178, 182
Hemingway, Ernest, 67, 69, 71, 212
Herakleitos, 268
Hermanitos de Jesus (abbey), 131
Herrero, Father Jacinto, 25
Hibakusha, 164
Hidden Ground of Love, The (Merton), 106
Hinduism, viii, xiii, xxii, 268; Vedanta, xiii
Hiroshima, Japan, xxii, xxvii, 93, 106, 164
Hitler, Adolf, 91
Hochland (magazine), 91
Holt, Rinehart and Winston (publisher), 104
Hopkins, Gerard Manley, xiv, 13
Huxley, Aldous, x, xiii, xxii; *Ends and Means*, xiii

Imbert, Anderson, 104
India, 141, 142, 267
indigenous peoples, xxii, 31, 32, 116, 119, 124, 142, 144, 146, 149, 151–52, 153, 154, 155–56, 160–61, 167, 168, 170, 186, 187, 189, 267–69

Indonesia, 241
Institute for the Study of Nonviolence, 222
Islam, viii, xxii, 73, 74, 120, 267
Israel, 91
Italy, xvii, 90

Jacob, Max, 32
Jaguar y la Luna (Cuadra), 90
Japan, xiv, 240, 241
Java, 240
Jehovah's Witnesses, 42
Jesuits, viii, xxviii, 11, 13, 20, 27–28, 45–46, 85, 105, 108, 128, 194, 234
John Birch Society, 85
Johnson, Lyndon B., 164, 192, 216
Journal for the Protection of All Beings, 68, 69, 72
Joyce, James: *Ulysses*, x
Jubilee (journal), 9, 24, 78, 79, 82, 83, 92, 95, 137; *Jubilee Pax* [*American Pax*], 80
Judaism, 91–92, 268
Justin, 268

Kennedy, John F., 75, 154, 164
Kentucky, vii, xv, xix
Khrushchev, Nikita, 50
King, Martin Luther Jr., xxvi, 149
Knight, Jim, xi
Kogi Indians. *See* indigenous peoples
Kowalski, Frank, 93

La antología de poesía Norteamericana, 90
La Ceja (seminary), 81, 87, 91, 128, 130, 153, 156, 166, 183, 219
La Dehesa (monastery), 220
La Grande Trappe (abbey), ix
Lamantia, Philip, 70, 72, 76
Lao Tzu: Tao Te Ching (trans. Wu), 146, 147, 159
La Prensa (newspaper), 88, 99, 104, 124, 174, 177, 197, 198, 230
La Revelación Cósmica Siguiendo a Daniélou (collection), 116, 124
Las cuatro plagas (Vasto), 126

"Las Cunas" (Cardenal), 151
Latin America, 75, 78, 87, 88, 94, 100,
 103, 115, 130, 134, 140, 141, 148, 149,
 151, 158, 160, 166, 171, 172, 176, 182,
 190, 191, 210, 213, 220, 227, 232, 236,
 237, 238, 239, 242, 245
La torre de Babel (Merton), 22, 146, 158,
 167, 171, 172, 179, 195, 199
Laughlin, James, xv, 17, 47, 49, 52, 55,
 68, 76, 78, 79, 80, 82, 86, 92, 99, 114,
 115, 119, 127, 146, 159, 173, 201, 204,
 222
La Universidad Nacionál, Nicaragua, 131
Lawler, Justin G., 140, 141, 143, 148
Lawrence, D. H., x
Lax, Robert, x, 9, 13, 17, 22, 64, 73, 79,
 80, 82, 85, 86, 159; *The Circus of the
 Sun*, 17, 64, 73, 76
Leclerq, Dom Jean, 74
Lemercier, Dom Gregorio, 10, 17, 20,
 21, 27, 28, 31, 32, 33, 35, 36, 37, 38,
 42, 43, 44, 47, 48, 51, 53, 54, 57, 68,
 87, 235
Lentfoehr, Sister Thérèse, 118
León, Nicaragua, xvi, 14
Le pelerinage aux sources (Vasto), 127
"Letter to an Innocent Bystander"
 (Merton), 109
"Letter to a Paéz Indian" (Cardenal),
 160
"Letter to Pablo Antonio Cuadra
 Concerning Giants, A" (Merton), 72,
 77, 78, 80, 86, 88, 91–92, 100, 127,
 140, 144, 267–69
"Let the Poor Man Speak" (Merton),
 100
Levertov, Denise, 78
liberation theology, vii, viii
Lima, Alceu Amoroso, 91
Lima, Peru, 25
Literary Essays of Thomas Merton, The
 (Merton), 112
Literatura Hispanoamericana (anthology),
 104
Literatura indigena americana: Antologia
 (anthology), 119

Little Brothers of Charles de Foucauld,
 128
Little Rock, Arkansas, xxi–xxii
Lopez, José, 123; "Marcan los relojes
 dolores similares," 123
Los Angeles, California, 135
Louisville, Kentucky, viii, 11, 12–13, 34,
 40, 42, 52, 53, 179, 192, 201, 206, 233,
 239
Louisville Carmel. *See* Carmelite
 Monastery of Louisville

"Macarius and the Pony" (Merton), 134
"Macarius the Younger" (Merton), 134
Madrid, Spain, 96, 107, 205
Malcolm X, 149
Managua, Nicaragua, xvi, xvii, 14, 89,
 91, 154, 155, 172, 182, 198, 233, 234
Mantero, Manuel, 79
"Marcan los relojes dolores similares"
 (Lopez), 123
Maria Laach Abbey, Germany, 100
Maritain, Jacques, 128, 135, 137, 216,
 219, 220, 222
Maritain, Raïssa, 127, 128, 135, 137,
 139, 220
Martínez, Father Ángel, 22, 23, 125,
 142–43
Martinique, 110, 164
Marxism, xxvi, 89, 130, 131, 236
Massignon, Louis, 74, 120
Mayapán (Cardenal), 241
McCarthy, Eugene, 241
Mejía Sánchez, Ernesto, 9, 13, 18,
 22–23, 29, 36, 42, 45, 49, 55, 58, 92;
 Poesía revolucionaria nicaragüense, 90, 117,
 118–19
Mennonites, 72
Merton, John Paul, xv
Merton, Thomas: *Antología de Merton*,
 158, 219, 228; "Art and Worship,"
 147, 149, 153, 156, 158, 161, 162,
 165, 167; *The Ascent to Truth*, xxii, 135;
 "Atlas and the Fat Man," 109, 118;
 The Behavior of Titans, 65, 96, 103, 105,
 109, 114, 161; "The Black Revolution:

Letter to a White Liberal," 148–49; "Boris Pasternak and the People with Watch Chains," 22, 100; *Bread in the Wilderness*, xxii; *Cables to the Ace*, 238; "Chant to Be Used In Processions around a Site With Furnaces," xxvii, 68, 69, 72; "Christian Action in World Crisis," 88, 98; "Christian Ethics," 104; *Clement of Alexandria*, 73, 85, 119, 124; Cold War Letter 98 to The Honorable Shinzo Hamai, 106; *Cold War Letters*, 82, 115, 128, 135; *Conjectures of a Guilty Bystander*, 200, 222, 229, 237; *The Courage for Truth*, 63, 186; *Disputed Questions*, 88, 89, 91; "D. T. Suzuki: The Man and His Work," 222; "An Elegy for Ernest Hemingway," 67, 68, 71; *El Espiritu Primitivo del Carmelo*, 88; *Emblems of a Season of Fury*, xxvii, 112, 127, 133, 140, 147, 154, 159, 185; "From Pilgrimage to Crusade," 176; "Gandhi and the One-Eyed Giant," 164, 166; "The General Dance," 83; "Gloss on the Sin of Ixion," 119; "Grace's House," 106, 110; "Guigo the Carthusian," 128; "Hagia Sophia," 110, 127, 128; *The Hidden Ground of Love*, 106; *La torre de Babel*, 22, 116, 146, 158, 167, 171, 172, 179, 195, 199; "Letter to an Innocent Bystander," 109; "A Letter to Pablo Antonio Cuadra Concerning Giants," 72, 77, 78, 80, 86, 88, 91–92, 100, 140, 144, 267–69; "Let the Poor Man Speak," 100; *The Literary Essays of Thomas Merton*, 112; "Macarius and the Pony," 134; "Macarius the Younger," 134; "Message to Poets," 168, 171; "The Moslems' Angel of Death," 74; *Mystics and Zen Masters*, xxvii; *The New Man*, 105, 147, 161; *New Seeds of Contemplation*, xxii, 83, 87–88, 90, 158, 161; "News from the School of Chartres," 119, 159; *Obras completas de Thomas Merton*, 85; *Original Child Bomb*, xxvii, 65, 67, 68, 73, 76, 79;

The Ox Mountain Parable, 83; *Peace in the Post-Christian Era*, 96; "Picture of a Black Child with a White Doll," 174; *Poemas* (Spanish translation), 58, 61, 63; "A Prayer for Peace," 93, 98, 100; "A Priest and His Mission," 176; "The Primitive Carmelite Ideal," 91; "The Prison Meditations of Father Delp," 131, 132; "Prometheus: A Meditation," 22, 100, 103; *Raids on the Unspeakable*, 222, 229, 237; "Religion and the Bomb," 92, 95, 100; "Respuestas sobre arte y libertad," 149; *Seeds of Destruction*, 180; *Selected Poems of Thomas Merton*, 63; "Seven Essays on Albert Camus," 222, 225; *The Seven Storey Mountain*, xi, xiv, xvii, xx, xxii, 171; "A Signed Confession of Crimes Against the State," 22, 109, 118; *The Sign of Jonas*, xxii, 38; *The Silent Life*, xxii; "Song for the Death of Averroes," 159; *Spiritual Direction and Meditation*, 161; "Teilhard's Gamble: Betting on the Whole Human Species," 231; "There Has to Be a Jail for Ladies," xxvii, 93, 101, 102; *Thirty Poems*, xv; *A Thomas Merton Reader*, 108, 119, 131, 186, 209, 228, 234, 237; "Time and Transition," 43; "To Alfonso Cortés," 93, 98, 138; "To Each His Darkness: Notes on a Novel of Julien Green," 148, 172; "To Friends of Victoria Ocampo," 92; "The Tower of Babel," 96, 99, 103, 118; *The Tower of Babel*, 65, 85, 107, 164; "Truth," 137; "Vida solitaria," 185; *The Waters of Siloe*, xxii; *The Way of Chuang Tzu*, xxvii, 73; "We Have to Make Ourselves Heard," 92; "Wisdom in Emptiness, A Dialogue: D. T. Suzuki and Thomas Merton," 78, 85; *The Wisdom of the Desert*, xxvi, 65, 109, 114; *Witness to Freedom: The Letters of Thomas Merton in Times of Crisis*, 43, 57; *Zen and the Birds of Appetite*, xxvii; "The Zen Revival," 137, 138, 148

Merton Annual (journal), 43
Merton Reading Club, 234
"Message to Poets" (Merton), 168, 171
Mexico, xxv, xxvii, 9, 10–11, 12, 14, 22, 24, 31, 32, 34, 37, 41, 45, 46, 49, 58, 59, 69, 70, 77, 78, 99, 139, 145, 160, 171, 198, 227, 235, 268
Mexico City, 12, 15, 20, 37, 45, 61, 76
México en la Cultura (newspaper supplement), 69
Middle Ages, 269
Miller, Henry, 105, 110, 126, 135, 143, 146; *The Wisdom of the Heart*, 105, 110, 146
Mistral, Gabriela, 92
Mito (magazine), 109
modernismo, xvi
Mollejones movement, 14
Monks Pond (magazine), 238
Montserrat, Lesser Antilles, 233, 234
Morales, Armando, 13, 18, 22, 25, 29, 36, 41, 42, 45, 49, 55, 58, 63, 86
Morales, Beltrán, 227
"Moslems' Angel of Death, The" (Merton), 74
Mott, Michael, xxi, 63; *The Seven Mountains of Thomas Merton*, 63
Mumford, Lewis, 92
Mystics and Zen Masters (Merton), xxvii
Mystic Theology, 97

Nagasaki, Japan, xxii, xxvii
National University, Mexico City, xvi
Native Americans/Indians. *See* indigenous peoples
Nepal, 240, 241
Neruda, Pablo, xvii, xviii, 13; *Canto General*, xviii
New Blackfriars (journal), 172, 200
New Directions (publisher), xv, 17, 23, 48, 65, 76, 78, 92, 119, 140, 147, 164, 166, 173, 201, 228; *New Directions 8*, 112, 114; *New Directions 17*, 64, 68, 69; *New Directions 18*, 127; *New Directions Annual*, 222
New Man, The (Merton), 105, 147, 161

New Mexico, 200, 209
New Orleans, Louisiana, 10, 11, 12, 15, 179
New Seeds of Contemplation (Merton), xxii, 83, 87–88, 90, 158, 161
"News from the School of Chartres" (Merton), 119, 159
New Voices of Hispanic America (Flakoll, Alegría), 131
New York City, xi, xiv, xvii, xviii, xxix, 79
New York Review of Books, 172
New Zealand, ix, 267
Nicaragua, vii–viii, xvi, xvii, xxii, xxv, xxvii, 14, 20, 25, 28, 30, 35, 45, 47, 61, 65, 69, 73, 75, 83, 87, 88–89, 90, 97, 98, 99, 100, 103, 104, 109, 110, 111, 114, 116, 124, 125, 129, 130–31, 134, 138, 143, 151, 153, 156, 158, 166, 174, 175, 178, 180, 181, 182, 183, 193, 194, 197, 200, 204, 205, 208, 227, 231, 236, 238, 240, 241, 242, 244
Nicholas of Cusa, 149
Niedhammer, Bishop Matthew A., 37, 40
Nivel (magazine), 123
non-violence movement, 163–64. *See also* peace movement
Norway, 192, 202, 203, 210
Nuestra Señora de Solentiname (monastery), 208, 210, 211, 212, 213, 215–16, 218–19, 220, 226, 229, 232–33, 234, 236, 237, 239, 241, 242–43

Oaxaca, Mexico, 38
Obras completas de Thomas Merton (Merton), 85
Ocampo, Victoria, 80, 86, 92, 127–28
Olama movement, 14
Ometepe Island, Nicaragua, 37, 40, 83, 89, 90, 97, 129
Oración por Marilyn Monroe y otras poemas (Cardenal), 189
"Organ" (Cortés), 113
Origen, 268
Original Child Bomb (Merton), xxvii, 65, 67, 68, 73, 76, 79

Oslo, Norway, 180
Our Lady of Gethsemani. *See* Abbey of
    Gethsemani
Oxford University, 122
Ox Mountain Parable, The (Merton), 61,
    69, 83

Pájaro Cascabel (journal), 168
Pakistan, 73
Pallais, Odilie, 47, 50, 86, 157, 197
Panama, 116, 151, 153, 167
Papeles (magazine), 220
Paris, France, 120, 214
Parra, Nicanor, xxix, 222
Pasternak, Boris, 9, 13, 22
Paz, Octavio, 73, 79, 173
Peace in the Post-Christian Era (Merton), 96
peace movement, 88, 92, 96, 108, 120,
    122, 145–46, 163, 200, 216, 239
Pearl Harbor, xiv
Pérez de la Rocha, Róger, 236–37
Perilla, Eduardo, 163, 166–67, 219;
    "Colombia machetada," 163, 166, 219
Perón, Juan, 25
Peru, xxviii, 18, 170
Pessoa, Fernando, 173
Philippe, Archbishop Paul, 242–43
Philippines, xvi
"Picture of a Black Child with a White
    Doll" (Merton), 174
Platform Sutra of Hui Neng (trans. Wu),
    147–48
Plumed Horn (journal), 99
Poemas (Merton), 58, 61, 63
Poemas de Ernesto Cardenal (Cardenal), 237
Poesía Hispanoamericana del 1900, 90
Poesía revolucionaria nicaragüense (Cardenal,
    Mejía Sánchez), 90, 92, 117, 118–19
Pope Francis, viii, xxviii
Pope John Paul II, vii–viii, xxvi
Pope John XXIII, 164
Pope Paul VI, 142, 180, 244–45
Pound, Ezra, xv, xvii, 100
"Prayer for Peace, A" (Merton), 93, 98,
    100
"Priest and His Mission, A" (Merton), 176

"Primitive Carmelite Ideal, The"
    (Merton), 91
"Prison Meditations of Father Delp,
    The" (Merton), 131, 132
"Prometheus: A Meditation" (Merton),
    22, 100, 103
Protestants, xvi, 83, 84, 93, 141, 148,
    156, 164, 180
Proust, Marcel, 21
Psalms of Struggle and Liberation, The
    (Cardenal), 230, 237, 238
Puerto Rico, xvi

Quakers, 93
Queens, New York, x
Quiroga, Vasco de, 119

Raids on the Unspeakable (Merton), 222,
    229, 237
"Raleigh" (Cardenal), xvii
Ramparts (magazine), 148–49
Razón y Fe (magazine), 108
Reflexiones Sobre la Historia de Nicaragua
    (Coronel Urtecho), 100, 124
Reinhardt, Ad, x
"Religion and the Bomb" (Merton), 92,
    95, 100
"Respuestas sobre arte y libertad"
    (Merton), 150
Restrepo, Father Camilo Torres, xxvi
Revista de la Universidad de Mexico
    (journal), 13, 22, 55, 98
Revista Mexicana de Literatura (journal), 13,
    22, 29, 55
Rice, Ed, x, 85, 204
Río San Juan, Nicaragua, 83, 89, 116,
    120, 125, 129, 136, 138, 156, 158, 170,
    181, 182, 198
Rise and Fall of the Third Reich, The
    (Shirer), xxii
Roman empire, viii, xxvi
"Roman Nocturne" (Alberti), 225
Rome, Italy, xxv, 32, 34, 35, 47, 48, 52,
    54, 55, 83, 188, 202, 203, 204, 214,
    219, 220, 225, 235, 245
Romero, Archbishop Óscar, xxviii

Romero, Sister Maria, 111, 125, 128, 134, 139
Roosevelt, Theodore, xvi
Russia/Soviet Union, 115, 164, 175, 177, 267

Sacred Pipe, The (Black Elk), 149
Saint Martin de Porres, 94
Salamanca, Spain, 20
Salesians, 111
Salmos (Cardenal), 121, 144, 146
San Antonio, Texas, 15
San Blas Islands, Panama, 153
Sandinistas/Sandinista Revolution, vii, viii, xxvi, xxviii
Sandino, Augusto, xvi
San Francisco, California, xviii, 68
San Salvador, El Salvador, xxviii
Santa María de la Resurrección, Mexico (monastery), 9, 10, 17, 19
São Paulo Biennial Exposition, 45
Sartre, Jean-Paul, 149
Second Coming (magazine), 95
Seeds of Destruction (Merton), 180
Selected Poems (Cardenal), 48
Selected Poems of Thomas Merton (Merton), 63
Selva, Salomón de la, 73
"Seven Essays on Albert Camus" (Merton), 222, 225
Seven Mountains of Thomas Merton, The (Mott), 63
Seven Storey Mountain, The (Merton), xi, xiv, xvii, xx, xxii, 171
Sewanee Review (journal), 137
Shakespeare, William, x
Sheen, Bishop Fulton J., 207, 209
Shick, René, 130
Shirer, William, xxii; The Rise and Fall of the Third Reich, xxii
"Signed Confession of Crimes Against the State, A" (Merton), 22, 109, 118
Sign of Jonas, The (Merton), xxii, 38
Silent Life, The (Merton), xxii
Silva, Ludovica, 187, 189–90; "BOOM!!!: Poema," 187, 189

Sitting Bull, 146
Socrates, 268
Solentiname Islands, Nicaragua, vii, xxviii, 181, 182, 202, 204, 205, 206
Somocistas, 26, 130
Somoza, Anastasio, vii, xvii, xviii, xix, xxviii, 13, 26, 75, 88–89, 130
"Song for the Death of Averroes" (Merton), 159
Sortais, Dom Gabriel, 48, 154
South America, 79, 108, 134, 160–61, 168, 202, 242, 267
Spain, xvi, xvii, 96, 104, 147, 163, 207, 216
Spender, Stephen, 29, 172
Spirit of Medieval Philosophy, The (Gilson), xi–xiii
Spiritual Direction and Meditation (Merton), 161
Squirru, Rafael, 168; The Challenge of the New Man, 168
Stadtagen, Roberto, 229
Stalinism, 148
St. Anthony Hospital, Louisville, 34
St. John's University, 54
Sudamericana (publisher), 96, 99, 103, 105, 107, 109, 116, 118, 132, 146, 147, 158, 161, 164, 166, 167, 171, 172, 179, 195, 198–99
Sufism, 73
Supplément de La Vie Spirituelle (journal), 47
Sur (journal), 9, 22, 80, 86, 92
Suzuki, D. T., xxvii, 34, 46, 64, 78, 85, 148, 173, 222; "Wisdom in Emptiness, A Dialogue: D. T. Suzuki and Thomas Merton," 78, 85
Switzerland, xvii
Szilard, Leo, 96

Tadié, Marie, 195, 207, 214, 216, 217, 223, 230
Taoism, xxii, xxvii, 73, 124
Teilhard de Chardin, 205, 231
"Teilhard's Gamble: Betting on the Whole Human Species" (Merton), 231

"Telescope in the Dark Night"
(Cardenal), xx
Teotihuacán (archaeological complex), 37
Texas, 164
Thailand, 240
Theology of Liberation, A (Gutiérrez)
"There Has to Be a Jail for Ladies"
(Merton), xxvii, 93, 101, 102
Thirty Poems (Merton), xv
Thomas Merton Reader, A (Merton), 108,
119, 131, 186, 209, 228, 234, 237
Thomas Merton Studies Center,
Bellarmine University, 43
"Time and Transition" (Merton), 43
"To Alfonso Cortés" (Merton), 93, 98,
138
"To Each His Darkness: Notes on a
Novel of Julien Green" (Merton), 148,
172
"To Friends of Victoria Ocampo"
(Merton), 92
To Live Is to Love (Cardenal), xxiii
Toranzo, Carlos, 25
Tower of Babel, The (Merton), 65, 85, 107,
164
"Tower of Babel, The" (Merton), 96, 99,
103, 118
Trappists, vii, viii–ix, xiv, xv, xix, xxv,
19, 21, 22, 24, 43, 59, 76, 119, 180,
188, 192, 240, 242
"Trip to New York" (Cardenal), xxix
Trllling, Lionel, x
"Truth" (Merton), 137
Tulane University, 12

Ubico, Jorge, xviii–xix
Uitotos Indians. *See* indigenous peoples
Ulysses (Joyce), x
United States, viii, xvi, xxviii, 12, 44–45,
50, 67, 71, 72–73, 75, 76, 77, 88, 89,
104, 115, 122, 125, 135, 141, 161, 163,
168, 192, 198, 203, 212, 219, 227, 228,
242, 244, 267
Universidad de México, 133
Universidad Iberoamericana, Mexico, 9,
10, 45–46

Universidad Nacional, Mexico, 11, 58,
61, 69, 90
University of Iowa, 148
University of Kentucky, 118
University of Oklahoma, 149
Uruguay, 92

Vallejo, César, 9, 106, 127, 227
Valverde, José María, 104, 217, 219, 230,
234
Van Doren, Charles, 49
Van Doren, Mark, x, xv, xvii, xxi, 49
Vasto, Lanza del, 126, 127; "4 Plagues,"
127; *Las cuatro plagas*, 126; *Le pelerinage
aux sources*, 127
Vatican Councils, 149, 165, 184, 198
Venezuela, 78, 222
Ventana (magazine), 121–22, 123, 131,
140
Vida en el amor (Cardenal), 81, 90, 104,
171, 205, 209, 223, 228
"Vida solitaria" (Merton), 185
Vie Spirituelle (magazine), 111
Vietnam War, 192, 239
Vitier, Cintio, 144, 145, 148, 175, 180,
184, 222

Washington, DC, 50
Waters of Siloe, The (Merton), xxii
Way of Chuang Tzu, The (Merton), xxvii,
73
"We Have to Make Ourselves Heard"
(Merton), 92
Whitman, Walt, xvi, xvii
Williams, Tennessee, xv
Williams, William Carlos, xv
Winandy, Dom Jacques, 164
"Wisdom in Emptiness, A Dialogue: D.
T. Suzuki and Thomas Merton," 78,
85
Wisdom of the Desert, The (Merton), xxvi,
65, 109, 114
Wisdom of the Heart, The (Miller), 105,
110, 146
"With Walker in Nicaragua" (Cardenal),
xvii

Witness to Freedom: The Letters of Thomas Merton in Times of Crisis (Merton), 43, 57

World War II, xiv, xxii, 93

Wu, John, 73, 146, 147–48, 159; *Lao Tzu: Tao Te Ching*, 146, 147, 159; *Platform Sutra of Hui Neng*, 147–48

Yabilinguina. *See* indigenous peoples

Zen and the Birds of Appetite (Merton), xxvii

Zen Catholicism (Graham), 141, 143

"Zen Revival, The" (Merton), 137, 138, 148

Zero Hour (Cardenal), 13, 58, 90

"Zero Hour" (Cardenal), xviii–xix

Zilboorg, Gregory, 54, 55

Zoo (Cuadra), 122

About the Authors

ERNESTO CARDENAL MARTÍNEZ (born January 20, 1925) is a Nicaraguan Catholic priest, poet, and politician. He is a liberation theologian and the founder of the primitivist art community in the Solentiname Islands, where he lived for more than ten years (1965–1977). A member of the Nicaraguan Sandinistas, a party he has since left, he was Nicaragua's minister of culture from 1979 to 1987.

A monk who lived in isolation for several years, and one of the most well-known Catholic writers of the twentieth century, THOMAS MERTON was a prolific poet, religious writer, and essayist whose diversity of work has rendered a precise definition of his life and an estimation of the significance of his career difficult. Merton was a Trappist, a member of a Roman Catholic brotherhood known for its austere lifestyle and vow of silence in which all conversation is forbidden.

Printed in the United States
by Baker & Taylor Publisher Services